POPULAR CULTURES

The Media, Culture & Society Series

Editors: John Corner, Nicholas Garnham, Paddy Scannell,
Philip Schlesinger, Colin Sparks, Nancy Wood

POPULAR CULTURES

Rock Music, Sport and the Politics of Pleasure

David Rowe

SAGE Publications
London • Thousand Oaks • New Delhi

SAGE Publications Ltd
6 Bonhill Street
London EC2A 4PU

SAGE Publications Inc
2455 Teller Road
Thousand Oaks, California 91320

SAGE Publications India Pvt Ltd
32, M-Block Market
Greater Kailash – I
New Delhi 110 048

British Library Cataloguing in Publication data

A catalogue record for this book is
available from the British Library

    ISBN 0 8039 7700 X
    ISBN 0 8039 7701 8 (pbk)

Library of Congress catalog record available

Typeset by M Rules
Printed in Great Britain by The Cromwell Press Ltd,
Broughton Gifford, Melksham, Wiltshire

For Patrick

Contents

Acknowledgements

I have always thought of the acknowledgements page as akin to the wedding invitation list in generating anxiety about who will be deliberately or inadvertently left off it. Then again, there are those embarrassing Oscar acceptance speeches . . . Oh well, all due care taken, no responsibility accepted.

Over the years a patchwork of friends, colleagues, students, research subjects and known associates have helped my work in diverse and inestimably valuable ways. The few that I select for honourable mention on this occasion are, in roughly chronological order, Jon Stratton, Claire Williams, Geoff and Dimity Lawrence, Jim McKay, Toby Miller, Ivor Gaber, James Curran, Glenn and Jill Albrecht, Colin Sparks and Deborah Stevenson.

Before all of them came my parents, Jean and Ken, and sisters, Susan and Mary, who gave unstinting support to what seemed a very peculiar educational and career practice. On the other genealogical branch, my children, Daniel and Madeleine, have provided enough agony and ecstasy for several lifetimes. It is hard to know what I would be without them, but it would certainly be worse. Finally, there is my son Patrick, who kept watch with me during the long, pre-dawn hours when many of the ideas contained in this book were taking shape. Alas, he wasn't in it for the long haul, but the brevity of a life is no measure of its worth nor of its persistence in sweet memory.

1

Introduction: Analysing the Popular

It is appropriate to begin this book about popular culture on an autobiographical note. This is not simply because of self-indulgence, although the subject matter does exert a strong auto-confessional pull for those who write on the subject, just as it encourages readers to tell their own stories about personally significant popular cultural styles, texts and identities. A conspicuous intellectual current is also running through *fin de siècle* social science which is preoccupied with the relationship between the theorist and the theorized. The sociological literature is now liberally peppered with self-reflexive examinations of what is variously termed identity, emotion, affectivity, auto/biography, subjectivity, selfhood, person formation, the somatic and the sublime (see, for example, Stanley, 1993). A postmodernist concern – either explicit or 'under influence' – with the proliferation of self-identities and with the repudiation of the rationalist grand narratives of modernist social theory is both symptom and cause of a re-evaluation of social life in its personal, political and academic domains. To acknowledge the impact of postmodernist thought is not, however, to embrace it as faith (even if in fakes). The political and intellectual shortcomings of what is broadly termed postmodernism have been well documented (see, for example, Callinicos, 1989; Frankel, 1993), although often in a manner that takes due account of its contribution to the overdue questioning of critical orthodoxies and to the opening up of new lines of intellectual inquiry (Hebdige, 1988; Norris, 1992; Squires, 1993b). It also cannot be ignored that, in a theoretical genre where the 'death of the author' has achieved mantric catchphrase status, the cool memories and travel stories of central figures in the postmodern canon (such as Baudrillard, 1990) have acquired the kind of powerful authorial cachet which can attract 3,000 of the initiated and the intrigued to a lecture by the embodied subject in an Australian university (Frankovits, 1984). The notion of postmodern irony here is stretched beyond its own improbable and vertigo-defying limits.

The major imprint that postmodernism in its various guises has made on contemporary social thought has been to emphasize reflexivity – a constant awareness that thoughts occur within discourses and that objects, irrespective of their ontological status, are gazed upon from a range of conceptual and perspectival positions. Such anti-universalism and rejection of the figure of the social scientist as all-knowing, all-seeing and unfeeling are by no means novel. A variety of theoretical positions over the last four decades has highlighted, in different ways and with varying levels of self-consciousness, the contingent nature of social thought. It is common, in elaborations of the renewed interest in selves and in embodied, interested knowledge, to invoke C. Wright Mills' (1970) classic assertion of the linkage between biography and social structure in *The Sociological Imagination*. The influence of Anthony Giddens' (1991) reformulation of structure-agency has now been extended to a re-appraisal of self-identity, just as post-structuralist feminism (Caine et al., 1988; Morris, 1988) has challenged the mind-body dualism of patriarchal rationalism. Michel Foucault (1980), whose theoretical *oeuvre* has been claimed by both modernist and postmodernist camps, has mounted a sustained challenge to determinist and monolithic theories of power by stressing its diffusion into multiple micro-circuits, while Michel de Certeau (1984) has provided an often-cited neo-phenomenological manifesto for the practice of everyday life alongside Pierre Bourdieu's (1977) more structurally determinist conception of the *habitus*. The British culturalist legacy of Raymond Williams (1966, 1975) has placed greater emphasis on the negotiation of power relations through symbolic, lived 'structures of feeling' (McRobbie, 1989; Nava, 1992; Willis, 1990). Finally, post-colonial writers have successfully exposed the imperialist foundations of the master concepts of western thought (Bhabha, 1990; Said, 1983).

These theoretical interventions, mentioned here in no particular order or priority, have (along with diverse other contributions from cultural studies) been important correctives to the 'structural supra-determinism' (Miliband, 1970), teleology and Euro-centrism that has dogged so much critical analysis in the political economic and Althusserian traditions. They have demanded a more reflexive and reflective approach to the analysis of popular culture and, indeed, to any other socio-cultural phenomenon. It is necessary, therefore, to situate this book in that most sociological of spaces – its social context. Authors, after all, as historically constituted human subjects, can hardly be exempt from the kind of explanatory framework they seek to impose on their research objects. The tension between writing and being history must be recognized rather than tranquillized.

Framing the subject

I first became interested in the study of popular culture after a standard 'high' cultural English literary education in school, with its Leavisite canonization of favoured authors and texts. While a good deal of cultural capital could be accumulated through the mastery of the prescribed analytical methods applied to the likes of Chaucer, Shakespeare, Byron, Wordsworth, Austen and the Brontës, there was something lacking both in the overall approach to the subject matter and in the material itself. In regard to the former, textualist myopia combined with a conservative appropriation of the literary canon in producing a thoroughly idealist orthodoxy. The ferocity of current debates concerning, for example, the historicity of the Shakespearean *oeuvre* and deconstructive methodology (Hawkes, 1992) is testimony to the deep and resilient ideological investment in a transcendent, universalist (and in this case English) great tradition. As for the cultural material being subjected to such intense scrutiny (a term so beloved of the Leavises), the much-derided concept of 'relevance' could not be bypassed. The post-war emergence of the teenager, youth culture, the pop industry, psychic and behavioural experimentation, political dissent and personal politics made little mark on late sixties and early seventies cultural education in schools. At the very moment when contemporary culture, politics and society were experiencing major convulsions, English Literature carried the torch for continuity, certainty and the eternal aesthetic (Docker, 1984a; Eagleton, 1990). Constructing a sustainable *habitus* out of this massive disjunction between the institutionally legitimate and the experientially compelling was a contradictory process for those many 'grammar school kids' caught between elite and common cultures.

Universities (especially of the 'red brick' variety), polytechnics and colleges were the privileged (in a variety of senses) spaces where a certain latitude was extended to the exploration, celebration and, it should be conceded, institutional re-appropriation of popular culture. I will expound later on how popular culture may be defined, but here it can be delineated historically and discursively in terms of its intellectual illegitimacy. That is, popular culture (especially emerging forms of youth culture) was largely seen as the domain of simple, bodily pleasure which could – indeed, must – be readily differentiated from the complex, cerebral forms of culture which could only be commanded and understood after rigorous training. The zero-sum implication of Denys Thompson's (1964) influential collection *Discrimination and Popular Culture* was enthusiastically accepted by many on the Left and Right alike (Swingewood, 1977). In challenging this cultural hierarchy, the new 'cultural materialists' (Milner, 1993) employed the various intellectual tools at hand in the then emerging strands of the sociology of culture, including historical materialist, semiotic, structuralist and culturalist approaches. Sociology (which later ceded its disciplinary hegemony to the more diffuse field of cultural studies) both symbolized and mobilized the systematic study of popular culture. Open, personal identification with a sociological perspective (especially after the coming of Thatcherism to Britain) was itself a gesture of resistance to academic tradition and political hierarchy, just as the exaltation of popular culture ran counter to the received values of the stratification system of high culture. While it is possible to romanticize and exaggerate the oppositionality of the sociology of popular culture, it is important not to underestimate the antagonism which it engendered among conservative forces.

Well before the organized assault on the discipline during the Thatcher years in Britain, a series of moral entrepreneurs (including clergy, newspaper columnists and comedy writers) ridiculed and fulminated against the 'soft option' of sociology and its insidious ideological 'looniness', just as they railed against youthful affluence and the 'degeneracy' of youth culture (Cohen, 1980). In this manner sociology and contemporary (youth) popular culture became conceptually linked by apologists and detractors alike.

Indeed, even within the discipline there were attempts to restore a degree of pre-sixties academic legitimacy and reactionary detachment (Gould, 1977). In much the same way as heavy-handed proscriptions of indulgence in alcohol, tobacco, marijuana, LSD and sex often stimulated the very behaviour they were designed to prevent, so the stigmatization of sociology by the guardians of education and morality helped to invest it with an attractively resistive *frisson*. This ideological and intellectual tension made it possible for sociologists of youth culture to address questions which were simultaneously the subject of moral panics in the parent culture and the substance of lived experience within youth culture. Youth behaviour and the cultural tastes of the young had a mutual fascination for the generations as a 'metaphor for social change' (Hall and Jefferson, 1976). For young (predominantly white and male) sociologists of youth who were both subject and object, this led to a degree of 'self-centredness' in a period when narcissism and exploration of the self were encouraged at the behest both of the politics of experience and of the economics of the culture industries. It also presented a problem of generalizability and of ventriloquism in over-extending specific, historical experiences into abstract, de-historicized categories of 'youth' (Tait, 1993). A fascination with the expressive practices of spectacular (predominantly British and working-class) male youth cultures was, therefore, a manifestation of the search for 'imaginary' solutions to contradictions of class, culture and gender experienced by an emergent, self-consciously progressive male intelligentsia (McRobbie, 1991; Turner, 1990).

Bodies like the Centre for Contemporary Cultural Studies (CCCS) and the National Deviancy Symposium were influential as a British strain of the sociology of youth and popular culture rapidly developed a significant body of literature which contested conservative analyses of youth, culture and disorder (for example, Hebdige, 1979; Taylor et al., 1973; Willis, 1977; 1978). Where cultural conservatives (of Right and Left) saw only decadent young people obsessed with the manufactured trivia of the youth industry and the cheap, anti-social thrills of gang violence and vandalism (Davis, 1990), radical sociologists of youth saw expressions of alienation, unconscious resistance and a defiant assertion of autonomy and difference. The flowering of youth cultural studies accompanied the development of youth both as an ideological and as an economic category. Hence there was a great deal of interest in youth from a variety of political groupings with very different motives. The reactionary Right and the orthodox Left wanted to 'save' it from itself and from capitalist exploitation, the pragmatic Right wanted to capitalize on it, and the New Left wanted to re-direct its energies and to re-educate it. This ideological contestation over the categories of youth and youth culture represented, above all, an attempt to come to terms with broad and profound changes in the alignments of social groups and cultural identities. The commodification of youth culture, for example, became a test case for the much wider proliferation of the commodity form. If Hebdige's (1988) *Hiding in the Light* signalled the end of this dynamic period of youth studies from one of its major exponents, the questions which surround and constitute the subject remain alive. Youth as a social category no longer dominates the field, although the mythology of youth and youthfulness is no less central. There has been a progressive detachment of the concept of youth from that of popular culture, not least because of the widening age spread of many contemporary taste cultures and the chronological aging of many of the established researchers in the sociology of culture. If the study of popular culture is now less 'youthful', it is also more established by virtue of its institutional incorporation.

Debates about culture, politics and pleasure take place today in an atmosphere of some, albeit tentative respectability, not least because of the 'market power' of cultural studies in the universities compared to more established humanities disciplines such as literature and history, which have undergone a degree of modernization as a result (Grossberg, 1988). Outside (and sometimes within) academe there is still resistance to the notion that anything save high culture with a capital K is worthy of deconstruction. The academic study of popular culture can still draw the ire of those elite and lowbrow agencies who patrol the cultural frontiers. One British tabloid paper, for example, was provoked by an Australian popular culture conference (at the University of London in 1992) into a full-page diatribe against the '150 international boffins gathered in Britain to try to answer this extremely perplexing question: "Why is [the Australian television soap opera] *Neighbours* so popular [in Britain]?"'. It solved the mystery by means of an enlightened injunction: '*Next time just stay at home and switch on the telly, clever clogs*' (McIntosh, 1992: 9).

While allowing for a degree of jaundiced (post)colonialist disdain (Rowe, 1994b), this response reveals the extent to which the popular media themselves often willingly sustain the split between high and popular culture. For all the interpenetration of high and low cultural forms celebrated by postmodernists, with opera singers in the charts, vernacular styles of architecture on the street, avant-garde filmic techniques in television advertisements, and art exhibitions hyped like pop festivals, there remains a widespread ideological enforcement of cultural hierarchies. The initial project for many sociologists of popular culture was to function as apologists for lowbrow cultural forms (Bennett, 1986), asserting that modern popular music, literature or film could be every bit as rich, complex and expressive as the aesthetic objects endorsed by the academies and their fellow travellers in the cultural elite. It also sought to extend the concept of culture to a much wider range of symbolic objects and practices, organized according to generative grammars of style. Neither task obliterated judgements of taste and value. Instead, new forms of distinction were produced – rock not pop, Kerouac before Cartland, *nouvelle vague* over Hollywood, tie dye instead of drip dry. The situationist-inspired celebration and aestheticization of everyday life (Hebdige, 1979; Willis, 1990) also entailed the careful grading of cultural forms and practices. Under the sway of postmodernism, the toleration and promotion of 'difference' have shaped the rhetorical field, inducing a reluctance to articulate evaluative responses to texts. It is, however, precisely through selection and judgement that culture works. Even if absolutist pronouncements of the transcendental value of particular texts carry less authority today, more provisional forms of aesthetic, social and political evaluation continue to be made. As the following chapters seek to demonstrate, this ideologically loaded dimension of culture (which is so close to the surface in its popular form) guarantees that it is an endlessly productive source of inquiry into the constitution of society and its formations of power.

Reflective treatments of popular culture, like cultural forms themselves, betray (in both senses) their origins and histories. This book and its author bear the inscriptions of the conditions of their production, but no text or historical subject is a mechanical product of delimited time and space. What is described and analysed here will resonate in different ways with the experiences of readers – if only through radical contrast. What has come to be called the 'Birmingham school' (CCCS) has been of formative importance to this work for the historical, geographical, social and cultural reasons outlined above. A critical–analytical work should not, however, be a hostage to its influences, and the weaknesses of the Birmingham project have been forcefully and persuasively advanced (Hebdige and Stratton, 1982/3; McRobbie, 1991; Turner, 1990). The positive legacy of the CCCS is that its sustained concentration on the relations between culture, social structure and everyday life has been adapted to contexts far beyond the narrow confines of spectacular male youth cultures. Many roads lead out of Birmingham – and even more do not pass close by. Imaginary solutions to social contradictions look different from California, Sydney, Berlin, Bombay, Naples or Tokyo (Stratton, 1985). Time and space, in whatever state of compression (Harvey, 1989), create their own theoretical revisions. The British intellectual diaspora (Marshall, 1990) in the Thatcher years, of which I am a part, has produced a very particular 'critical distance' from previous theoretical and political positions (see, for example, Bennett, 1992). There is some consistency and resilience, however, in the popular cultural problematic. For all the supersession of naive concepts of resistance and meaning, and the proliferation of the 'hybridities' of the high, the low and the middle-brow, pivotal questions are still canvassed concerning the nature and extent of the relationships between cultural practice and social power. The concepts of 'the popular' and of 'popular culture' have been crucial to these debates, and must now be given more detailed consideration.

Looking for the popular

It would be possible to expend a good deal of time examining the utility and validity of the concept of popular culture. From a postmodern perspective this would be a fruitless task, given the fluidity and inter-textuality of cultural forms and the promiscuity of signs (Crook et al., 1992: 75). If we assume, however, a degree of 'discursive regularity', then it would be possible, in Foucauldian terms, to see popular culture in relation to certain forms of 'governmentality', by which the bodies of urban populations are managed and controlled through disciplinary regimes of pleasure (Mercer, 1986). Alternatively, popular culture may be approached empirically as a set of leisure practices and texts or defined ideologically in terms of either exploitation and pacification or 'productivity' and resistance. These tasks have been performed elsewhere (Bennett et al., 1986; Fiske, 1989; Mukerji and Schudson, 1991) and I do not propose to replay them here. In this book popular culture is treated as an ensemble of pleasurable forms, meanings and practices, whose constituents are neither static nor unambiguous, and which cannot be insulated from the social processes and structures in which they are imbedded. As indicated above, the use of the term culture is in accordance with the expanded configurational definition (Williams, 1977) which views it as more than the notion of bourgeois refinement and its legitimized texts. Nonetheless, the forms of culture that are being discussed and the social relations they entail are deeply implicated in the process by which cultural objects are bought, circulated, exchanged and sold. If there is a primary focus here on cultural commodities of various kinds, be these recorded music, rock stars, sporting spectacles or celebrity athletes, then it is because the popular culture that I am describing is quite literally unthinkable without a full appreciation of its existence in the context of advanced capitalism.

What I call popular culture should not be confused with rival formulations like folk or mass culture. The former can be best characterized as essentially pre-industrial, pre-capitalist sets of symbolic practices which have been progressively destroyed by the erosion of non-commodifiable and unrationalized forms of culture. The latter concept is essentially chimerical, given its founding assumption that the industrialization of cultural forms and their systems of production inevitably constructs a Pavlovian relationship between addressor and addressee, created out of the manipulative potency of stimulatory, trivialized and inorganic texts. The idea of 'the popular' is deceptively complex. It refers to things, acts and institutions that are of 'the people', immediately proposing a cleavage between the official and the popular or, as Hall (1981: 238) puts it, between the 'people' and the 'power-bloc'. The immediate question to be raised by this formulation is – which people and what power-bloc? Highly differentiated articulations and uses of culture by different social groups – or by the same members of those groups – problematize the concept of the people (Sparks, 1992). Furthermore, what looks like the culture of the people for one group may resemble that of the power-bloc for another (a simple example is racist situation comedy). The power-bloc itself is in need of examination – the notion of hegemony with which Hall works requires that formations of power are negotiated, unstable and contingent, rather than uncompromising, solid and absolute. Both the people and the power-bloc exist in a state of flux, albeit one in which underlying structures (especially of class, gender and race/ethnicity) constrain social relations and cultural patterns.

Popular culture is, then, regarded here neither as an effect of discourse – that which is interpellated as popular in specific moments by specific groups (as, for example, is suggested by Wickham, 1990) – nor as an empirically unproblematic set of stable and predictable symbolic practices and meanings. Popular culture is regarded as those shifting sets of social and cultural relations, meanings and texts which in varying ways emerge as contemporary forms of pleasure, leisure, style and identity, and which are linked to personal and expressive politics, aesthetic address and cultural economy. There are many ways in which we can approach popular culture, as noted above, including the industrial processes of cultural production, the meanings of popular cultural texts, the ideologies of popular discourses and the pleasures and uses of cultural commodities. In most appraisals of popular culture the principal explicit or implicit question has concerned whether in its various forms popular culture can be characterized as resisting or abetting hegemonic domination in modern capitalist societies. In other words, does popular culture function as a means by which people can hold material and ideological oppression at bay, or does it activate and reinforce that oppression? The debate has, therefore, turned on the meanings and uses of popular culture. Where it once took the form of critiques pitted against defences of popular cultural forms, cultural analysis is now more specific, relativistic and provisional. Neo-Marxist, postmodernist, receptionist and liberal pluralist perspectives jostle in a much less theoretically and methodologically polarized field as part of what James Curran (1990) calls the 'new revisionism in mass communication research'. This current spirit of eclecticism and critical tolerance must, however, be tempered by a concern to avoid a descent into incoherent, *laissez-faire* and subjectivist treatments of the subject. It is in the space between intellectual flexibility and critical focus that a workable analysis of popular culture can emerge.

Popular culture: rock and sport

This analysis addresses simultaneously the social, economic, cultural, political and ideological dimensions of popular culture. For this reason, political economic analysis and textual interpretation, interviews and cultural readings are all used in developing an understanding of the production and meaning of the popular. Popular cultural production, distribution, exchange, consumption, interpretation and response can be broken down into various constituent parts. Each can be studied separately to good heuristic effect, but the compartmentalized study of popular cultural practices, processes and institutions cannot provide the kind of intimate relational analysis necessary for a productive movement towards a desirable combination of 'thick description' (Geertz, 1973), empirical generalization and theoretical explanation. The book addresses general debates about popular culture as well as providing more detailed analyses of two crucial forms – rock music and sport. The dimensions and elusiveness of the subject matter make futile any attempt at achieving comprehensiveness and theoretical closure, but it is intended at least to analyse productively the dialectics of similarity and difference in popular culture. The ways in which forms of popular culture come to converge and diverge is a running theme of this work. The two case studies of popular culture are highlighted not only because of their raw popularity and economic significance, but also because each is devoted to the body and its pleasures by means of both participation and spectatorship. Rock and sport are key cultural industries of the body, constantly replenishing the stock of corporeal images which also function as metaphors of social and cultural change.

Of all the cultural forms that constituted the emergence of post-war youth culture, rock music and its associated elements of style are the most conspicuous and influential. I employ the term 'rock' rather than the more inclusive word 'pop' because of its specific discursive positioning against the twin 'evils' of legitimate high culture and illegitimate commercial pop culture (Frith, 1978). Jimi Hendrix or Cream, *qua* rock, could in the sixties and seventies be celebrated at the expense of both the western art music of Mozart and Beethoven and also the overtly commercial pop offerings of The Monkees or Lulu. Hence the rock era, which has recently been pronounced dead by Simon Frith (1988: 1) and is, if not entirely defunct, unquestionably less vibrant, can be characterized as a moment in which youth culture and ideology were pitted, in openly contradictory manner, against the society and economy that had produced them. Frith (1978; 1986) has previously proposed that rock and capitalism are intimately linked in contradiction, with the rationalized, technologically sophisticated sale of youthful expressivity framed within an ideology of romantic, anti-commercial dissent (Stratton, 1983a). Rock has been instrumental in placing the sexualized body in a rather more ambiguous relationship to capitalist society than the decorative corporeal imagery of mainstream advertising or the graphic representations of the body in pornography. Bernice Martin (1981: 184) argued over a decade ago that:

> It [rock] has certainly acted as the single most important vehicle for the spread of the hedonistic messages of the Expressive Revolution, passing them up and down the age and class hierarchies in ways which have become so normal that we no longer even notice the radical nature of the change which has occurred in our cultural presuppositions over these last three decades.

Although rock does not in the nineties occupy such a prime position as '*par excellence* the cultural medium through which young people explore[d] and express[ed] the symbolism of liminality' (Martin, 1981: 154), it nonetheless remains a significant site at which the symbolic dimensions of the sexualized body are tested and extended. In the task of constructing and asserting new inflections of sexuality and body image, rock is increasingly being shadowed by sport. Sport and rock music are incontestably two of the most significant forms of popular culture and share a preoccupation with the physical display of youth. Yet in the sixties and seventies, with some signal exceptions (see Chapter 7), sport and rock, as institutions, were on largely divergent paths. This is not to argue that young people did not play or watch sport in this period or could not enjoy both pursuits, but rather that there was a quite definite split in the ethos of rock and sporting culture. The major source of this schism was their differential relationship with the parent culture (interpreted here, following Hall and Jefferson, 1976, as both dominant and generationally distinct). Rock in this period was the quintessential youth cultural form, even if its infrastructure was largely owned and controlled by 'adults'. As Robert Palmer (1985: 13) has argued, 'Rock was the sound of young people talking to each other.' This statement could never be applied to sport because, in spite of its fetishization of youth, sport was much more severely compromised by its fraternization with 'straight' society than rock. Unlike rock, sport was a cornerstone of the school curriculum (Hargreaves, 1986) and of official national state ideology (Hoberman, 1984), claiming the kind of edifying function that western classical music asserted against 'light' musical entertainment.

Sport's promotion of the notion of healthy minds, healthy bodies and self-imposed discipline was almost the antithesis of the dionysian ethic of rock culture (Pattison, 1987). Not only was sport a key component of some of the British Empire's most reactionary myths, but it was also consumed by older people as freely as it was played by the young. While rock derived much of its rhetorical force from its conscious alienation of other generations, sport could not be easily detached by the young from its older aficionados in the same way that rock differentiated itself from other post-war musical styles. In the early seventies, to declare an interest in sport, let alone to participate in it willingly, was often a little *infra dig.* for those who also adhered in some way to the resistive tenets of rock culture (Hornby, 1992). This relative unfashionability of sport prompted, apart from a degree of closet sports appreciation, attempts to link rock style and sport. In the case of football in Britain, for example, stylized gang violence, sharp terrace dress codes and identification with musical genres like ska and punk partially modernized the sports aesthetic. The residue of hippie culture, however, meant that organized sport was widely regarded (especially among women) as an 'uncool' product of competitive individualism, masculine aggressiveness and rule-bound behavioural patterns. To pledge allegiance to a football team, for example, required justification in class and community terms (sticking to one's real, imaginary or exaggerated proletarian roots) or needed to be situated within a general critique of the elite pretensions of bourgeois society. These self-justifications have to be made much less frequently and defensively in the nineties (Redhead, 1991). This cultural convergence of rock (now less conceptually distinguishable from pop) and sport can be explained in terms both of the decline of the generational and ideological coherence of rock culture and of a shift in the cultural and economic location of sport.

The economic, the ideological and the cultural

These trends cannot be situated within a monocausal framework, nor can they be regarded as arbitrary and random. Instead, even the most minute, temporary or apparently anomalous trends – or, conversely, surprising instances of resilience and stasis – are today produced under extraordinarily complex conditions of rapid technological change, proliferating forms of communication, transformations of economic processes, suddenly emergent social movements, and upheavals in seemingly orderly social relations (Lash and Urry, 1994). The explanatory and descriptive approach adopted here is relational rather than totalizing, seeking to make connections between super-ficially discrete processes without recourse to teleological or doctrinaire explanations. For this reason there is no attempt to privilege a single theo-retical position or overriding causal factor. Instead, it is intended to appraise aspects of contemporary popular culture in a manner sufficiently plausible to counter familiar pronouncements of its absolute debauchery, commercial-ization, manipulativeness and triviality or, alternatively, its irreproachable resistiveness, oppositionality, playfulness and elusiveness. This approach can be illustrated by reflecting on Marxist theories of culture which, since the late sixties, have been the reference points (both supportive and hostile) for most significant analyses of communication and popular culture (Bennett, 1986). Any Marxist approach to popular culture, irrespective of theoretical or polit-ical variation, must acknowledge that under capitalism culture is increasingly commoditized and that, at some level of determination, the social relations of production under capitalism will be favoured and reproduced. In this way popular culture is theorized as deeply linked with class and other formations of power. Marxism, in spite of its theoretical and political loss of favour 'after the Wall', has consistently supplied the critical underpinnings of the analysis of popular culture (Cunningham, 1992). To ignore or marginalize the economic and ideological dimensions of popular culture like, for example, the more anodyne, pluralistic 'the-public-gets-what-the-public-wants' models or the more ecstatic forms of postmodernism would be to paint too voluntaris-tic and Panglossian a picture. Yet, to reduce the study of popular culture to the ascribed logics of the culture industry would be unacceptably reductive, failing to demonstrate that culture may also be unpredictable, contradictory and subversive. While the Gramscian strain in theories of hegemony and subculture (Fiske, 1989) and the revisionist post-Fordist economic accounts (Murray, 1989) have sought to overcome these deterministic rigidities, they still invoke 'a traditional marxist explanatory prejudice: that the features of the production system can be used to characterize the wider society' (Hirst, 1989: 322). If traces of economic determinism are still evident even in 'New Times' accounts (Hall and Jacques, 1989), it is because its total suspension suggests a descent into a relativistic critical void (Harvey, 1993; Norris, 1993).

Steering a path between determinism and voluntarism is by no means easy, especially in the analysis of popular culture, with its dualistic history of intuitive resistance to academic explanation and attraction for high-flown critical rhetoric. The approach adopted here will seek to overcome these limitations by doing justice both to the structurally-induced (although not secured) continuities of popular culture and to the mercurial elements that present the constant possibility of surprise and re-alignment. Furthermore, while the conceptual separation of economics, ideology and culture is heuristically useful, it is impossible to separate them in the absolute for any other purpose. In the case of the relationship between economics and culture, the classical Marxist base-superstructure metaphor is predicated on an assumption that the former has a prior foundational status, with the latter essentially derivative and subordinate. This theoretical position has a paradoxical tendency to fetishize the economic, separating it in its primacy from the processes of social and cultural reproduction that are central to the activities of production, exchange, distribution and consumption, to the determination of use and value, and to the institutional maintenance of the state and the market. Even if earlier forms of capitalism based on primary and secondary mass commodity production were quite conducive to an economically determinist thesis, the later preponderance of capitalist practice conditioned by the command of information, the manufacture of image and the quickfire manipulation of the global financial system represents a highly developed imbrication of culture and economics (Harvey, 1989: 159–60; Lash and Urry, 1987; 1994). As Stuart Hall (1989: 128) has argued, it is necessary to:

> open our minds to the deeply *cultural* character of the revolution of our times. If 'post-Fordism' exists, then it is as much a description of cultural as of economic change. Indeed, the distinction is now quite useless. Culture has ceased (if it ever was – which I doubt) to be a decorative addendum to the 'hard world' of production and things, the icing on the cake of the material world. The word is now as 'material' as the world. Through design, technology and styling, 'aesthetics' has already penetrated the world of modern production. Through marketing, layout and style, the 'image' provides the mode of representation and fictional narrativisation of the body on which so much of modern consumption depends. Modern culture is relentlessly material in its practices and modes of production. And the material world of commodities and technologies is profoundly cultural. Young people, black and white, who can't even spell 'postmodernism' but have grown up in the age of computer technology, rock-video and electronic music, already inhabit such a universe in their heads.

The interpenetration of culture and economics parallels that of the concepts of ideology and culture. While their meanings and applications vary widely, they are frequently treated as synonymous or interchangeable, so that 'even the distinction between culture and ideology seems a strategic rather than a substantive one at times' (Turner, 1990: 197). Whether ideology is conceived in the traditional sense of a bundle of conscious political attitudes or in its Althusserian (Althusser, 1971) formulation as the unconscious relation of the subject to material reality, most uses of the term presuppose a fairly straightforward conversion of symbolic practices into political interests. Again, culture is presented as subordinate – this time to politics – in spite of the observation that only a passing acquaintance with contemporary issues reveals the deeply cultural nature of the political itself, not least through the rationalized deployment of political iconography. My argument is not that culture is unideological, but rather that ideologies cannot be 'read off' forms of culture in any unambiguous or coherent sense. The relationship between culture and ideology is not always neatly containable, just as that between economics and culture cannot be simply reduced to commodity logic or aesthetic freedom. The position adopted here, therefore, is that culture, ideology and economics are not discrete concepts, but their analytical maintenance and use are desirable in order to illuminate different features of complex and contradictory social phenomena. For the purposes of this book, the term culture stresses the significance of symbolic expressiveness, the construction of identities, the production of texts and the principles of pleasurable and aesthetic discrimination; the term economics emphasizes the ways in which material resources are deployed in the physical production and symbolic communication of cultural objects; and the term ideology stresses the links between these structures and practices and their associated (abstract and concrete) communities of interest and power. Above all, the connections between these ideas, objects and practices highlight the sociality of popular culture and the culture-bound nature of society.

Each chapter of this book emphasizes the economic, ideological and cultural features of rock and sport. Perhaps the treatment of economic relations first betrays Hirst's (1989: 322) aforementioned 'traditional marxist explanatory prejudice' that the 'production system' provides the key to other facets of society. If this prejudice exists, then it is present in the certain knowledge that, while cultural practices and texts have existed in diverse forms for all of recorded time, the large-scale sale and dissemination of cultural items on a global basis by specialized corporate and broad conglomerate organizations is historically unprecedented (Garnham, 1990: 163; Ryan, 1991: 10). Alongside these mega-organizations is a vast range of national, regional and local cultural organizations, the constituents of which stand in different relation to the cash nexus and to the state, but which are reliant on some form of material exchange for their existence. No adequate analysis of cultural production, however, can focus exclusively on profit generation and survivalism. The distribution of resources and power evident in the production of popular culture raises sharp questions concerning the kinds of politics that can be discerned in the engagements between the personal, the pleasurable, the popular and the commercial. These questions also provoke consideration of the texts and social relations of contemporary cultural production, and the symbolic exchanges between artist and audience which constitute what we call culture. These deliberations also prompt further questions about change and persistence, convergence and differentiation among popular cultural forms and practices. The problematization of the phenomena and of ways of seeing them lead, finally, back to the points raised earlier about who is doing the producing, gazing, interpreting, choosing, celebrating and denouncing and what is their agenda or interest in such activities? If, following Barthes, the critic should also be a lover, is not also the lover – in this case of popular culture – always in some sense a critic? Critical self-reflexivity, far from paralysing and degrading pleasure, is a condition of its existence. It nonetheless poses a problem in establishing critical authority.

Criticism and doubt

Self-doubt about the status of treatments of popular culture from within academe is longstanding. The established homology between high culture and high criticism demands few apologies or disclaimers about the function of criticism, its appropriateness for specific audiences and its manifest limitations in representing texts and the experience of reading and using them. A 'canonical' subcultural or popular cultural work like Dick Hebdige's (1979: 139) *Subculture: The Meaning of Style* typically worries, however, that:

> It is highly unlikely, for instance, that the members of any of the subcultures described in this book would recognize themselves reflected here. They are still less likely to welcome any efforts on our part to understand them. After all, we, the sociologists and interested straights, threaten to kill with kindness the forms which we seek to elucidate.

There is a range of anxieties present in statements of this kind about the relationships between academics, forms of popular culture, members of subcultures, and fans. These include that academic analysis and criticism are no more authoritative than that of any other observer or, worse, that the 'serious' commentator may be constitutionally incapable of doing justice to the subject. Even more corrosive of critical purpose is the idea that popular cultural analysis is ideologically recuperative, that its apparently innocent or progressive attempt to 'account for' the popular is part of the denial and repression of difference that characterizes the Enlightenment project (Lyotard, 1984). This latter strain of thought, which is broadly postmodernist, underlies the contemporary fashion among cultural critics (mentioned above) to assert their autobiographies, subjectivities and idiosyncrasies, in this case by eliding posited differences between the critic and the fan. Anthony May and Alec McHoul (1989: 181), for example, argue that the 'problem of the fan' can be countered 'through an examination of the self' which informs readers of the 'intersection of cultural practices and social/textual history'. There is, perhaps, an understandable irony that those who have chosen the formal written word to render cultural forms usually deeply inimical or indifferent to it are also seeking to evade the burdens of rationalism and logocentrism. This Nietzschean impulse encourages an imaginary constitution of the object of academic popular cultural inquiry as a 'fantasy land, but the fantasies are those projected onto it by (male) intellectuals themselves, intellectuals longing, daring, fearing to transgress; intellectuals wondering what it would be not to be an intellectual' (Frith, 1990: 235).

While fantasizing about elemental, unmediated and unreflective action may be common among the sedentary, professional middle classes, it cannot be permitted to supplant critical practice any more than the 'dream of a pop-ulist–mimetic writing able to capture and render the surface of the things it now so alienatingly (and self-alienatingly) describes', which forgets the lesson 'that any act of criticism necessarily relocates, remakes, rewrites the objects and practices it purports (neutrally) to explain' (King, 1990: 83–4). The posi-tions of intellectual and fan are neither mutually exclusive nor coterminous (Grossberg, 1988: 63), just as 'multilingualism' (Morris, 1990: 479) can be found within and between texts and other sites of criticism. This book is nei-ther a simulacrum nor a dissimilation of popular culture. It is the product of quite specific conditions of production and is intended largely for an institu-tionally defined audience. Like any other cultural product, 'popular' or not, its origins, however, shape without ultimately fixing its meanings and uses.

Structure

The two case studies employed here examine the industrial, ideological and cultural forces which broadly shape the popular, as well as indicating areas specific to particular cultural forms in determinate historical contexts. Chapter 2 examines the economic and industrial dimensions of rock music, which is viewed as both a product of and a reaction to the emergence of the culture industries, particularly those catering to the comparatively modern concept of youth. The tension between cultural and economic structures is revealed in analysing patterns of ownership and control in the rock music industry, with specific emphasis on major and independent record companies and the concept of 'independence'. This discussion is first situated within the familiar setting of the commerce versus culture debate, which is shown to remain significant although often re-cast by cultural producers in an era increasingly characterized by post-Fordism (or reflexive/flexible specializa-tion/accumulation). Attitudes to the commerce–culture nexus are, of course, conditioned by ideology, and Chapter 3 interrogates the volatile politics of pleasure and entertainment in popular culture. Rock's relationship to ortho-dox politics is shown to be complex and uneven, ranging from direct political interventions to repudiations of its political significance. This chapter reviews a range of ways in which ideology is manifest in rock, including the more orthodox politics of 'protest' music, populist politics (such as Live Aid) and the cultural politics of, for example, sexuality or consumerism. The 'British independent moment' is given particular prominence in exploring ideologies of production. There is also an appraisal of the bureaucratic politics inherent in the formation of cultural policy and in the regulation of relations between rock and the state. Questions of rock ideology, state subsidy and censorship problematize how relationships between producers and audiences are con-structed. Rock has drawn much of its power from the mutual identification of artist and fan, and, on occasions (as in the case of punk), has claimed to oblit-erate the distinction between performer and spectator. It also has a particularly strong association with pleasure and the body, for musician and listener alike. Chapter 4 examines the extent to which the relationship between artist and audience can be called 'organic' in considering the creation of rock stars, the concepts of amateurism and professionalism among rock musicians, the classification and targeting of audiences, and the ideas of authenticity and simulation in rock's use of technology (again employing the independents as a key test case). The linking and positioning of producers and consumers in a commercial environment are, ultimately, shown to undermine any notion of 'cultural purity', but it is also argued that there is no corresponding subsumption of the cultural by the commercial.

The arguments made in the analysis of rock music may be specific to it or transportable to other cultural forms. A second case study of sport is performed in tracing the contours of the universal and the particular in popular culture. In Chapter 5 the enormous expansion of the global sports industry in the twentieth century is examined. Pre-capitalist forms of sport and their attendant social relations are shown to have been substantially replaced by the domination of the 'sports–media complex'. The roles of sponsors, advertisers and the media in the maintenance and exploitation of modern sport are presented as founded on the creation and exchange of the 'athlete worker'. In Chapter 6, this discussion is expanded to embrace ideologies of sport, which are seen to be marked by a contradiction between the denial of politics in sport ('sport and politics don't mix') and the political mobilization of sport (sport as an index of national progress). While there are often overtly political issues in sport (for example, the sporting isolation of South Africa and the various Olympic boycotts), the everyday construction of sports ideologies of class, gender, nation and race/ethnicity are shown to be of greater significance. The politics of sport, which embrace such disparate phenomena as sports metaphors in political language and the determination of state sports policy, are tied closely to its cultural expression both as a physical activity and as a spectatorial practice in which a diverse audience gazes on other performers. Chapter 7 examines the circulation of sports texts under mass-mediated spectatorship and the consequent separation of elite and grass-roots sports culture. Sport is shown to have its own media 'independence movement' in the form of the fanzine, which, it is argued, attempts to reconstruct the relationship between the sports writer and the fan. The meanings of sport and, in particular, iconic images of the body are also shown to be crucial cultural resources which draw on and shape social consciousness and practice. This process does not, however, operate in isolation, and it is suggested that popular cultural forms like rock and sport are converging in their stylish bodily display, disciplined 'performativity' and (hyper)commodification. At the same time, the increasing fluidity of the structures and relations of cultural production, and the accelerated mobility of capital and images, are shown constantly to propose new popular formations and different combinations. Contemporary popular culture is made out of these contending and dynamic processes of convergence and divergence.

Conclusion

No book can legitimately claim to command the field of popular culture. Its scale and mutability are such that any account can make only limited inroads into a subject over which expertise is claimed by everyone who has heard a record or watched a televised sports event. This academic work on popular culture aims to be critical without being self-righteous, and respectful of its subject matter but not seduced by it. At some level it is designed to be useful, to show that analysis and pleasure are not inimical to each other, but that each (although not always simultaneously) illuminates and defines the other. If it is conceded that 'Even sociologists fall in love' (Jackson, 1993) and that there are manifold pleasures in the 'ecstacy of communication' (Baudrillard, 1983b), it is also submitted that some critical reflection and reflexivity over our regimes of pleasure are in order. Even the most hedonistic and abandoned fan of popular culture must step out of the sublime sometime.

2

Rock Industry: Song and Business Cycles

While legions of people across the globe experience popular music as pleasurable sound and stimulating style, it is also a multi-billion dollar industry. Expenditure on musical hardware (such as high-fidelity sound reproduction equipment), software (including tapes and compact discs), music-related products (T-shirts, magazines, books and so on) and attendance at musical performances represents a large component of contemporary leisure consumption. By the early nineties, world sales of (non-pirated) recorded music alone were worth over US$24 billion (Negus, 1992: 160). When due account is taken of the role of popular music in the television, radio and advertising industries, its economic significance becomes even more apparent. The industrialized character of much contemporary musical production is not, however, without its contradictions and tensions. The dual activities of formulating music and generating capital have produced continuing disputes over the nature and control of popular music. These material and ideological conflicts have been particularly vigorous in the sub-category of popular music which, since the late sixties, has been called 'rock'. This term is used less frequently in the nineties to describe what was once regarded as 'young pop' (Frith, 1978: 14) and, as was noted in Chapter 1, the author of the seminal *The Sociology of Rock*, in the light of the proliferation of musical styles and the erosion of aesthetic–ideological hierarchies and certainties, opened a new work a decade later with the statement 'I am now quite sure that the rock era is over' (Frith, 1988: 1). Today, it is the knowing postmodern pop of singers like Madonna (Schwichtenberg, 1993), the urban rap polemics of black groups such as Public Enemy (Costello and Wallace, 1990), the sounds of 'Otherness' in so-called world music (Manuel, 1988), and the digitally-sampled sound collages of 'techno' dance ensembles (Redhead, 1990) that are more likely to be celebrated as genuinely subversive than the more orthodox hard rock and 'grunge' music of groups like Guns and Roses and Nirvana (Grossberg, 1993). Even attempts to define rock as a particular musical style are undermined by the diverse musics which claim the rock label or have had it affixed to them, so that today rock increasingly appears to be more of an expedient market niche than a deep-rooted, significant cultural form.

Nonetheless, I will, against the grain, predominantly employ the term rock here because of the discursive history imbedded in the rhetorics, practices and organizations signifying overt youthful dissent in post-war musical culture (Street, 1986; Whiteley, 1992). The now more widely used term pop is connected only weakly to notions of generational resistance through music which have been regularly invoked in treatments of the relationship between commerce and culture in the music industry. The term pop is used here to describe contemporary youth music at its most general, although the widening age spread of audiences/performers and the diversification of the pop charts (which now somewhat improbably admit the likes of Gregorian Chant and The Three Tenors) makes even the most vague of classifications difficult to operationalize. If I am stubbornly retrieving a cultural category which looks increasingly obsolete from the perspective of the nineties, it is primarily because of its historical tradition of critique of the music industry. In this chapter I will examine the economics of rock and debates about commercialism and music making. The nature of work in the rock labour market is given brief attention, but is developed more fully in Chapters 3 and 4. There will be a specific focus on the shifting balance between major and independent record companies in terms both of organizational structures and of competing ideologies of cultural production. This discussion is given an historical dimension in a detailed consideration of what I call the 'British independent moment' of the late seventies and early eighties, when the rise of the 'punk independents' threw into sharp relief the nature of economic competition and ideological contestation in rock. The chapter concludes with an assessment of the changing shape of the rock music industry in response to the emergence or refinement of post-Fordist production regimes (also referred to as flexible/reflexive accumulation/specialization) and of new organizational structures and relations in the rock music industry.

Songs for sale

There is no sphere of human activity which can entirely transcend the mundanely material imperative of commanding sufficient resources to be able to perform, repeat and persist. Even the most seemingly private and non-monetized relationships, such as those within families and peer groups, are conditioned by the necessity of exercising some control over the means of life and, through them, the lives of people. In capitalist societies, the reach and visibility of overtly economic (especially commodity) relations are unprecedented. Cultural producers under the regime of capitalism are implicated in a peculiarly strong way in the process of generating rewards through performances and texts. Making, combining and disseminating symbols through expressive practices such as speaking, drawing, interpreting and singing are everyday human activities not necessarily subject to direct economic exchange. Under a 'modernist' division of capitalist cultural labour (Lane, 1980), however, a relatively small number of people and organizations become remunerated specialists in symbol making. Most of these cultural workers and enterprises will barely garner the resources necessary to live off this form of work, but a very few will emerge as amongst the most conspicuous examples of the super rich, especially when their humble origins, as in the case of Elvis Presley or The Beatles, have turned them into ready vehicles for the promotion of the myth of social mobility through talent, motivation and hard labour.

The close and often uneasy link between cultural and economic activity under capitalism provokes its own kind of critique of market relations, with film-makers regularly being accused of capitulating to Hollywood, novelists of going middlebrow and painters of pandering to the gallery system. Rock discourse has, from its inception, addressed and circled the question of the relationship between making music and making money. Critiques tend to take the form either of totalizing political economic denunciations of any musical practice seen to be tainted by the cash nexus or of strategic arguments which seek to discriminate, for example, between commercial pop and rebel rock (Street, 1986). Both positions condemn what is seen as a harmful concentration of ownership of record companies and the increasing centrality of the profit motive in the making of music. For example, Chapple and Garofalo (1977: 222–3), in their classic polemic *Rock 'n' Roll is Here to Pay*, state in a representative passage that:

> In addition to interlocks with other businesses, institutions, and political parties, and ownership by larger conglomerates, the major networks and record companies are tied in with long standing banking interests . . . The media-record company conglomerates work in tandem with the major continuing finance institutions in American business, which themselves are based on the first fortunes of the robber barons. There is a full integration of the media conglomerates into the fabric of US industry and capital.

Such critical accounts construe rock history as the continued subordination of singers, musicians and composers to the imperatives of capitalism (Harker, 1980). The drives to generate profit, to sell recorded music and 'acts' (which, according to Lash and Urry (1994: 137) are increasingly analogous to 'brands') consistently to a large market and to rationalize artistic creativity, are held to have specific aesthetico-political consequences –standardized 'formula' music, pseudo-rebellion, consumerist individualism, inauthentic values and manipulated taste. This kind of mass cultural critique pre-dates the rise of rock music. Adorno and Eisler (1979: 22–3), for example, bemoan the emergence of 'mass' radio and film music in the thirties and forties thus:

> The greater the drabness of [this] existence, the sweeter the melody. The underlying need expressed by this inconsistency springs from the frustrations imposed on the masses of the people by social conditions. But this need itself is put into the service of commercialism . . . Today indolence is not so much overcome as it is managed and enhanced scientifically. Such a rationally planned irrationality is the very essence of the amusement industry in all its branches. Music perfectly fits the pattern.

The Frankfurt School or Left Leavisite critique of mass culture, in combination with more orthodox Marxist critiques of class relations, and also right-wing nostalgia for a pre-capitalist past, have been applied to diverse print and electronic forms (Frith, 1978: 191–2; Swingewood, 1977), but post-war popular music's close association with a conception of 'youth as a metaphor for social change' (Clarke et al., 1976: 17) encouraged especially

severe condemnations of youth subcultural styles and their associated musical genres from commentators at opposing ends of the political spectrum
(Brake, 1980). Youth music has been the subject of particular attention from
Left and Right thinkers searching for the most vivid instance of debased
contemporary cultural values. From a position on the (pro-folk cultural)
Left, for example, Dave Harker (1980: 111) is contemptuous of virtually all
forms of 'electric' music:

> Under capitalism, it will remain the case that most artists (if not most of the audi-
> ence) will have to be content to succumb to the commercial sausage machine, and
> be compensated with cash ... Those who 'make it' will continue to be, by and large,
> the mindless, spineless creatures that pop stars have traditionally been.

In this way, rock and pop are represented as irredeemably commercial and
so subjugated to the economic imperatives of the cultural production line, the
ideological consequences of which are the co-optation of youth into dominant institutions and systems of thought. Expressions of anti-commercialism
from within are seen to be self-serving or deluded. The tone of such critique
is unremittingly hostile in mounting an absolutist assessment of the behavioural and ideological consequences of the industrialization of youth culture.
As Simon Frith (1988: 12) puts it, this perspective declares that 'What is bad
about the music industry is the layer of deceit and hype and exploitation it
places between us and our creativity'.

Immediate objections can be lodged to such comprehensive condemnations of rock and pop, in particular the assumption that an entire
constellation of institutions, signs and practices is reducible to an over-determining economic regime and its functional ideologies. The subsumption of
the cultural sphere by the economic produces a curiously undialectical theoretical posture which renders contestation over the forms and meanings of
culture as alternatively epiphenomenal or epic. The chaotic and auto-destruc-
tive nature of much cultural exchange under advanced capitalism (Berman,
1983) is thereby subordinated to a disabling teleology. Furthermore, the uni-
linear assumption of the inevitable and inexorable 'progress' towards
monopoly capitalist domination (only to be dramatically terminated by its
own excesses) plays down the level of capitalist disorganization and instability (Lash and Urry, 1987; 1994). Unreflexive grand theorization of the nature
and impact of capitalism across all the spheres of cultural production denies
the specificity and unpredictability of its processes and outcomes. The
advancement of a simple base-superstructure or mass cultural model ignores
not only the differences between 'national formations', but also means that:

> the social relations of production and consumption are reduced to the struggle
> between the recording artists to express their 'natural' creativity, and the record
> company to maximise profits. The complex of relations between musicians, pro-
> ducers, engineers, executives, accountants etc., with all their divergent views on
> what will sell, what sounds 'good', etc., are passed over. (Hustwitt, 1984: 91)

This kind of argument, while not denying the deep significance of economic relations in cultural production, asserts that to treat the complex of

social relations entailed in the making of pop and rock as simply subject to the immanent logic of commodification is misguided. To reduce, as do many critiques of the cultural industries, dynamic social and cultural processes to a specified set of economic structures, exchanges and functions (usually conceived as transnational cultural corporations exploiting and pacifying the proletariat or 'the people') not only does little justice to the possibilities of resistance and 'escape', but also seriously misunderstands even those economic factors which it seeks to propose as ultimately determining. For this reason, as will later become clear, the emergence of small independent record companies in an industry dominated by majors can only be explained by at least modifying the more mechanistic features of the political economic and ideological critiques of popular culture.

That rock and capitalism should be deeply entwined is no great cause for surprise. Yet, just as radical (including academic) books cannot simply be dismissed because they might emanate from multinational commercial publishing houses, the politico-cultural potential of music is not wholly determined by the organizational set within which it is produced and communicated. As Frith (1978: 209) states:

> The industry may or may not keep control of rock's use, but it will not be able to determine all its meanings – the problems of capitalist community and leisure are not so easily resolved.

There are few areas of cultural production, however, where the idea of 'selling out' has a deeper resonance than in rock music, which, much more than pop, is deeply inscribed with a resistive ethos. The discourse of rock music, as historically constituted, is explicitly linked to ideas of rebellion and transgression (Street, 1986; Pattison, 1987). Rock music is simultaneously a product of capitalism and a reaction to it. The distinction between pop and rock rests, in the first instance, on the idea that some forms of culture are purely commercialized, while others, although operating in the commercial sphere, are essentially antithetical to it. The potency of the idea of 'selling out' (invoked and satirized, it should be noted, in early rock albums by The Who and Frank Zappa and the Mothers of Invention) lies not simply in the selling of recorded music, charging for performances and the marketing of fan merchandise, but in professed attitudes and symbolic responses to the process by which resources are transferred from the 'buyers' of rock to its sellers. It is notable that, as the idea of rock's inherent capacity for resistance became harder to sustain in the face of the continued centrality of capitalist practice to music making during and after the hippie and punk eras, the conceptual distinction between rock and pop began to disappear. Not only did this entail a constant slippage between the terms, but it also led to a preference for the term pop and the use of the neologism 'rockist' to characterize and lampoon attitudes to youth culture and youth music which were regarded by key cultural gatekeepers (such as the music journalists Paul Morley and Ian Penman of the *New Musical Express* during its period of style leadership in the late seventies and early eighties) as outmoded and reactionary (Frith, 1988; Redhead, 1990).

One of the key distinctions between rock and pop hinges on assessments of cultural labour. In the case of rock, the emphasis on integrity and authenticity has likened a musical career to (in an echo of Weber, 1965) a 'calling', in which remuneration is held to be of secondary importance and where there is an integral linkage between behaviour in the public and private spheres. The persona adopted and the values articulated by rock stars (like Bruce Springsteen) in the conduct of their 'musical duties' are generally expected by fans to be in close accord with their personal identity, ideology and conduct. In the case of pop, there is a much greater tolerance of a disparity between image and identity (except perhaps in the area of the 'teen idol's' romantic availability and respect for fans) and much less sensitivity to their politics. As John Street (1986: 5) suggests, 'Rock and pop stars play to different rules', so that while a 'radical' group like The Clash has been subject to accusations of selling out, such a term has little relevance to pop stars like Madonna, whose fans:

> are wholly indifferent to her wealth; if anything they enjoy it vicariously when they dress up like her or together sing 'I'm a material girl, living in a material world', and she is under no pressure to justify it. For pop musicians the politics of work resemble the politics of enterprise. (p. 142)

Within the discourse of rock itself there is also a concern with the kind of organization in which cultural labour is performed. Too close an identification with corporate bureaucracies is seen undesirably to align music making with the manufacture of more utilitarian commodities like soap and cigarettes. It is for this reason that, as we will see below, organizational independence is a widely shared index of cultural integrity. Unlike highly specialized corporate personnel who are often regarded as bureaucratic time-servers, musicians and other workers in independent companies are believed to be more committed and more personally involved in the musical 'product'. Suspicion of the industrial production and capitalist expropriation of rock is formative in its discourse, while in the case of 'postmodern pop' it is the star's capacity unashamedly to celebrate and control business and its profits – to be the cynical exploiter rather than the naive exploited – that invites admiration.

Irrespective of whether the master concept is resistive rock or ironically postmodern pop, the taking up of a position in relation to corporate capitalism nevertheless remains of pivotal concern. A pervasive and resilient image of crass commercialism is still attached to the sign of the cultural corporation (Ryan, 1991). The idea of large, differentiated, multi/transnational corporations controlling and manipulating musicians and their audiences has been vital to rock as an ideological (and economic) formation. Corporations have simultaneously sought to dominate the industrialized production of music culture and functioned as the principal *bêtes noires* of the rhetorics of its producers since the emergence of 'protest music' in the mid-sixties (Belz, 1969; Denisoff and Peterson, 1972; Eisen, 1969; 1970). Under the rubric of the commerce–culture debate, a multi-dimensional contest over control, authenticity, affect, community and reception has been played out. One notion has been of particular significance in operationalizing and signifying the idea of producing rock that is organic, non-corporate and resistive, if not entirely free. This enduring concept is encapsulated in the term independence.

Independents and majors

The idea of independence in rock and pop is distinct from, though closely related to, notions of freedom and autonomy. The term independent (often shortened to 'indie') is most commonly deployed as both noun and adjective in representing the relationship of an organization (such as a group or a record company) to its discursive opposite, which is usually referred to as a 'major', itself generally a synonym for a corporation. The quality of independence is often celebrated because of a posited distance between itself and the undesirable values associated with the production of music in its most rationalized form – what is called here corporate cultural capitalism. The music industry, like other culture industries such as film and publishing, has in the twentieth century undergone a pronounced and increasingly globalized concentration of ownership and control (Mattelart, 1979; Schiller, 1969; Williams, 1968) and a commensurate increase in the size and complexity of its constituent organizations. This development has produced a negative response among those cultural producers and consumers who see the corporation as representing the triumph of profiteering, instrumentalism, control and manipulation over music making, romanticism, artistic freedom and unmanaged pleasure. In contrasting independents and majors, the former's apologists (such as Gillett, 1971) do not necessarily see the 'indies' as entirely insulated from capitalist practice, but rather suggest the possibility that, by operating on a different scale, according to different motives and under different social relations of production, independent aesthetics and politics will be more 'authentic' and progressive than is possible under a corporate regime.

A bipolar structure of major and independent does not, however, exist in any empirical sense. A complex weave of licensing and distribution arrangements creates a high degree of interdependence between major and independent companies, while in the non-corporate sector the scale of companies may range from substantial organizations whose turnover is measured in millions (such as the formerly independent Virgin Records) to 'backyard' and 'garage' concerns, with several grades of company size in between. Qualitative distinctions may also be made within the corporate world itself, as is evident in the recent court case between the pop star George Michael and Sony Music. Michael wished to terminate his contract with the company on the grounds that, when in 1988 the Japanese Sony Corporation took over the American CBS major with which he had previously signed, the company became less warmly personal and artistically sympathetic. As Ellison and

Donegan (1993: 5) describe it, 'Michael believes that he has been treated as software rather than a creative artist' by Sony, as opposed, presumably, to more humane treatment by CBS. Court cases of this kind invoke a considerable degree of anti-corporatism and anti-capitalism in pop (and especially in rock), re-tracing the commerce–culture debate along the lines of the small, personal and committed versus the large, 'anonymous' and detached.

While the rhetorical claims on behalf of majors and independents need to be examined and tested, the split between them has been important in fashioning histories of the emergence of post-war youth music and its industry. Charlie Gillett (1971: 15), for example, in *The Sound of the City*, his classic history of the emergence of rock and roll in the United States in the early 1950s, states that:

> Faced with a continuous broadcast diet of melodrama/sentiment/trivia over the major radio networks, the more adventurous members of that popular music audience had been twiddling their dials in search of something better for several years. And in many areas of the country they had been rewarded with one and sometimes two specialist stations, playing either country and western music or rhythm and blues, each recorded mainly by independent companies.

For Gillett (1971: 78), the difference in the quality of the musical output of the majors and independents was stark:

> The overwhelming majority of both the best (musically and critically) and the most successful (commercially) rock 'n' roll records were produced by independent companies.

In recounting the development of the popular music industry from the birth of rock and roll in the United States in the mid-1950s, most versions trace the transformation of the production of pop from its original institutional setting in small-scale, regional independent companies to its domination by vast, multinational conglomerates (Denisoff, 1975; Palmer, 1977). Commentators on rock music frequently develop this critique by arguing that rock's shrinking organizational base (that is, its conditions of material production) has had serious ramifications for its output (its quality as a cultural product). For example, Gillett (1971: 308) contrasts the vibrant rock and roll period of 1954–58 to the 'blight of the late sixties [which was] "bubblegum", music planned entirely as a product, not as anybody's art'. Similarly, Chapple and Garofalo (1977) point to a higher level of creativity amongst independent producers, while Peterson and Berger (1975) propose a structured association between competition, diversity and creativity in which periods of 'consolidation' and 'concentration' under the majors are intermittently broken up by critical periods of creativity analogous to the crises of paradigms which recur in the natural sciences (as proposed by Kuhn, 1970). According to this 'pro-independence' line, bursts of creativity occur when the audience becomes increasingly disaffected with the tendency of the majors to minimize risk and uncertainty by turning out standardized, bland and formulaic musical fare. Innovative musical material, it is claimed by Gillett (1971; 1974), Laing (1969) and others, emanates from the small companies

which are prepared to take risks and which sometimes manage to break the
major companies' market domination of popular music. While it is usually
conceded that the majors will ultimately regroup and utilize their superior
resource base to dominate in whatever new style has been developed by the
independents, it is argued by apologists for the independents that the majors'
control is neither total nor entirely secure. From such perspectives, musical
credentials are problematic when control is in the hands of corporations or
transnational conglomerates rather than independent enterprises. This distinction between majors and independents is both political and aesthetic.
Indeed, affiliation to a major is seen as politically undesirable even where the
music itself may claim to be more radical and challenging than that produced by many independents. Gillett (1971: 309), in following the ebb and
flow of the fortunes of majors and independents, argues that by the late sixties the majors had triumphed and that this development heralded the
collapse of rock's political credibility, so that:

> While the contrived bubblegum sound was recorded by independent companies,
> rock was almost entirely under the control of majors, confirming the impression
> that, despite the vaunted political implications of the music, this was a formulated
> product, whose audience was often more, rather than less, gullible than the bub-
> blegum and soul audiences they sometimes belittled.

Lydon (1970: 54) is similarly critical of the apparent disjunction between an
avowedly revolutionary cultural form and its operation in the service of
capitalism:

> While the White Panthers talk of 'total assault' upon the culture by any means nec-
> essary, including rock and roll, dope and fucking in the streets, Billboard, the music
> trade paper, announces with pride that in 1968 the record industry became a billion
> dollar business.

Peterson and Berger's (1975: 160) study of the number of firms and their
share in the American pop singles market reveals that the four-firm concentration ratio (the market share of the four leading companies) rose from 38
per cent in 1966 to 51 per cent in 1970, a period when rock music's connection
to political dissent (through the anti-Vietnam War and hippie movements) is
normally regarded as reaching its apogee. Chapple and Garofalo (1977: 92)
also argue that independent record companies did not play a major part in
the production of rock music in the late sixties, thereby presenting the paradox of ideological rebellion and industrial orthodoxy. The enhanced
opportunities for corporate involvement in the popular music industry, it is
argued from such a position, had the effect of destroying the diversity, radicalism and 'authenticity' of popular youth song, so that the cyclical swings
between concentration and standardization fail to disturb the orderly
rhythms of corporate control under conditions of 'repressive tolerance'
(Marcuse, 1972).

The late sixties seem anomalous when appraised within the analytical
framework of concentration/standardization and diversification/creativity.
Peterson and Berger (1975), whose argument is reliant on the model, resort to

describing the period as one of paradoxical reconcentration coupled with diversity. A contrary position, which views the independents in a rather less favourable light and which explicitly links creativity to corporate resources, was advanced in the immediate pre-punk era by Frith (1976). Reviewing what he saw as the undistinguished musical output of the independents in the seventies, Frith (1976: 42) challenged the independence-equals-creativity 'orthodoxy' of Gillett and other anti-major rock critics:

> One of the few laws of pop sociology says that the quality of the music is in direct proportion to the number of record companies producing it . . . But the emergence of the new pop labels in Britain over the last few years has not improved anything. I admire Rak and the early UK, Bell and Magnet, for their success, but in musical terms their output is rubbish, lowest common denominator pop, they've hardly issued a single between them that I've kept. The same goes for all those independent producers, these days people go out on their own not because they can't make it with the majors, but because they can make it only too well – what's at issue, isn't taste but profit. And so my new law goes: the bigger the company, the more likely it is to sign someone original, issue something interesting.

Frith, therefore, inverted the equation by suggesting that independents (or at least those independent record companies he is addressing) are (in the highly judgemental terms of the times) likely to produce less worthy music than the majors. This argument runs counter to the more usual assumption that it is the majors that are more economically oriented, stressing instead the profit imperative of entrepreneurial cultural capitalism among the British pre-'punk independents' (Frith, 1981). Harker (1980) takes this point further by arguing that the independents may often be more exploitative of their artists than the majors. Unlike Gillett, who regards the emergence of rock and roll among the independents of the American south as a sign of their openness and innovation, Harker judges this development as little more than racial exploitation and sharp business practice which actively colluded with the majors. He says, for example, of Elvis Presley's first label:

> Like any other so-called independent record company, Sun Records survived by having a captive local market, by doing one-off recordings for individuals (such as the job which first brought Presley into the studio), and by selling masters of promising material to the majors. 'For most black artists, in the early 1950s, there was no place in the South they could go to record. The nearest place where they made so-called 'race' records . . . was Chicago, and most of them didn't have the money or the time to make the trip' (quoted in Hopkins, 'Elvis'). They were, therefore, at the mercy of men like Sam Phillips, as indeed were the majority of hillbilly artists. (p. 55)

The essential rationale behind American record production in the 1950s is presented here as being pragmatic and commercial. The innovations of the independents are viewed, therefore, in much less heroic terms. As Frith (1981: 157) states:

> In the heyday of small R and B and rock 'n' roll labels in the 1950s, the impetus came from unmet consumer demand: jukeboxes, radio stations, and stores all wanted music the majors weren't making, and the object was to find, record, and

sell that music (financially, the independents probably treated their musicians worse than the majors would have done).

Harker (1980: 55) and Gillett (1971: 78) similarly point out the entrepre-neurial and opportunistic motives and operations of the American independents, while Wallis and Malm (1984: 111) observe, when comparing the operations in the Third World of large transnational record companies with smaller independent companies, that 'Small is not always beautiful. Some local companies can be more evil to local musicians than the trans-nationals.'

This dispute over the respective musical quality, politics and ethics of inde-pendents and majors is a clear inflection of the culture–commerce debate, in this case setting up a distinction between cruel and caring cultural capitalism. It reveals an under-theorization of the relationships between the independent and major spheres which tends both to de-historicize and to polarize them into homogeneous opposing camps. The most straightforward perspective, directly or indirectly theorized, presents independents and majors as essen-tially inimical in both competitive market and in philosophical terms. An alternative perspective, which rejects the idea of such endemic struggle, is that independents are largely serviceable to the majors – what Keil (1966) calls 'fattening frogs for snakes'. Gillett (1974: 269) also acknowledges this prac-tice, describing, for example, how the former independent company Atlantic did not expand its United Kingdom branch in the early seventies, 'apparently preferring to wait for other British companies to go through the teething troubles of putting a first album together, and then paying the asking price if it sounded good'. In conceptualizing independent and major enterprises as other than necessarily competing institutions, it is possible to see the former functioning as 'nurseries' which enable the major record companies to extract from the field only those acts which have been market 'pre-tested'. Indeed, Vignolle (1980: 83–4) regards this arrangement as a 'structural duality' which is beneficial to all sectors of the music industry:

> Far from being accidental or residual the existence of 'independent' producers is backed up by the integrated firms, for the small firms would be unable to survive without the willingness of the large firms to act as subcontractors. This relationship is by no means an indication that the large firms dominate or maintain unilateral control over the small firms, but rather that they are mutually interdependent. The small firms are not at the mercy of the large firms on which they depend for the manufacturing and marketing of their products; the conditions they obtain are actually favourable to them in terms of turnover, their net profit margin is often higher than that of the integrated firms. The large firms, in turn, draw extra prof-its from distributing the products of outside customers, whom they support because they can neither supplant them in their own domain nor turn their backs to them for fear of strengthening the position of their own competitors or else of opening the door for the entry of fresh rivals. Socio-historical analyses have shown that the number of small producers and their share in the market can vary noticeably over a long period depending on the prevailing socio-cultural and musical circumstances. But whatever the circumstances may be, this duality within the record industry has the character of a permanent structure, regardless of the variability of its outer forms and extent.

In this account of a symbiotic relationship between majors and independents – what in contemporary corporate jargon is called 'synergy' (Negus, 1992: 4) – a seemingly eternal struggle gives way to a functional interdependence (Middleton, 1990: 39). It is apparent, then, that the 'major–minor' split may be characterized as representing a linkage founded on conflict, subordination, mutual reliance and many positions in between, just as their respective output may be evaluated as superior, inferior or qualitatively varied. While clearly these different 'ways of seeing' are substantially governed by different vantage points (for example, of the musician, record company executive, fan, music journalist), the objects under investigation do not fall into convenient and static polarities. As Wallis and Malm (1984: 91) point out, 'the majors are not homogeneous colossi made up of totally programmed human nuts and bolts', and the view of the independents as playing David to the corporate Goliath: 'is too simplistic. There are the large and the small, but except in extreme cases, size doesn't tell us much about the exact relationship involved' (p. 109).

Analysts and rhetoricians, for purposes that are heuristic and strategic, tend necessarily to produce bipolar oppositions in representing an ensemble of relations which, strictly, obeys no conveniently dualistic logic. In conducting a critique of contending positions that portrays mobile cultural practices and aesthetics as unproblematically determined by organizational size, form and motive, it is possible, however, to overcompensate and so to underestimate the degree to which such factors do clearly have a major impact on what is produced, by and for whom. As was argued above, while it is not possible simply to read off a ready-made set of meanings from economic and organizational relations and forms, it is important to demonstrate how structures, practices and the values ascribed to them interact. The material and the ideal interpenetrate, therefore, in a manner that does not self-evidently privilege economic, organizational or cultural factors. To do justice to the complex interactions of majors and independents demands an analysis which is not preoccupied with finding the singular causal, explanatory mechanism underlying all popular cultural production, and yet is not perversely dismissive of those extra-textual phenomena that have a considerable bearing on the manufacture, communication and consumption of rock music. As Andrew Goodwin (1992: 166) has argued in his study of music television, attempts to handle the concept of ideology in cultural studies have increasingly displayed a sterile polarization of perspectives which has worked to:

> conflate political economy and cultural pessimism, so that any attempt to understand contexts of production (and the wider issues concerning how political and economic forces shape these contexts) is thought to be reductionist (not giving sufficient autonomy to the materiality of the text), disempowering of the audience, and elitist (implying a link between economic analysis and personal taste). Reversing this logic, text and audience analysis has increasingly been associated with finding sites of resistance in popular culture (thus, the loss of ideological critique).

The approach I am adopting attempts to combat this analytical divergence by appreciating more comprehensively and dialectically the mutually articulating processes which constitute cultural production. The different ways in which rock production is managed and the varying relationships between organizations and people represent a shifting (but not random) set of historical conditions. At specific moments or conjunctures, considerable flux and re-positioning of elements can be demonstrated, often with quite unexpected outcomes. The period of the late seventies and early eighties in Britain can be assessed as an era in which a surprising fragility was displayed in the seemingly solid structures and predictable routines of rock production and consumption. It is not accidental that the relationships between major and independent record companies were central to the articulation and resolution of a crisis in rock economics, culture and politics. It is useful, then, to examine this transformative period in rock history, but first some theoretical and conceptual elaboration of the meaning of independence is required.

Indicators of organizational difference

It is possible to select one key indicator of an independent/major distinction – for example, scale – and to treat it as a defining characteristic. However, the mutability and diversity of institutions involved in rock production and distribution make such an approach unsatisfactory in accounting for the constant ebb and flow of expansion, contraction, diversification and concentration. The categorization offered here is neither conclusive nor exclusive, but reflects the tendency of key indicators to be consistently associated in the form of a pattern or configuration. Four 'economic' measures of the major/independent division (ownership, scale, integration and market share) help to give some conception of typical differences between majors and independents. Rock is industrially communicated culture which by various means is created, translated into particular forms, distributed and sold. Raymond Williams (1968: 31) notes that the two major trends in the modern history of communications are the 'remarkable expansion of audiences' and a concomitant development in which:

> The ownership of the means of communication, old and new, has passed or is passing, in large part, to a kind of financial organization unknown in early periods, and with important resemblances to the major forms of ownership in general industrial production. The methods and attitudes of capitalist business have established themselves near the centre of communications.

This corporate domination of the communications industry is frequently identified by sociologists as the process of concentration, integration and diversification (Ryan, 1991). We might, therefore, suggest that the major/independent structural opposition lies in the contrast between corporate or conglomerate ownership and what may be termed entrepreneurial ownership patterns. In the case of the former, responsibilities such as financial support and executive decision making lie within a bureaucratic corporate structure in which the institutions of rock production and distribution are divisions of the organization, rather than comprising the entire structure itself. In contrast, independents tend to be 'specialist' enterprises which are involved solely or predominantly in the musical field. This distinction may be illustrated by pointing to the extra-musical commitments of those companies regarded as 'majors'. Harker (1980: 88), for example, notes how, by the late seventies, Britain's largest record company, EMI, was also involved in films, computers, guided weapons, printing equipment and many other commercial activities, while also pointing to the (then) American music corporation CBS's substantial involvement in the defence field alongside its music 'portfolio'. Similarly, Chapple and Garofalo (1977: 203) indicate the extensive extra-musical involvement of the American major RCA in the seventies and describe the takeover of Warner Brothers by 'the Kinney Corporation, a funeral and cleaning services conglomerate'. These multi-operational, multi-divisional conglomerates may be distinguished from companies which have a largely singular function – the production and sale of rock music. Of course, such a distinction is not absolute and is subject to change (witness the movement of the Virgin music retail and record company into wider leisure activities and, ultimately, into transatlantic air travel, only later to sell off its musical operation to EMI), but it remains a useful indicator of institutional form in the rock music industry. The broad separation of monopoly/corporate and competitive capital has clear ramifications for the structure of the industry. One such is the scale of the operation.

Recorded rock and pop are produced in different quantities by institutions of different proportions and characters. This variation in organizational dimension is often ignored in critiques of the corporate 'dominance' of the music industry. In Britain, for example, there emerged in the late seventies a plethora of small batch releases (often in quantities of no more than 1,000 units). This scale of production can be readily contrasted with the 'break-even' figure of 23,000 copies for singles and albums described at the time by the British Phonographic Industry (1979: 140) in its role as representative of 100 of the larger record companies then operating in Britain. The quantity produced and the projected break-even sales figure is, then, a useful though not absolutely reliable yardstick of major/independent status. Small-batch production, involving a relatively low capital outlay by enterprises with commensurately low overheads, inevitably has a far lower break-even figure on sales. The more modest infrastructure of non-corporate enterprises does not, unlike its corporate counterpart, require a constant stream of 'mega hits' to underwrite high overheads under conditions where only one in nine singles and one in sixteen albums is profitable (British Phonographic Industry, 1979: 140). In the late seventies and early eighties, a period when the aforementioned 'punk independents' were in vogue and before the widespread availability of digital sampling technology, it was possible in countries like Britain (where relatively cheap recording, cutting, pressing, labelling and distributing arrangements could be made) 'to press 500 records, sell them and cover all your costs' (*Grapevine*, 1980: 19). Similarly, Wallis and Malm (1984: 158) reveal how a British independent rock band with slightly greater resources and ambitions could in the early eighties break even on a (vinyl) LP record by selling just over 4,000 records with a total outlay of £7,200, while Lash and Urry (1994: 120) note that, at the end of the eighties, it was possible for a rock group to construct a functioning home studio and issue 2,000 copies of a single record for a total of £4,000.

These broad differences between large/medium-sized companies and very small, often 'cottage' organizations demonstrate how the former have been reliant on selling large quantities of recorded music in an uncertain 'task environment' (Hirsch, 1970) in which most musical products will not provide a return on investment. The result is an impetus to generate a widely spread 'product line' in which a few successful (in market terms) items cross-subsidize the many more which are unsuccessful. Independent enterprises are rarely willing or able to produce musical commodities in such profusion, and for this reason tend to rely on a smaller 'product' range, the profitability of which can be achieved at much lower levels of turnover. While such differences should be represented as a continuum rather than as an absolute break, the level of output, total costs (both fixed and variable), break-even figures and the size and quantity of overheads are all useful indicators in differentiating major and independent enterprises – as are degrees of horizontal and vertical integration. Horizontal integration, briefly, describes the processes of merger, takeover, subsidiary expansion and so on which extend the influence of large corporations (and sometimes smaller enterprises) in a given field of economic activity. Vertical integration refers to the level of control established over each stage of production, distribution, retail and 'product exploitation'. The post-war popular music industry has seen several cycles of integration. Chapple and Garofalo (1977: 83), for example, describe the increasing incidence of 'vertical mergers' in America in the sixties thus:

> Vertical mergers allowed companies to keep middleman [*sic*] profits for themselves, and to control the selling as well as the manufacturing end of the industry. These mergers often had a defensive, snowballing effect. Other manufacturers moved to protect themselves from their competitor's [*sic*] monopolies by buying outlets of their own – distribution companies in the case of manufacturers, rack-jobbing firms or retail chains in the case of distributors.

More recently, a series of global mergers has seen more musical 'hardware' manufacturers like Sony become involved in the 'software' also sometimes referred to as music and musicians. At the same time, even the most entrepreneurial of the independents – such as Virgin and Island in Britain and Tamla Motown in America – have been taken over by conglomerates and corporations. Complete control over the whole 'record cycle' (Vignolle, 1980), from production through recording and manufacturing to distribution and retail, has been strategically important in the quest for market dominance. This economic strategy was pursued in the 'Fordist' phase of rock's industrial development, where scale and organizational stability were regarded as the prerequisites for global power in the cultural marketplace, although, as is discussed below, in recent years smaller and more flexible production units have emerged which are outside formal, bureaucratic commercial organizations under the regime of 'post-Fordism'. The level of resource command required for an organization to achieve complete or even substantial integration is in any event the preserve of only a few large corporations. For this reason, a pronounced structural polarization has occurred between the so-called 'Big Five' multinational music corporations and nationally, regionally and locally-based enterprises. The ability of the majors to exert power and influence over recording, manufacturing, distribution, promotion, publishing and retail means that independents often have to enter into contractual relations with the majors for these functions to be carried out. Indeed, as Wallis and Malm (1984: 109) argue, it is paradoxical that '*independents* are normally *dependent* on someone else'. 'Separatist' independent networks, such as the ironically named Cartel in Britain, were set up in the eighties in order to lessen this dependency and to circumvent the major distributors, but these are necessarily limited in their impact and, as in the case of the above-mentioned Cartel, prone to disintegration under the weight of under-capitalization and shifts in consumer preferences.

It is, finally, in calculations of market share that the depth and scope of the major/independent division is revealed. It can be illustrated by examining the four-firm ratio – that is, the share of the market of the leading four firms in the music industry. Establishing how many recorded musical products are actually sold is not a straightforward task, and independent sector sales are likely to be substantially underestimated in calculations of the size of the music market. Nonetheless, the collected sales statistics provide a useful record of the market power of a small number of large corporations in the popular music field, as is revealed by a consideration of estimated market shares in Britain during the period prior to, during and immediately following the rise of the 'punk independents' mentioned above and more fully discussed below.

Statistics from this period (taken from the British Phonographic Industry's *Yearbooks*) are particularly instructive because they cover, as noted above, the period when the 'independence movement' was emerging in the United Kingdom. The four-firm ratio did not drop below 40 per cent for either singles or albums in the period 1972–83, with corporations such as EMI, CBS, WEA and Polydor consistently dominating the market. Several mergers were achieved and attempted at this time between Phonogram and Polygram, Polygram and Decca and, later, WEA and Polygram. Although this was also a period when the accustomed rise in record/tapes sales was slowing (ultimately to fall by 1980), the statistics reveal the high market share achieved by four (relatively 'stable') transnational corporations and also how this share declined after peaking in the late seventies. The leading company in 1979, EMI, had a 20 per cent share of the singles market and a 22 per cent share of the full-priced album market, with 15 and 17 companies (respectively) accounting for 94 per cent of the 'singles' and 'long player' markets, leaving only 6 per cent for 'Others'. By 1983, the (then) leading company (CBS) had only a 15 per cent share of the singles market and a 16 per cent share of the albums and cassettes market, while the share of the top 15 companies had fallen to 85 per cent for singles and to 82 per cent for the 17 main producers of albums. These figures reveal not only the heavily concentrated nature of the popular music industry (a condition that persists today, if less dramatically) and the high market shares of the leading companies, but also, in the period under examination, a downward movement. By 1982, the remarkable expansion of independents meant that they had taken over '18 per cent of British record sales' (Leonard and Shannon, 1984: 27). Thus, although the independents had clearly made an impression on the market structure of the music industry, they still lagged far behind the majors in market share. In view of the estimate that by 1982 there were over 4,500 independent record and tape labels in the UK alone, the concentration of market power in a small number of multinational musical corporations is readily apparent (although much independent output and sales went 'officially' unrecorded).

A number of other criteria help to delineate a broad distinction between majors and independents. I have defined majors as predominantly multi- or transnational in character. Independents, however, tend to be national or indeed local enterprises, servicing delimited areas of 'targeted' taste groupings. Similarly, while the majors have the capacity to produce a diverse range of music and to service mass markets, independents are likely to be more highly specialized and coherent in musical output. This closer relationship of independents to a narrower range of audiences has garnered a good deal of critical approval. Wallis and Malm (1984), for example, suggest that independents and majors can often (particularly in small countries) be located on a commercial continuuum, with the latter more profit-oriented and concerned with high sales turnover at the expense of musical quality. While, as discussed earlier, there is no necessary difference in cultural and ideological orientation between those operating within major and independent organizations, it is only to be expected that small, spatially-fixed record companies will display greater commitment to local styles and identities. Majors and independents are also usually distinguished in terms of the highly professionalized division of labour which exists in the case of the former, which may be contrasted with the relative 'amateurism' of the latter. Similar contrasts may also be made in terms of the privileged access to high technology and 'hardware' of the majors. It is necessary to monitor these differences between majors and independents because, as Negus (1992: 16) points out, there is a strong incentive for majors, given the resilience of anti-corporate commercialism in rock, to disguise their ownership and control of many nominally 'independent' record companies and artists.

I have attempted in the above discussion to establish a broad, relative distinction between those rock institutions which can be roughly classified as major and independent. This analysis can produce no more than ideal typifications which empirically reveal a considerable degree of convergence, change and complexity. It is, nonetheless, important to recall and record that the institutions of rock are not all as monolithically 'mass' based as is frequently suggested in accounts of the rock music industry, while the independent/major distinction is pivotal in a discursive formation which, it is argued below, has its own specific institutional and rhetorical history. If we examine the British experience in what is generally called the punk and imme-diate post-punk eras, some understanding is gained of the conditions under which different organizational forms emerge, collide and interact in rock and pop.

Cycles in rock production: the British independent 'moment'

Demonstrated above were both increasing levels of independent production and a concomitant prominence of the concept of independence in Britain in the late seventies and early eighties. These developments, at least *prima facie*, run counter to theories of the inevitability of (the fundamentally Fordist) dominance of a global music industry. This period saw an efflorescence of independent activity in a depressed overall musical market. Denselow (1980: 8), having noted the crisis of the British record industry due to falling sales, indicates the expansion of independent record production at a time of music (and wider) industry recession:

> Yet there are still record labels, distributors and even record stores where it's claimed that business is actually booming – as long as you have 'an ear for the streets' . . . Rock music has always thrived on a mixture of idealism and anarchy, and the financial problems and corporate politics of the majors has [*sic*] given the 'indies' a tremendous boost. They have already built up a sizeable underground market that has never fully registered in official sales figures. *Music Week*'s latest market survey prepared from statistics from the British Market Research Bureau gives 12.6 per cent of the market of 'Others' (which includes the independents). But the independents would claim that some of their records now out-sell the majors' hits, though this is rarely reflected in the charts.

By 1984, the estimated component of the British market attributed to 'Others' had, as noted above, risen to over 18 per cent (Leonard and Shannon, 1984: 27). There are, of course, considerable difficulties encoun-tered in accurately estimating the levels of sales of independent (and, indeed all other) records, a position which is exacerbated by their lack of represen-tation in or influence on industry organizations (in this case the British Phonographic Industry). However, John Bassett (1982: 5) of the (now defunct) Independent Labels' Association estimated in the early eighties that '1500 indie labels account for at least 40% of the records released in the UK' and about 4,500 companies registered at that time with the Mechanical Copyright and Protection Society. The 'grass-roots' magazine *Zig-Zag* strug-gled to monitor and record this constantly shifting independent scene by issuing a series of frequently-updated Independent Label Catalogues which demonstrated high levels of formation, dissolution, recombination and pro-liferation of independent labels and acts. If the precise economic significance of the independents is difficult to gauge, their centrality in the discourse of rock music at key moments can be readily demonstrated. In the period in question, articles concerning independents appeared in a range of British media, including the mainstream daily press (such as Denselow's *Guardian* feature quoted above) and the national Sunday newspapers. A significant article in the *Sunday Times Magazine* by Cynthia Rose (1981), for example, stated that:

> Up until 1977, our nations' juke-boxes were stocked by the record companies known as 'the majors' – conglomerates whose modus operandi was transatlantic, monolithic, and inflexible . . . Three years later, Britain can boast an entire network of independent labels.

Coverage of independents in the non-musical press was largely garnered from that of the weekly music press, which championed the expansion of independents. The *New Musical Express* (*NME*), in particular, championed and celebrated independent rock music in spite of the comparative lack of advertising revenue from that source. Paul Morley and Adrian Thrills (1979: 23), in a fairly representative passage of the time, stated that:

> As the powerful established record companies sink ever deeper into 'crisis', small independent record labels reach unprecedented heights of activity, and success, providing the major labels with tomorrow's signings and the rest of us with some of the best and most radical rock music of the times . . . The majors' control of the new music – which eventually must come – will be nowhere near as total and as strict as they're used to. A real shift has occurred.

This position, which was rather less quixotic than many adopted in that period, was also prescient. The majors did regroup, but do not now, at least in Britain, exercise the degree of market dominance they achieved in the period from the mid-fifties to the mid-seventies. The greater fluidity, freer market access and looser division of labour which fostered and accompanied the rise of the independents, it should be noted, is symbolized by Morley's own move from journalistic mediator and interpreter of rock's stylistic trends to founder of ZTT, a label that was successful in the eighties with acts such as The Art of Noise and Frankie Goes to Hollywood.

Much of the coverage of independent labels during the 'heyday' of the British independents did propose a more dramatic economic, cultural and ideological shift, particularly in their literary equivalents – 'fanzines' – which emerged as small-scale, locally-based music rock papers and magazines and were established as alternatives to the major music papers (such as the IPC-owned *NME*). For example, the fanzine *Common Knowledge* (1980: 18) remarked in an editorial that:

> The single most important aspect of an independent label, the one thing that none of the major labels can supply is total freedom. Freedom to control a band's output and approach . . . On both sides of the coin headway is being made. There is the non-compromising attitude of bands such as the Mekons (only signing a 3 album contract with Virgin as opposed to the normal 8 album contract) and The Specials with their own 2-Tone label, entirely run by themselves yet funded by Chrysalis. On the other hand, the success of the debut Stiff Little Fingers album on the Rough Trade/Rigid Digits Label has shown that it is possible to break through into the Charts on a small label. Now is the time that more discourse is needed on this

subject. The Gang of 4 ought to reveal to all exactly <u>what</u> their contract with EMI is. Individuals and bands everywhere – get together and converse.

The independent ethos was also widely promoted through publications designed to be of practical use for musicians and other music industry operatives. In the *Music Business Yearbook*, for example, Gee (1981: 9) stated that:

> At the beginning of the 80s, as the transnationals fight for an increasing share of a rapidly decreasing market, the only way forward is by way of quality, originality and widely varying styles of music. The new independent labels, with a greater intimacy between artist and label, promise the most exciting development in pop music for twenty years, and as artists realise their artistic integrity is more important than their commerciality, independents tread where the majors had forgotten there was a path.

Leonard and Shannon (1984: 27) are similarly favourable to the expansion of independent recording activity in the late seventies, describing it as 'a backlash against the virtual monopoly of modern music by a handful of major record companies'. Such assertions concerning the genealogy of the 'independent revolution' and its impact on the structure of the music industry are legion in the journalistic and 'trade' literature of the period, while in the electronic media, independent record production also received similar (albeit limited) exposure. In radio, the late evening programmes of John Peel on the BBC were important showcases for independent music. In television, the broadcast of a BBC *Grapevine* programme on independent rock was accompanied by the publication of a free booklet (more appropriately described as a 'how to' independent record label manual) compiled by the pioneering independent rock group Scritti Politti. In the scholarly field, the writings of sociologists like Dave Laing (1978) and Simon Frith (1981) also endorsed independent rock. Frith (1981: 156), in recanting his earlier 'pop law', states that:

> At a time when British rock companies were in trouble, the punk independents, however small, had the authority of their own idealism. They moved attention back from the markets to musicians, to the way music works to symbolize and focus communities. They articulated an explicitly anti-professional attitude to record making, a concern for music as a mode of survival rather than as a means to profit. They brought a new tension into rock practice, a new concept of ambition, a new challenge, particularly for those musicians – the majority – who continue to sign with majors, to abandon local love for mass success.

This interpretation of independent activity as providing an explicit or implicit critique of the rock music industry and, by extension, of broader social conditions under late capitalism meant that the 'punk independents' were not seen as simply re-asserting entrepreneurial practice in the industry (as many argued of the 1950s American independents), but as questioning the foundation of the culture industry itself. It is evident, then, that the idea of independence, which as we have seen was already imbedded in the discourse of rock and established in its institutional structures, professional ideologies and practices, became prominent at a time when many critical media theorists were emphasizing the economic dominance of the music corporations. The emergence of independent singles and albums charts in the weekly music papers and the establishment of a nationwide network of independent record/tape production, distribution and retail in the early eighties at least demonstrated that the stairway to corporate heaven was not an escalator. The British independent moment (which, it should be stressed, was not simply replicated in other countries) questions some of the more mechanical theories of unbroken and unstoppable transnational corporate dominance. It does not represent the triumph of culture over commerce – such a formulation is theoretically and politically naive – but nor does it demonstrate the ineluctable ascendancy of capital over art. Instead, it is a salient reminder of the continued contestation of the practice and meaning of cultural production under capitalism.

To conceive, as do many cultural critics, 'units of rock' as flowing uninterrupted through a series of established corporate task environments gives to the rock industry an apparent permanence and a uni-directional, functionalist logic which belie the more chaotic (material and cultural) struggle which typifies the making and re-making of rock culture. To a considerable degree critical sociologists and cultural studies scholars have displayed and replayed the commercialist biases of business economists, concentrating on large-scale formal organizations and more easily measured economic and cultural activity. Subcultural theory has, all too commonly, lacked interest in the more self-conscious institutions of cultural production, preferring to concentrate instead on 'grounded' mediations of established power structures (for example, Willis, 1990). It is, however, in the complex and multifarious relations between cultural producers, 'relayers' and consumers (many of whom themselves occupy multiple roles) that rock is made manifest. Outlining the importance of the major/independent split in rock discourse and its historical significance at specific moments does not, however, explain why and how such organizational differentiation occurs within the rock music industry. It is necessary, therefore, to address the conditions under which stability, change, transformation and re-establishment occur.

Conditions of change

The most common explanations given for the great increase in independent rock activity in the late seventies (as discussed above) concern 'consumer' dissatisfaction with the output of the majors and the spread of production capability following the development of cheap recording technology. Denselow (1980: 8), for example, states that:

> the advantage of the independents was their awareness of stylistic change and their willingness to follow and encourage the rapid twists of musical fashion, and [they] don't rely on the fast-disappearing vast profits from the seventies' best-sellers. According to Steve Melhuish, who runs the fast expanding Bonaparte chain around London 'the majors are slow, dull and 18 months behind what is going on. They

should have realised what happened in '76 when music changed.' Many of the records that he stocks are by the 'indies', the independent labels like Stiff, Rough Trade or Factory, and Melhuish predicts the growth of a massive independent scene.

This is a familiar argument which echoes the cyclical theories which propose that there is a periodic crisis in the process of 'symbol production' engendered by over-concentration and standardization. In extending the deployment of Kuhn's (1970) theory of scientific innovation (or perhaps returning it to its origins in the history of artistic movements), we might suggest that, just as 'normal science' undergoes a 'paradigm crisis' on occasions, so 'normal rock' as transmitted through the majors was challenged by comparatively marginal enterprises which were prepared to make and sell what to the majors were risky styles and uneconomic quantities of rock music. Yet public demand for 'alternative' rock through different channels is not, in itself, a sufficient condition for its production. Such an explanation is founded on a functionalist consumer sovereignty argument, representing rock as a self-correcting industrial system based on market equilibrium. It is necessary for circumstances to be favourable if independents, with their weak resource base, are at any time to do more than operate in highly-localized environments or to service the majors' product-testing requirements. Where production capacity is limited and demand is strong, the majors are likely to monopolize facilities and so make it difficult for independents to have their records manufactured. For example, Frith (1978: 113) points out that the vinyl shortage of 1973 (caused by the oil crisis) left many independents temporarily without access to raw materials, while the majors could rely on their long-term contracts with petro-chemical companies. Similarly, priorities in manufacturing and distribution schedules favour record companies with greater 'throughput'. Establishing a high degree of vertical and horizontal integration, or, to put it another way, an intensified penetration of conglomerate capital into the rock production process, will in times of market expansion constitute a huge commercial advantage. The corporate share of profits from a global business which until the mid-seventies was growing faster than almost any other (Chapple and Garofalo, 1977: 172) was immense. However, control of fixed capital can be disadvantageous in periods of consumer recession, when the considerable spare productive capacity in corporate-owned record plants and recording studios facilitates the entry into the productive process of those comparatively small enterprises formerly restricted or excluded. The low level of capitalization and institutional flexibility of independents may, in these circumstances, enable them to get a tenuous foothold in the marketplace.

The majors, with their considerable fixed and variable costs and their need to generate large-scale sales to offset them, displayed considerable vulnerability and took substantial losses at the end of the seventies and in the early eighties. As Hardy (1984: 7) notes, in the period 1978–83 trade deliveries in Britain of vinyl singles fell by 17.4 per cent and of albums by a huge 36.8 per cent (although there was a large, but insufficiently compensatory, 73.7 per cent rise in the trade deliveries of audio cassette tapes). The outcome was that existing jobs in the manufacture, distribution and administration of recorded music were almost halved. The sense of crisis among the larger record companies in this period was dramatically expressed by Peter Scaping (British Phonographic Industry, 1982: 7) in pleading in a music trade publication that 'Every reader should bear in mind that the information describes an industry which is threatened as no other. It may have an image of affluence which is a relic of past decades.' The problems of the majors – over-capacity, falling sales, rising costs, high overheads and organizational rigidity – were not so much shared by the independents as exploited by them. Indeed, Hardy (1984: 10) noted that 'the new independents took advantage of cracks in the monolithic structures of manufacturing and distribution to carry the new music of Britain to its audience without the assistance of either the transnational or the domestic media'. This lesson was well learnt by the music corporations which, as is discussed below, imitated the independents' flexibility and engaged in increasingly fluid contractual arrangements for the provision of a wide range of productive, licensing and distributive services.

There are two kinds of development being described in these analyses of the condition of the British rock music industry in this period. One is limited in that it may be referred to as the entry of independents into the rock marketplace, utilizing (that is, purchasing) the majors' facilities of manufacture, recording and distribution at times of spare capacity. The other development goes further because it represents the 'seizure' of the means of musical production, however limited and temporary, by small enterprises which then set up alternative or parallel institutional networks. The extent to which the operations of the independents may be regarded as relatively permanent and oppositional features of the music industry is, as we have seen, subject to contestation. Whatever evaluative position is adopted, the mere fact of organizational re-alignment is insufficient to explain why the idea and practice of independence re-surfaced with such force in the period 1978–83. Certainly, some propitious market conditions did exist for the 'independent renaissance', in particular the increasing availability of cheap recording technology, which, when combined with a widespread consumer recession, inhibited the seemingly inexorable expansion of corporate power over the making of rock music. Yet economic and technological factors cannot solely explain why large numbers of records and tapes were produced for limited audiences in this period, or why there existed the aforementioned gulf between the music of the majors and that of 'the street'. If the independents were simply holding their share of a shrinking market and producing rock music which was identical in form to that purveyed by the majors and with similar motivations, then the development would be of little more than passing interest. At the level of market economics, the gradual decline of the majors' market shares after a peak in the late seventies was significant, but this development reflected more than a simple re-distribution of sales to a larger number of companies. Trade deliveries of albums in Britain, for example, fell from a peak of 91.6 million units in 1975 to 54.3 million units in 1983 (a fall of 40.7 per cent), while singles, having peaked at 89.1 million units in 1979, had fallen to 74.0 million units in 1983 (a drop of 16.9 per cent). What needs to be explained, then, is not only whether conditions were favourable to the entry of the independents into the rock arena (and, in spite of greater availability of recording and manufacturing technology, the overall fall in production and sales suggests that they were not propitious), but also what differentiated the majors and independents in terms of the music they were producing. In other words, the shift in the economic balance of forces within the rock music industry was also a significant cultural and ideological transformation. Any explanation of the musical change in this period must, then, take account of the cultural rupture of punk.

The culture and economics of punk

The intimate connection between the independents and punk has been alluded to above. As Leonard and Shannon (1984: 27; see also Frith, 1981; Wallis and Malm, 1984) argue:

> It was the punk boom that really put the independents on their feet. It completely revitalised the flagging 70s music scene. They compensated for lack of money and experience with tremendous hard work, enthusiasm and a sense of adventure. By ignoring convention, doing things on their own terms rather than the major labels' terms, they rocked the music industry from top to bottom.

It is suggested here that punk had an important institutional effect in stimulating new arrangements and networks in the rock production process. It is further proposed that punk was influential in the whole rock music industry, even among those rock acts which did not sign up with an independent record label or which quickly signed to a major label. This is an important distinction because it is clearly the case that punk had wider ramifications than simply spawning a new independent network – indeed, many seminal punk and 'new wave' bands, like the Sex Pistols, The Clash and The Jam, signed to major record companies (respectively, EMI, CBS and Polydor). The influence of punk, then, should not be taken too literally as somehow immediately and uniformly translatable into rebellious action across the entire field of popular music. Punk should, rather, be regarded as providing an 'informing spirit' which challenged the then dominant rock values and practices from within a significantly dissenting 'structure of feeling'. The independent labels and punk style may even be judged as having, in a Weberian sense, an elective affinity, or, in neo-Marxist terms, a fundamental homology (of the kind suggested by Willis, 1978). Punk, as a musical style and rhetorical posture, was the cultural dynamic which overlay, directed and capitalized on the favourable structural conditions which made possible the (re)emergence of the independents. These features of punk are briefly traced below.

The material and cultural conditions of the mid-seventies out of which punk arose have been widely canvassed. Youth unemployment and alienation;

low-technological development; the remoteness, pretentiousness and high-technological obsession of rock musicians and their corporate record companies; the resurgence of situationism in forging alliances between bohemian and working-class youth in inner-city areas; and sundry other factors combined to produce a rock style that was nihilistic, minimalist, anti-corporate and, above all, devoted to the idea of do-it-yourself cultural production (Chambers, 1985; Frith and Horne, 1987; Hebdige, 1979; Laing, 1985; Marsh, 1977; Savage, 1991; Wicke, 1990). The inchoate anarchist political stance of the early punks fed upon a conception of musical production which was technically rudimentary and which repudiated a specialized division of cultural labour, and it was this attitudinal shift which provided the ideological foundation of independent record production. This rugged pragmatism, it should be noted, was as often a case of expediency as of ideological conviction – the means of record production were now available to those groups which did not or could not secure major record contracts. It is misleading to suggest, therefore, that the growth of the independents was simply due to the idealism (in both senses) of art for art's sake (see Chapters 3 and 4). The aetiology of 'rock independence' is complex – a highly interdependent combination of social, cultural, economic and political phenomena producing, over time and space, a range of disparate outcomes. The social malaise of seventies Britain, manifest in rising teenage unemployment and deepening alienation from the parliamentary democratic apparatus, fuelled and found expression in punk's dissident stance (as Stratton (1985) notes, punk in the USA was connected rather differently to the social formation). Furthermore, the very forces that perpetuated the concentration of ownership and control of rock music and that made entry into the industry difficult were also those which drove a wedge between an emergent 'amateurist' ethic and the specialization and high capitalization of so-called 'progressive' rock. In an early and influential article, Dave Laing (1978: 124) noted punk's hostility to the industrial, aesthetic and ideological status quo – an antagonism which took the form of:

> a challenge to the 'capital-intensive' production of music within the orbit of the multi-nationals, a rejection of the ideology of 'artistic excellence' which was influential among established musicians, and the aggressive injection of new subject-matter into popular song, much of which (including politics) had previously been taboo.

The argument here is that punk challenged how rock was organized, played and lyrically focused. It has often been pointed out (for example, by Hatch and Millward, 1987: 152; Moore, 1993: 127) that the form of rock music which was dominant prior to the inception of punk required an enormous investment in high technology which could only be funded by trans/multinational record companies. In such accounts, punk is presented as a reaction to the music of the likes of Emerson, Lake and Palmer, Yes and Rick Wakeman, music which, according to Coon (1977: 10, 13), 'smacks of higher education and technical expertise' and which 'uses an increasing amount of technical apparatus, has become increasingly quasi-orchestral and quotes liberally from the classics'. The 'progressive' rock music regarded as aesthetically dominant in the mid-seventies was widely portrayed as pompous (so-called 'pomp rock'), indulgent and distant both from its audience and from the pool of aspiring professional rock musicians who were increasingly intimidated by its exacting entry requirements. Punk was an overt reaction to this rock style in that it favoured simple and short rather than complicated and lengthy songs (that is, three-minute singles rather than long-playing albums) and, in its presentational codes, was rudimentary rather than sophisticated in its recording, marketing, packaging and performance (Savage, 1991). The rhetoric of punk moved to make technical sophistication positively undesirable, thereby offering encouragement to independent rock enterprises which saw themselves as no longer disadvantaged – indeed, as positively advantaged – by their lack of access to 'state-of-the-art' technology and to large recording and performing budgets. Yet the relationship between punk and the independents should also be seen as substantially reflexive – the tentative independent release of records by early groups like The Buzzcocks and The Desperate Bicycles both reflected and in part constituted emergent punk culture. The punk stress on low overheads and basic technical production and performance standards also fostered an amateurist ethic favourable to under-capitalized and loosely-formed independent record companies.

Peter Marsh (1977) indicates that an integral part of the rejection of what I have called the 'normal rock' of the early and mid-seventies was a challenge to the idea of competence and professionalism in the production of rock music. This calculated amateurism reflected an egalitarian ethic which sought to overcome the barriers between performers and audiences. The relationship is strikingly represented by the often-quoted example of the diagram of three basic guitar chords in the punk fanzine *Sniffin' Glue*, which demonstrated how punk music could be played and then exhorted readers to form their own punk rock band. This egalitarian ethic threatened the institutional and financial barriers erected by corporate interests by also challenging conventional ideas of a difference in competence and status between performer and audience. As Marsh (1977: 113) states:

> Whatever else it may be, punk rock is **access** music. Despite the fact that the Pistols are headline material, there is no distance between them and people who regularly support them. You could even stand next to Johnny Rotten in the urinal.

Integral to punk mythology was the idea of the fan who moved from front-of-stage observation to on-stage participation. This attempted transcendence of the division between the performer and the consumer substantially fostered an heroic vision of the punk independents. The highly routinized and rationalized procedures of the majors systematically separated performers, support staff and audiences. The independents, however, by choice and necessity enlisted punk artists and their followers alike in such tasks as affixing labels, carrying out visual artwork and publicizing performances and recordings. This close contact between musicians, record companies, retail outlets and local audiences entailed a degree of mobility and interchangeability impossible in the majors' world of contracts, advances and promotional budgets. Hebdige (1979: 110–11), for example, shows how:

> Examples abounded in the music press of 'ordinary fans' (Siouxsie of Siouxsie and the Banshees, Sid Vicious of the Sex Pistols, Mark P of Sniffin' Glue, Jordan of the Ants) who made the symbolic crossing from the dance floor to the stage. Even the humbler positions in the rock hierarchy could provide an attractive alternative to the drudgery of manual labour, office work or a youth on the dole. The Finchley Boys, for instance, were reputedly taken off the football terraces by the Stranglers and employed as roadies.

This blurring of distinctions and interchangeability of function is distinctive of independent rock production, both as ideology and as practice, and was given an oppositional twist by punk's anti-professionalism. It presented a different model of unalienated cultural labour quite distinct from the hyper-rationalized work structures and routines associated with the majors. This involvement in making the whole product rather than its component parts is more recognizable as craft or artisanate labour, while the frequently informal settings in which production was often haphazardly conducted was more redolent of 'cottage' industry and 'hobbyism' than professionalized work. As will be argued in Chapter 3, much of the claim to the radicalism of the punk independents was founded as much in organizational structure and production process as in oppositional content.

The influence of the twin features of rudimentary technology and basic levels of skill on punk music has been acknowledged above, but it is important not to omit the third facet of punk outlined by Laing – its often explicitly political subject matter. While the rock lyrics which immediately preceded punk tended to be 'about goblins or outer space' (Laing, 1978: 125), punk lyrics concerned 'high rise flats, dole queues and white riots' (Brake, 1980: 81) and displayed a 'tremendous focus on social criticism and concern' (Lewis, 1983: 139). This oppositional aspect of punk frequently fitted with the 'alternative' nature of the independents in challenging the rock corporate establishment, just as punk lyrics chided the political power bloc (first and most conspicuously in the Sex Pistols' ridicule of the British monarchy in the Jubilee Year of 1977, but extending, also, to the Dead Kennedys' excoriation of the Reagan presidency in the United States). In this manner, a general, expressive critique of the capitalist state and civil society fused with a specific, expressive and instrumental critique of the power structure of a rock music industry which was itself often at the heart of the subject matter of punk. The Sex Pistols song 'EMI', for example, was a vitriolic attack on a major record company which had expelled the group because of its unacceptable 'public behaviour' (Matlock, 1990; Savage, 1991), while another prominent punk band, The Clash, recorded in 1980 a paean to the British independent labels entitled 'Hitsville UK'.

The two examples immediately above indicate, however, the problem of making straightforward assumptions about the politics of punk. Both the attack on the majors and the celebration of the punk independents came from groups who were not signed to punk independents. The Sex Pistols, after an equally acrimonious split with the large American independent A and M, recorded on Virgin, an entrepreneurial independent founded in the early seventies and later sold, ironically, to EMI. The Clash signed to the American corporate CBS label (which was later, as we have seen, acquired by the Japanese Sony Corporation) and, in spite of some well-publicized disagreements with the company, did not succumb to the lure of independence (Street, 1986: 146). It is important, then, to differentiate between the adoption of a particular rhetorical public posture and actual practice, just as it is necessary to be sceptical of claims that the independents are in eternal structural and ideological opposition to the majors. This acknowledgement, however, is not intended to support a self-righteous and self-defeating purism which, as noted above, regularly prompts ritualized accusations of 'selling out'. It is rather to counsel scepticism both of extravagant claims of a quantum shift in the distribution of power in the rock music industry towards greater equity through independence and of fatalistically circular pronouncements of the inevitable triumph of business as usual. In briefly tracing this instance of historical change in the ideological mediation and industrial organization of rock music, it is evident that such developments are produced out of simultaneously generated (though not necessarily consistent) trends in the increasingly interpenetrating spheres of the economic and the cultural. One such trend, which calls into question the historic division between majors and independents, is connected to the claimed expansion of post-Fordism or flexible/reflexive specialization/accumulation in the culture industries.

Post-Fordism, post-punk

The discussion of the rock music industry has so far concentrated on the longstanding discursive antagonism between majors and independents. This conflict, it was shown, has been grounded both in orthodox market competition between corporate and entrepreneurial organizations and in ideological–aesthetic contestation over the politics of music making, the progressivity and authenticity of musical texts, and the nature of the relationships between rock musicians, musical organizations and consumers/fans. These questions are still of pressing importance, not least because in its many guises the culture–commerce debate is still central to the everyday discursive strategy of ascribing differential value to cultural objects, practices and institutions. Jon Stratton (1983a) has argued that the art-industry cleavage which marks out rock culture, in drawing heavily on the philosophic legacy of nineteenth-century aesthetic romanticism, has been central to the symbolic resolution of the paradox of expressive creativity and industrialized cultural production. More recent re-conceptualizations of these questions, including those which have been influenced by the postmodern emphasis on simulation, identity politics and semiotic elusiveness, continue to stress (directly or indirectly) the possibilities and difficulties of symbolic escape through music, of 'living out the fantasy of participation with "global culture" whilst being subject to what is in fact a transnational economy' (Murphie and Scheer, 1992: 173). The figure of the transnational cultural corporation has, as we have seen, been pivotal in debates about commodification, resistance and control in the rock music industry. Bill Ryan (1991: 105), in outlining the political economy of what he calls 'the corporate form of capitalist cultural commodity production', states that:

> the primary empirical assumption of my argument relates to the market domi-
> nance of the corporations of culture across the culture industry especially in the
> decades since World War II, and the distinctiveness of the form of cultural pro-
> duction which operates inside them.

Ryan argues (1991: 106) that the 'corporate form [of cultural production] may also be found in some of the smaller firms operating in the semi-periphery of the industry', having "imperialised" other sectors to a greater or lesser extent'. The aforementioned 'nursery' and research and development functions of independents are presented here as 'necessary evils' in the cultural corporation's management of innovation:

> The appeal of freelance and independent production creates problems for the cor-
> porations who have problems holding their project teams together. Nonetheless, the
> corporations can live with the system, since it provides a constant flow of innova-
> tion and novelty which is the necessary foundation of any cultural commodity,
> without paying for the cost of gestation. (p. 260)

In such analyses, the corporate form is described as both dominant and institutionally contagious in its insistent drive to rationalize cultural production and capital accumulation. We might suggest, however, that the corporate blueprint is itself undergoing substantial transformation and that the Fordist attachment to large-scale units of production, formal divisional structures and vertical integration characteristic of the transnational corporation is being supplanted by a post-Fordist embrace of niche marketing, 'down-sized' business enterprises and 'sub-contracting' of productive tasks (Harvey, 1989). Keith Negus (1992: 1) observes that the expanding 'Big Five' music corporations (EMI Music, Polygram, Sony Music Entertainment, Warner Music International and the BMG Music Group), which in recent history have 'produced, manufactured and distributed' around 70 per cent of 'the recorded popular music sold in the world', have, since the early eighties, sought to counteract the problem of corporate inflexibility and unwieldiness in the management of risk by:

> dismantling hierarchical working practices and devolving tasks; spreading the deci-
> sion-making across small units within the corporation . . . These patterns of
> organisation enable the corporation to adapt and respond more quickly to local cir-
> cumstances, languages, laws and markets. In the recording industry it means that
> staff in large companies confront less daily bureaucracy and can concentrate more
> of their energy on artistic decision-making. (p. 15)

This devolutionary reorganization of music corporations has been accompanied by engagement in 'collaborative arrangements, joint ventures and licensing deals with small companies' (p. 16). Under these circumstances, the formal organizational independence of non-corporate enterprises becomes increasingly elusive, while the majors' exploitation of the independents' cultural cachet in contriving to present 'phoney indies' in the rock marketplace has eroded further their distinct identity. Negus is, therefore, critical of the romanticization of the independents, seeing (like Vignolle, 1980) a high degree of interdependence between majors and independents. These 'organizational webs' work by loosening 'operational control' (Murdock, 1982) over semi-autonomous units while simultaneously exercising tight 'allocative control' over resources through rigorous performance monitoring. This 'loose–tight approach' seeks to combine high levels of creativity with considerable financial stringency. Negus argues that in this way the majors have learnt from the independents and minimized the economic vulnerability they displayed in the early eighties – to the extent that the major/independent split has become obsolete. He prefers a major/minor classification which eschews the notion of the independents as 'oppositional mavericks on the margins' in favour of the conception of:

> Majors increasingly split into semi-autonomous working groups and label divisions, and minor companies connected to these by complex patterns of ownership, investment, licensing, formal and informal and sometimes deliberately obscured relationships ... Which companies are owned, part owned or licensed becomes difficult to ascertain. If it can be done, what it means in terms of working practices becomes equally hard to infer, as the distinctions between an inside and an outside, and between centre and margins, has [*sic*] given way to a web of mutually dependent work groupings radiating out from multiple centres. (Negus, 1992: 18)

In their appraisal of developments in the culture industries, Scott Lash and John Urry (1994: 120) similarly argue that a process of 'vertical disintegration' has taken place in which 'Fordist arrangements have been transformed'. In the popular music industry, they argue, the combination of musicians and writers within royalty-earning groups rather than outside as wage earners, the movement of producers 'out of house', and the 'externalization' of studios have meant that over the last twenty or thirty years new flexible and reflexive post-Fordist production arrangements have been installed. The ease of market entry of small independent companies has, according to Lash and Urry (1994: 130), meant that the 'British "indie" sector, proportionately dwarfing its American counterpart, provides groups for the majors, while continuing itself to thrive'. At the same time, many a contracted artist now 'appropriates all the functions of the production process, and just presents the final tape which he/she brings and, so to speak, "leases" to the record company' (p. 120), so that the 'record company buys the intellectual property, packages the artist and then sells the artist as a brand' (p. 137). These adaptations are significant in that they represent a post-Fordist or flexibly specialized response to the rigidities of Fordism in the commercial cultural sphere. They do not so much signal the decline of cultural corporations and the rise of independents as indicate a dynamic re-drawing of the

boundaries between them. Indeed, as Lash and Urry (1994: 123) note, the
emphasis on innovation and design in the culture industries always limited
their embrace of Fordism and meant that they were 'post-Fordist avant la let-
tre', disputing the orthodox Marxist judgement that:

> culture production is becoming more like commodity production in manufacturing
> industry. Our claim is that ordinary manufacturing industry is becoming more and
> more like the production of culture. It is not that commodity manufacture provides
> the template, and culture follows, but that the culture industries themselves have
> provided the template.

The increasing emphasis on intellectual property and the rights attached to
it in the popular music and other (increasingly connected) culture industries
has re-structured the network of institutions involved in the production of
rock. It has engendered a productive 'flow of signs' which, according to Lash
and Urry (1994: 143), 'opens up and helps reproduce a space disintegrated
from the culture-industry behemoths from which meaningful aesthetic critique can be launched'. It is the 'culture-intensive' nature of this production
which, while certainly not licensing a neglect of its institutional–industrial
foundations, resists the mechanistic application of models of capitalist corporate omnipotence.

These new flexible organizational relations of production do not, however,
transcend the stark realities of corporate power and the necessity of assessing
the relative strength of the majors and the independents. Nor do they excuse
the general paucity of detailed research on rock's independent operations. The
neglect of independent cultural activity is, according to Raymond Williams
(1981: 66), mainly due to the banal fact that large, formal organizations, with
their established procedures and structures, are much easier to analyse than
'relatively informal associations which have been so important in modern
cultural life'. The problems specific to the study of independents are the:

> relatively small numbers involved . . . [their] relatively, often extremely, short dura-
> tion . . . the rapidity of formation and dissolution, the complexity of internal breaks
> and of fusions, [which] can seem quite bewildering. Yet this is no reason for ignor-
> ing what, taken as a whole process, is so general a social fact. (p. 68)

It is these largely unexplored cultural forms which, on inspection, provide
rich data about the workings of rock and the wider popular music industry.
Their persistent significance, as demonstrated not only by their operations
but also by the subterfuge involved in producing a (corporate funded) image
of independence, is a sign of continuing unease about the rationalized manufacture of music as a commodity. The imbrication of the economic, cultural
and ideological reveals how an economistic and functionalist preoccupation
with large corporate organizations and their assumed control over cultural
production, consumption and exchange delivers only a teleological explanatory account of rock culture and industry. While the culture–commerce
debate, in its various formulations, remains a crucial reference point for socio-
cultural analysis and critique, it is imperative that it is cast in a manner fully

responsive to the dynamic, quixotic and sometimes contradictory character of the cultural production it seeks to explain.

Conclusion

In this chapter I have attempted, by means of theoretical, institutional, empirical and historical analysis, to demonstrate that a concern with the rock music industry, while crucial to any understanding of rock as contemporary popular culture, must be accompanied by an appreciation of the complex interplay of culture, economics and ideology in the making of music (Breen, 1994). I have also tried to show that the complicated, shifting nature of the industry constantly poses questions about the politics of cultural production. These political considerations embrace questions about who gets to make rock, in what kinds of settings and according to which motives. They also address the ideological character of rock texts in covering both the process and the content of rock as cultural production. The discourse of independence has been shown to be important by throwing into sharp relief alternative models of cultural production. It is to this politics in and of rock that I turn in Chapter 3.

3
Rock Ideology and Sound Politics

Rock's relationship to orthodox politics is complex and uneven, ranging historically from direct political interventions to repudiations of its political significance. The less tangible but more extensive concept of cultural politics has been more consistently associated with rock music and culture, although here the political dimension is tied more closely to personal rather than programmatic politics. As a consequence, ideologies of symbolic resistance and identity are open to much broader, often conflicting interpretations. This chapter encompasses various articulations of rock and politics, including the direct political engagement of 'protest music', the cultural politics of 'world music', the single issue-based populist politics of campaigns like Live Aid, the cultural politics of identity and style, and the intervention of the state in the conduct of cultural policy. The principal focus develops out of the discussion of major and independent rock organizations in the previous chapter. The 'British independent moment' is assessed as a test case of the political potential of rock, proceeding by means of a discursive analysis of interviews conducted (over the period from the late seventies to the late eighties) with a range of participants in the making of independent rock. This discussion highlights the ways in which ideologies of cultural production are formed and articulated through the institutional structures and practices that constitute rock as a discursive formation.

Music and movements

The politics of rock have been the subject of intense disagreement for decades. In the previous chapter the commerce–culture debate was demonstrated to be pivotal, with rock alternatively positioned as dominated by consumer capitalism or as subversive of capitalism (and also often of moral rectitude). In overt treatments of politics, rock and pop have been condemned by the proponents of various forms of 'folk culture' as unauthentic and insubstantial, especially in its posited failure to represent and engage with structural (for example, class-based) interests. This dispute is satirically captured in *Absolute Beginners*, Colin MacInnes' classic novel of the rise of British teenage pop culture in the late fifties. The following exchange between the narrator and his half-brother is representative:

> You could hear his brain racing and grinding behind his red, crunched face, till he cried excitedly, 'You're a traitor to the working-class!'

I took the goon's forefinger, which was still prodding me in the torso, and shook it away from me, and said:

'I am *not* a traitor to the working-class because I do *not* belong to the working-class, and therefore cannot be a traitor to it.'

N –h'n!' he really said, 'You belong to the upper-class, I suppose.'

I sighed up.

'And you reject the working-classes that you sprung from.'

I sighed some more.

'You poor old prehistoric monster,' I exclaimed. 'I do *not* reject the working-classes, and I do *not* belong to the upper-classes, for one and the same simple reason, namely that neither of them interest me in the slightest, never have done, never will do. Do try to understand that, clobbo! I'm just not interested in the whole class crap that seems to needle you and all the tax-payers – needle you all, whichever side of the tracks you live on, or suppose you do.'

He glared at me. I could see that, if once he believed that what I said I really meant, and thousands of the kiddos did the same as well, the bottom would fall out of his horrid little world.

'You're dissolute!' he suddenly cried out. 'Immoral! That's what I say you teenagers all are!' (MacInnes, 1986: 41)

This tension between decadence and political engagement is even more integral to rock as a pleasure complex. The folk-based 'protest music' of the sixties associated with the civil rights movement provided one model of resistance through music (Denselow, 1989), echoing in places the earlier form of the industrial 'folksong' (Harker, 1980; Lloyd, 1975; Rosselson, 1979). This model of musical progressivity encountered a series of objections, not least on account of its prescriptions of form, content and (principally acoustic) technology, and its reliance on rationalist decodings of ideology. The presentation of music as the song of politics is consistently confronted by irrationalist, expressive corporeal pleasure which exceeds lyrical meaning irrespective of formal content, and by the multiplicity of contexts in which rock and other musical forms are experienced. As Street (1986: 60) argues in his critique of 'left "folkism"':

> The difficulties are most neatly highlighted by the problem of musical criticism: what distinguishes the good from the bad in music? When are we hearing the sound of 'working class creativity'? . . . The politics of the music becomes linked (and confused) with the occasion at which it is performed – Ray Charles playing at a Rock Against Racism rally somehow makes the performance 'radical'.

The uneasiness of combining overt politics with rock music is well illustrated by the experience of Red Wedge, which in the mid-eighties tried to mobilize the British youth vote in favour of the Labour Party and against the strident right-wing politics of Margaret Thatcher. While acts like Style Council and Billy Bragg had substantial followings, political divisions between participants and discomfort at 'proselytization' through entertainment were evident (Denselow, 1989: 220). The concert tours were well attended and (perhaps not coincidentally) Labour's electoral performance improved, but the Thatcher government was still returned to power and rock's role in the electoral process failed to be clarified. This, presumably, must remain the case if a simple-minded exchange of music-for-votes is conceived as the limit of rock's political potential.

It is apparent, however, that the conception of rock and its relationship to politics are not exhausted by endorsing political manifestos and articulating specific political values. The complex of relationships that comprises rock culture creates the conditions for more diffuse but often compelling political discourse. One of the sharpest political debates in popular music, for example, is concerned with its cultural origins and impacts. Iain Chambers (1985: 9–10) describes how:

> Black American music has been crucial to developments in white popular music and dance since the beginning of the century, from ragtime through dance bands to 'swing' and rock 'n' roll. But until the 1960s, with the rare exception of Louis Armstrong or Duke Ellington, its direct presence remained in the barely acknowledged undergrowth of the popular music industry.

This perspective traces substantial elements of western popular music to 'the subordinated traces of black Africa' (p. 10). The black contribution is shown to be largely uncredited, with white pop stars appropriating elements of black music and style in order to make it palatable to an overtly or covertly racist white audience. This white-dominated popular music, suitably sanitized, is then 'played back' to the people from other countries who have helped to create it, as well as to those with strong indigenous musical traditions, thereby turning them into consumers of their own transformed cultural products. The outcome of this one-way musical export arrangement is seen to be the creation of a culturally imperialist apparatus through which western capitalism can garner profits from the 'Third World' at the same time as it promotes western 'supremacist' ideologies. As one appraisal of the relationship between popular music and global cultural diversity notes:

> Many observers of the 1960s and 1970s one-way flow of cultural products feared world cultural homogenization. They noted that, when Anglo-American rock 'n' roll 'invaded' countries, an enormous number of people in those places began listening to it, sometimes as a substitute for their own endogenous genres of music. (Robinson et al., 1991: 261)

From such a position popular music functions as a key agent of Americanization and globalization. Just as the seemingly benign cartoon figure of Donald Duck, for Dorfman and Mattelart (1975), masked a deeper purpose of ideological co-optation, so the musical video figures of Michael Jackson, Bruce Springsteen, Prince and Madonna, or the panoply of western musical genres from disco to country and western, can be seen to operate against cultural self-determination, ideological independence, musical autarky and economic self-sufficiency. This kind of argument rests on a 'corruptive' model of culture, one that is increasingly difficult to sustain in any straightforward manner in the light of the complexity of global cultural flow. As Frith (1989b: 3) states:

> Popular music in the USA, the sounds that now echo round the world, were shaped by the powerless, by black musicians and poor white communities, by migrant tunes and rhythms coming in from Latin America and the Caribbean, by old forms being played back by new audiences. If nothing else, popular music study rests on the assumption that there is no such thing as a culturally 'pure' sound.

The spread of reproductive musical technology also has consequences that often interrupt the one-way flow of music from the western to the non-western world. Peter Manuel (1988: 3), for example, argues that the development in the seventies of analogue cassette technology 'extended recording production and consumption potential throughout the world', contributing simultaneously to the expansion of control by transnational music corporations and the proliferation of 'smaller record and cassette outfits', which were able to make 'local music under local control for local audiences'. In his examination of the production of music in Indonesia, Manuel (1988: 207) notes that the spread of western-originated popular musics and musical technologies has not rubbed out traditional musical styles or led to the homogenization of sounds and musical preferences. He argues instead that cassette technology has had the effect of disseminating regionally-based music and so has created, for the first time, national popular styles, fostering the rise of 'new syncretic genres', and extending the 'control of mass media music production to small, backyard outfits throughout the country', a not inconsiderable feat in a country of over 150 million people living on more than 13,500 islands. Similarly, Jeremy Marre and Hannah Charlton (1985: 87), in their interview with the Nigerian pop star Sunny Okosun, point out his awareness of the irony of the influence of western music on his own music and that of other Nigerian musicians, whilst also being 'only too aware of how the drum rhythms of West-African slaves became the basis of popular western music'. On an organizational level, Roger Wallis and Krister Malm (1984: 285) record wide variations in how large transnational 'phonogram' companies operate in small nations, with some giving considerable latitude to their local employees in determining national musical priorities (subject, of course, to financial viability). While none of these arrangements could be reasonably described as autonomous, they could also not be appraised as unalloyed examples of media and cultural imperialism.

These significantly political questions are bound up with the cultural and economic developments described in Chapter 2 under the rubric of post-Fordism. Instances of the reversal of cultural and economic flows from the core to the periphery, more flexible production regimes and the shift from mass to niche marketing (Robinson et al., 1991: 264) have some potential to shift the international balance of forces in the circulation of sounds and musics. Political debates about control over cultural content and form parallel those of a more directly industrial character, with local musics, both rhetorically and organizationally, claiming the ground of 'independence' against the assimilationist incursions of the multinational corporations. One of the most keenly contested issues has concerned musical charity events like Live Aid's attempt to alleviate African famine in the mid-eighties, international cooperative political interventions such as the anti-apartheid Sun City Campaign, and the incorporation and 'showcasing' of African music and musicians by white pop stars like Paul Simon (in his top-selling *Gracelands* album). Several years after they appeared, Live Aid, Band Aid (with its hit single 'Do they know it's Christmas?') and USA for Africa (and its own hit song 'We are the World') still stand collectively as a key disputed symbol of popular music's political efficacy. Stuart Hall and Martin Jacques (1986: 10), for example, have argued in favour of 'Band Aid/Live Aid/Sport Aid' as popular resistance to Thatcherite selfishness and individualism, and Simon Frith (1989b: 198) has observed that '1985's charity rock moves affected people in ways that a detached analysis didn't always acknowledge'. Robinson et al. (1991: 269), however, are more drawn to the cynical conclusion that 'many musicians seek to participate in these demonstrations primarily to benefit their own careers', and Stan Rijven (1989) and Will Straw (1989) have characterized the Live Aid project as misconceived, naive, patronizing, imperialist and opportunistic. In a polemic against the USA for Africa Campaign, Greil Marcus (1989: 278-9) criticizes the 'subliminal' Them-and-Us message of 'We are the World', arguing also that it served to distract Americans from their own domestic poverty and provided an excellent opportunity for the soft-drink corporation Pepsi to promote its products in Africa (and elsewhere) through the involvement of 'the Pepsi-contracted songwriters, Michael Jackson and Lionel Richie'. John Street (1986: 79) concludes, in sceptical vein, that Band Aid, in requiring only a small investment in time and resources on the part of producers and consumers, 'raised few awkward questions of ideology, commitment and action'. Even the record companies which had foregone substantial income through the distribution of profit to African charity, he argues, gained long-term exposure and kudos for their artists. Nonetheless, Street concedes the existence of a 'passionate conviction' on the part of many of the participants which is not reducible to 'the smug sounds of Western self-satisfaction'.

Such arguments not only focus on the effectiveness of these and other campaigns which mobilize rock and pop culture in meeting their avowed goals according to their publicly expressed aims, but also give prominence to the achievement of other latent and unacknowledged goals by the same means. These points of view are not incommensurate, given the multi-dimensional nature of social action. Perhaps the most significant political impact of 'altruistic' campaigns like Live Aid is not the raising of money to alleviate suffering (however laudable a task that might be) but the raising of a 'collective consciousness' (and conscience) among its participants. In this sense, the ultimate object of these 'international "forums for change"' (Robinson et al., 1991: 263) is the recovery of a lost communality, if only momentarily, in the aggressively and individualistically competitive world of advanced capitalism. It is the idea of common purpose and identity so central to rock mythology that is 'magically' restored by 'charity' work. Arguments of this nature give priority to social functions, but, as Street (1986: 69) indicates in contrasting the financial triumph of Band Aid's 'Do they know it's Christmas?' (£7 million in sales) with the comparative failure of two records released by Council Collective and the Enemy Within to raise money for the 1983/4 British miner's strike (£1,300 in sales), not all 'politically progressive' campaigns deploying popular music are financially (let alone politically) successful.

The causes of such success and failure are, as in the wider sphere of the popular music industry, not simply a function of transcendent musical quality. Many a 'charity' record, however good or bad according to listener taste, will fail to make a substantial return because of the absence of corporate resources to fund, promote and market it. The resources of CBS, which were placed at the disposal of USA for Africa, and the star status of the singers and musicians on 'We are the World' gave it the kind of advantage that the latest releases by the likes of Michael Jackson, Prince or Dire Straits have over music issued by small independents or by comparatively under-exposed acts signed to majors. The lavish 'gratis' or at-cost services which enabled Live Aid to be seen by an estimated one billion viewers in 150 countries by means of seven telecommunication satellites, and which saw singer Phil Collins fly by supersonic passenger jet in order to attend the shows in London and Philadelphia on the same day, substantially secured a 'triumph'. While this point may seem self-evident, it is also significant in that it reveals that pop altruism comes at a price, and that the strategic harnessing of corporate cultural capitalism does not so much negate entrenched economic power as spectacularly reflect it. Another way of seeing Live Aid would be to observe that, if it could raise £50 million for Ethiopian famine through the agency of pop stars and their record companies, how much is routinely and daily accumulated by them when it is business as usual? The Live Aid story also clearly reveals that certain causes are more 'pop event friendly' than others. Whereas famine relief can be readily universalized as an issue (in contrast to the less spectacular but ultimately determinant geo-politics of development, aid and food production; see George, 1976), a bitter struggle between members of the working class and an antagonistic government in a single country is likely to be perceived as a local and specifically political issue which is unamenable to a mass campaign of popular support. Vague statements about being children and making days brighter are, by the nature of their elusiveness, readily stripped of any potentially disruptive political sting. Concrete declamations of hostility to Tories and in defence of the industrial proletariat cannot have their specific ideological content so easily evacuated. These variables are important in determining the ultimate economic success of disaster benefits and other fund-raising pop and rock activities. The music itself is, of course, also a relevant factor in the fate of a charitable and/or political initiative, yet it is not immediately apparent how musical form and lyrical content mesh with the securement of donations and the development of political sensibilities.

The fit between music and politics cannot be established by the simple device of reading off the latter from the former – the rules governing the 'decoding' of lyrics and the sharing of political sensibilities are by no means universally binding. There are many permutations of 'good' and 'bad' politics and art which are heavily reliant on the judgements of human subjects deeply embedded in social, cultural and ideological structures not of their own making. Marcus (1989: 278) addresses these disparities in stating that:

> Bad politics, which can be based in real desires, can produce good art; bad art, which can only be based in faked or compromised desires, can only produce bad politics.

Such oracular statements, however, as Marcus himself partially acknowledges, do not close off definitions of good and bad politics and art, but problematize them. They send us in search of the progressive musical text, a journey which is historically fraught with danger in its attempt to 'fix' the politics of signification. John Docker (1984b: 193) has criticized this tendency for self-consciously radical intellectuals to believe that the:

> primary – indeed sole – criterion for interpreting culture is 'political': is such and such a piece of culture 'progressive' or 'reactionary'? That is they collapse culture into politics, rather like the Althusserians collapsed all culture into ideology. They cannot see that popular culture is constituted by forms and conventions that give pleasure and that are not in themselves necessarily ideological or political. Rather such forms and conventions are constantly being inflected or used ideologically in specific historical and social situations.

This frequently espoused antinomy of politics and pleasure/entertainment and the subsumption of culture within politics is often reinforced by a negation of the political effectiveness of rock. Thus, Leon Rosselson (1979: 50) argues that:

> Songs never converted anyone. That is not what they are for. They are for sharing ideas, hopes, feelings about what is sad, funny, ridiculous, horrifying. They are for making a community out of the already converted.

For Rosselson (1979: 46), music cannot be politically efficacious in any determinate way and rock, because of its reliance on expensive technology, high overheads and operation within the music business, is incapable of mounting a political challenge to corporate capitalism, so that the most rock forms (such as punk) can hope to communicate is simple-minded slogans. John Downing (1976: 132), similarly, points to the political impotence of rock and asserts that, when it does directly address the political, more harm than good results in that it 'polarizes societies into identities rather than courses of action, and by this very act of providing a counterfeit social identity, exorcises the urge to act'.

Here rock's dependency on style means that it can provide no more than 'a spurious sense of solidarity which has no common purpose or direction' (p. 132), thereby diffusing political activity by giving a false unity to its practitioners and audiences. Dave Laing (1969: 175–76), from the vantage point of the late sixties (when claims of a rock revolution were most frequently heard), similarly criticizes the political naivety of those who saw rock as being the sound of a world being turned upside down:

> The trouble with the 'revolutionary' pop groups is that they seem to think that the crucial translation can be achieved by music which, in the final analysis is defined by, and contained within, the commercial structures of the society to which they are opposed.

These dismissive comments about rock's political potential contrast with those contributions which, especially from the British subcultural tradition (Turner, 1990), see popular music 'as part of the generation of alternative style, and as part of continuing political and ideological struggle' (Birch,

1984: 517). Fredric Jameson (1979: 140), in a somewhat different vein, also argues that a potent political progressivism can be found on the cultural margins, where the commodity form is not yet in the ascendant:

> The only authentic cultural production today has seemed to be that which can draw on the collective experience of marginal pockets of the social life of the world system: black literature and blues, British working-class rock, women's literature, gay literature, the roman quebecois, the literature of the Third World; and this production is possible only to the degree to which these forms of collective life or collective solidarity have not yet been fully penetrated by the market and the commodity system.

These latter arguments, in a qualified manner, see rock as the site of political struggle, standing as it does at the confluence of symbolic expression and material exploitation. They are rather more sanguine that 'revolt into style' (Melly, 1970) or the formation of dissenting socio-cultural 'communities' can have tangible and desirable political ramifications. There are, as is no doubt to be expected, deep divisions over the politics of rock, but both detractors and supporters are prone to exaggerate the opportunities for and barriers to the enlistment of its affective power in strategically effective political interventions. Those who have asserted rock's political impotence, its tendency towards sloganeering and the commercial exploitation of protest have tended to set up an intrinsically irrefutable argument by pointing to the absence of any revolutionary transformation through rock values, attitudes and practices. This rather disengenuous idealism projects utopian ambitions onto rock and pop which are destined to be unfulfilled. As Herman and Hoare (1979: 53) argue in answering Rosselson:

> Rock 'n' roll, folk-protest, reggae and punk have all left their mark. Their impact has not been revolutionary in itself – but then, Marxists do not expect ideological products to bring about that sort of change. We would not imagine that the directors of EMI might plump for socialism just because the Beatles stop selling records.

It is unfair and theoretically inconsistent to expect rock to be massively politically effective or even politically homogeneous in its progressivism, while those radical writers who bemoan its lack of political clout tend to echo the crude 'hypodermic syringe' model which is normally associated with conservative empiricism. The idea that an injection of radical politics into rock ought effectively to transform the consciousness of its performers and audiences often appears to be latent in such critiques. Not only is this an unreasonable expectation, but it also rests on an unduly narrow view of the politics of rock, which tend to be reduced to its lyrical content, its association with subordinate social groups, and to the degree of its enmeshment with the commercial domain. Even if the lyrics are seen to be politically progressive, Paul Hirsch (1971: 378) argues that audiences may not 'hear' them in the way that the author(s) intended. His study of listener decodings of self-consciously socially engaged rock songs found many:

> unable to interpret the messages these records allegedly contained in the same terms as research scholars and social critics. That is, most teenagers made no reference to drugs, sex, or politics when asked to interpret the meanings of songs which *we* believed said a great deal about each of these subjects.

Furthermore, audiences may be more than cognitively resistant to the 'politicality' of rock lyrics – they might be quite literally deaf to them. George Lewis (1983: 139), for example, notes a high degree of 'technical' noise obstructing punk's critique of social issues:

> And yet, their very energy precludes one from hearing their often stinging lyrics concerning society. Punks create a potent message on one level, yet destroy it in its musical translation.

Even if politically progressive lyrics are heard and understood, rock remains (for the more 'folk-oriented' critics) crucially hampered by its existence as a 'commodity in the market' (Rosselson, 1979: 47) and by the inevitable corruption of the 'committed artist' who is, according to Harker (1980: 211), in an 'invidious position in capitalist society, unless his [*sic*] commitment is to the system, and to his own success within it'. This kind of critique, while an important corrective to overly optimistic claims of deep structural transformation through the politics of song, represents only a highly circumscribed politics in and of cultural production (Breen, 1994). Rock may be more fruitfully conceived as a site (or as a range of sites) of conflict which is inevitably produced in an arena where 'chaotic' signifying practices encounter rationalized procedures of commodity production. As Jacques Attali (1985: 90) argues in his historical appraisal of the political economy of noise and music:

> Music, transformed into a commodity, gives us insight into the obstacles that were to be encountered by the ongoing commodification of other social relations. Music, one of the first artistic endeavours truly to become a stockpileable consumer product, is exemplary. However, we must avoid reading this as a global plot of money against sociality. Neither money nor the State entirely understood or organized this mutation of music and its recording.

It is this tension between musical and monetary 'mutation' that requires open examination. In the previous chapter I focused on the site of independence where, within rock discourse, the opportunity for a highly politicized self-consciousness is maximized and where direct integration into monopoly capitalism is minimized. Yet, although independent organizations stand in varying (material and ideological) conditions *vis-à-vis* the majors, the availability of a space within advanced capitalism which can be fully insulated from its effects and determinations is implausible. This does not render the task of further analysis of independent rock production futile, but rather compels a closer inquiry into how its politics are articulated, negotiated and mediated.

Rock politics in the making: independence and ideology

In tracing the relationship between major and independent rock enterprises as constituents of the popular music industry, it was argued in Chapter 2 that, while operating within a non-corporate organization by no means guarantees any particular orientation to economic practice, the concept of independence remains rhetorically powerful and suggests a predisposition to treat music-making as cultural-expressive before economic-accumulative. This independent ethos can be readily translated into an overt or implied anti-corporate capitalist ideology. In pursuing rock ideologies through a consideration of independent production – particularly where the politics of song and of making songs were made unusually conspicuous by the punk independents during the British moment of the late seventies and early eighties – some of the more pressing dilemmas of engagement are revealed. In raising the issue of music and politics with British musicians and record company personnel, a series of discursive antagonisms emerged, the most significant of which is between the idea of making 'serious' statements of an orthodox political nature and the idea of music as fun or entertainment which cannot be anchored directly to any political function or meaning. The concept of pop is able to accommodate this divergence more effectively because of its closer attachment to the idea of unmotivated pleasure, but rock, especially 'indie rock', is conceptually distinguished by its refusal to be subsumed under the banner of 'pure' (and industrialized) entertainment. Over the last decade, the celebration of postmodern playfulness and the rejection of programmatic politics in favour of parody, pastiche, evasion and refusal (Baudrillard, 1988) have been common responses to the crisis of cultural critique and effective political challenge to 'existing systems of oppression and injustice' (Squires, 1993b: 9). As has often been pointed out (Goodwin, 1992; Jameson, 1991; Norris, 1992), this embrace of reckless *jouissance*, for all its existential appeal, has not produced an adequate model for the politics of resistance in rock or in any other cultural or social domain. Most obviously, this shortcoming is revealed in the failure of postmodernists to deal satisfactorily with the economics and ideologies of cultural labour. In the following discussion, the attempts of various 'independent' cultural workers to negotiate their way through the minefield of political engagement, economic viability and pleasures of the musical-text-in-production illustrate the resilience and continuing centrality of these dilemmas within contemporary cultural production.

As this analysis of interview research demonstrates, politics in the independent rock sector, especially of a populist kind, is never far from the surface. It is by claiming closer connections to the people and so to the politics of everyday life that independents assert a certain moral authority over the majors. This association is, however, a finely-balanced one, and too close an identification with politics may be seen as detrimental to the future of a band or label. In part, this political caution is caused by new relations which the state has forged with the rock industry in order to capitalize on its economic (especially export) potential and its social reach into the lives of the young and the disadvantaged. Supporting independent studios and labels in areas of high youth unemployment, for example, has been one strategy employed by the (national, regional and local) state in countries such as Australia, Britain and Holland to assuage youthful alienation in the form of crime, vandalism and drug-taking (Bennett et al., 1993). This newly enthusiastic and uncensorious liberal–democratic state intervention, with its echoes of the state-sanctioned and subsidized rock of former state socialist regimes (Ramet, 1994; Troitsky, 1987), presents some difficulties for a cultural formation shaped by an ideological tradition of dissent and a nakedly market-based economics. It is in the independent sphere that state-fostered municipal initiatives, with their emphasis on post-industrial economic reconstruction, have the greatest and most loudly welcomed impact (Frith, 1993). The involvement of government, however, brings with it new pressures which counterbalance relief from straightforward material deprivation. One outer London suburban studio and label funded by central and local government, for example, found that the articulation of 'extreme' political positions might jeopardize both state funds and audience appeal:

> U: But if someone wants to bring out a National Front song, for instance, that would be totally out of order, but equally someone who wants to bring out a very, very socialist song, I suppose, would be out of order also.
> V: But on the other hand if someone wanted to bring out a reggae version of the Red Flag we'd probably fall over backwards to record it, because it would be hilarious. In fact, I'm going to do it tonight. But that's different, that's fun!

Sensitivity to the articulation of lyrical 'extremism' by means of a state-subsidized facility is founded here both on a traditional philosophy of 'liberal moderation' and on a fear that the facility would be closed down by a Conservative government which had waged war on 'radical' manifestations of the local state (such as the Greater London Council). This question of setting limits to the range of ideological positions which can be associated with independent projects is not confined to those supported by government. The integration of political partisanship with musicianship is frequently held to be difficult and ill-advised, even in an independent sector that draws much of its legitimacy from the radical potential created by its isolation from dominant institutions and its proximity to the 'grass-roots'. One common way of dealing with the 'problem' of politics in rock is to set up an antinomy between 'politics' and 'fun', with one independent label owner, for example, stating:

> S: I've travelled a lot around the world and I've found that music is the greatest bringer together of people that exists – it doesn't matter what language you speak. Music should be there to bring people together, it should be there for people to enjoy, to relax to, to escape with. I don't think it should be as a political message to ram something home, at all. I very strongly do not approve of that.

This belief that politics and music should be separated (which echoes, as we will see in Chapter 6, similar sentiments in regard to sport) rests on the notion that music should be a haven from political division. Music is seen to be a unifying force which could link disparate social groups by means of shared musical tastes or through participating (as spectators) in performances. To introduce politics at any level other than in the very general task of exhorting people to unite through music frequently receives strong disapproval, as the following exchange with two members of an independent group (which had just released their first single) demonstrates:

Q: You yourself don't see your music as being political?

L: No, not at all.

H: No, I think the whole point about music is, well for me anyway, people who would find it strange or very difficult to communicate on a social level normally, you will get together at rock gigs. They go there for the mutual pleasure of enjoying a band, that's why, it's great. We went to a Slade gig recently, I mean there were skinheads, rockers, students, hippies, I mean you name it. That's great – it gets the whole spectrum under one roof. You're all there to enjoy yourself, I mean you really can't wish for anything else. I'm sorry in a way that music does get such a lot of politics involved in it.

Views of this kind tend to be expressed by the more pragmatic and commercially-oriented personnel in the independent 'scene'. Those who are more idealistic in their hostility towards the commercial aspects of rock music also take a generally more favourable view of rock as a political force. These value clusters are not unexpected, except for commentators who regard the independent network as being exclusively opportunistic or exclusively altruistic. They represent a series of ideological negotiations which are revealed as the subjects attempt to situate themselves within a complex discursive matrix. Thus, the notion of rock as harmless fun does not sit easily with the idea of its political potency, yet those who have an overt political orientation rarely wish their cultural production to be reduced to its political dimensions, nor do they wish to exclude audiences who do not share their political persuasion. On the other hand, most pragmatists involved in the independent network are aware of rock's post-sixties, ideological 'heritage' of liberation and the requirement to differentiate their form of cultural production from rival, mainstream forms. The result of such difficulties is frequently political inconsistency and confusion. For example, another member of the band quoted above condemning the expression of politics in music also made the following statement:

Q: Do the independents damage the majors in any way?

V: I hope so. Because the majors were . . . they didn't give a toss about the music, they're in it to make money which is what all business is about . . . The disgusting thing, really on some scale, is the way you never get any new artists appearing on certain labels.

This position can be construed as in some ways connected with the culture–commerce antagonism described in the previous chapter. The assault on the excessively economic orientation of the majors and their *modus operandi* echoes the statements of those who have a deeply-held political repugnance for corporate cultural capitalism. Yet critiques of the music industry are often not carried over into a general political position on power, culture and material inequality, resulting in a compartmentalized radical condemnation of the domination of the majors in the rock music industry which is not linked to the wider socio-economic system of which they are key representatives. The specific nature of this politics of the music industry (viewed largely in a vacuum) is generated by the rhetorical necessity of positioning independent production as qualitatively different from that of the majors – a distinction which is, however, made largely on the grounds of creativity and flexibility rather than of politically-inflected struggle between cooperative, small-scale production and monopoly-capitalist mass production. Independent rock production does, however, also attract musicians and other cultural 'workers' who view their practice within a broader political framework, especially where social conditions provoke direct political interventions. In regional Britain in the late seventies and early eighties, social conditions of industrial economic decline, racial/ethnic tension and deep political opposition to central government in the regions were fertile ground for politically-engaged music-making. For example, as one independent group which had formed their own label in the depressed north-western city of Liverpool (shortly before an outbreak of urban disorder in the migrant-dense district of Toxteth) stated:

> I: Actually, the guys we've just got together to form the band, we're the only ones who've got any slight yearnings towards politics or anything slightly radical at all. Because like we want to make inroads into a lot of things, like Liverpool's got a really big black population, you know, really, really big, and it's so insular that nobody can make any inroads into them at all ... And the places where we go, we're going to be the first ones to maybe bring some of them out from where they are. We know they do produce music and some of them are pretty radical, like.

These musicians, in complaining of the lack of political commitment among other local independents, viewed their activity as quite explicitly political, in this case forging a link with some of the black population of Liverpool. This initiative was seen not simply in terms of the previously-described goal of temporarily unifying audiences, but also as providing a vehicle for the musical 'voicing' of an oppressed and marginalized social group. It might be noted here that one major group under-represented both in the independent network and in its political preoccupations was women. This gender inequality is evident also in academic research and writing (Bayton, 1993) and has only partially been redressed by some 'recuperative' works (for example, Bayton, 1990; Greig, 1989; Johnson, 1992; Steward and Garratt, 1984). While gender issues were addressed by male, female and 'mixed' bands of the period (such as Gang of Four, Scritti Politti, the Raincoats, the Slits and Au Pairs), the dominant form of overt politics among the 'punk' independents was race and class-based. One musician, for example, who was deeply involved in the aforementioned Red Wedge and Rock against Racism initiatives, described his energetic commitment to class politics in rock thus:

> P: Being from a very early age immersed in politics, it would have been difficult for me to write songs that were not political, because I see things in that way, you know. And this is going to sound like a cliché but I've always considered myself a socialist and would be incapable of writing a song that didn't reflect a certain amount of commitment to socialism . . . Maybe there's a tiny area of personal life that's vaguely non-political, but virtually everything is political, yeah.

Accompanying this uncompromisingly political orientation (which had resulted, for example, in the writing and performance of a song which he described as 'propaganda against the National Front') was the maintenance of an orthodox conception of entertainment and an acknowledgement that it might conflict with an explicitly political project:

P: If you're talking about a political band, then I suppose you certainly won't enlighten people in pop music if you don't hold their attention, so you've got to entertain them as well, and I wonder who's doing that, you know?

The idea of entertainment and of broad musical appeal is linked with a corresponding conception of popular politics. Thus, the Rock against Racism organization (Widgery, 1986) was seen by this musician to be sufficiently broadly-based even though it:

P: was in part a front organization for the SWP [the Socialist Workers' Party], right, but I was willing to take that while the SWP were being populist, you know, in that they weren't being cliquey, vanguardist Marxists, shut in the upstairs room of a pub discussing what Lenin would have done about something, and by the time they've decided what Lenin would have done, it's all over, you know.

Evident here is a concern that independent rock, irrespective of its overtly political orientation, should be free of elitism and obscurantism. This attitude is produced fundamentally in response to a felt tension between 'mass pop', which is seen to be democratic in its availability but often deficient in terms of quality and interest, and 'small-scale rock', which is seen to be provocative, thoughtful and politically progressive, yet too restricted in its circulation and appeal. It is, therefore, necessary from this perspective to overcome wilful obscurity without surrendering differentiating qualities of intelligence and interest. As a lyric writer with one independent band stated:

W: One thing that worries me actually is that I think we assume an intelligent audience, we assume that the average person who would buy our records and listen to us would be intelligent in the sense that they'd realize that there is a bit of depth to it. But, one thing that I think we all realize . . . If you look at the Top Twenty singles and albums the general standard is pretty pathetic and we realize that and when you see what gets in the charts it does get pretty disheartening . . . In a way it's a bit idealistic because you assume an intelligent audience and yet the evidence is that they're not intelligent. That sounds elitist, but that's the way it seems to me.

The concern not to appear 'elitist' and yet to encourage a discriminating audience is pervasive in rock. The separation between rock and pop is frequently made on the basis of an aesthetico-political hierarchy of the critical/oppositional and self-consciously 'cerebral' over the collusive/passive and unashamedly 'corporeal'. However, running counter to this distinction (which from the perspective of the nineties looks increasingly inadequate) is the requirement that rock ideology preserves the 'belief that classical music is elitist' (Moore, 1993: 20; see also Bennett, 1980; Shepherd, 1987) and that 'popular music has stayed especially close to "the body" – compared to the art music of the European aristocracy and bourgeoisie – and that this intimacy has increased in the twentieth century, particularly since rock 'n' roll'

(Middleton, 1990: 258). This elective affinity between rock and corporeal pleasure (discussed further in the following chapter) is an important check on what is seen as the excessive rationalism of overtly political and intellectually 'inaccessible' rock. For this reason, conceptual combinations of seriousness and pleasure are forged, as the above-quoted rock lyricist went on to emphasize:

> W: . . . what we're trying to get over, it's as [independent producer] Bob Fast once said, Bob Last sorry, 'serious fun's' the phrase sort of thing, that's the idea, serious fun . . . I wouldn't like the idea that people go away happy, in the sense that they've been reassured that everything is fantastic, I'd like them to have enjoyed it and been stimulated . . . I once introduced, when the group had been going a few months and nobody had ever thought of it before, and I suddenly said, 'Can anybody dance to our songs?' And in fact you couldn't at that stage, but I think that's improved quite a lot. But we wouldn't like people to sit there and think, we would like to get some instant reaction, and then perhaps people would talk and think later on, especially about the words.

This re-assertion of the phenomenology of the body and the function of dance is evidence of a particular tension within an independent rock genre self-defined as antithetical to mainstream corporate rock and chart pop. Simon Reynolds (1989: 254) notes this unease within what he calls the 'indiepop' of 'white-middle-class bohemianism'. Here, 'in today's independent label music, diverse as it is, we can find a common impulse to rise above the body', thereby producing a music characterized by its 'undanceability' in its encouragement of 'bodily passive contemplation'. Where movement does occur, it 'strictly demands physical responses that contravene the norms of dance and sexual attraction, that involve a *sacrifice* of cool' (p. 246). The ascension of the body as the explicit locus of desire in the hedonistic consumerist hegemony of late capitalism has, according to Reynolds, produced an anti-corporealism within white 'indiepop' which divides it from 'pop's body culture', which:

> is all about dance and spectacle, not meaning; about fascination, not interpretation . . . What's disliked about black pop and its white imitators that fill the charts is its notion of sophistication (a flashy lifestyle, reflected in a *class*-y sound) and its 'vulgarity' (a hypersexuality foreign to most indie fans' experience) . . . Chart pop foregrounds sexual passion, specific body need . . . But indiepop love is a cerebral affair . . . constituted/consummated not in the flesh and its throes, but in intense exchanges of *language* – the *unique* details of courtship, confidences, the scene. (Reynolds, 1989: 246–7)

Jim Curtis (1987: 307), in viewing punk as the complementary 'other side of disco' equally dedicated to 'celebrityhood as amateurism', proposes a similar racially-inflected split over rock's commodified body:

> If disco often flaunted sexuality, much of punk rock denied sexuality or feeling of any kind . . . If disco had roots in black music, especially Motown, punk renounced black music – it was the whitest music ever. (This was the principal reason why you couldn't dance to it.) If disco enjoyed great commercial success, punk did not, by and large.

The dualities of immediacy and thought, like the combination of seriousness and fun, and also intellectual stimulation and dance, are represented in rock discourse as qualities and practices which only intermittently connect and which exist in uneasy combinations. This 'teeth gritting harmony' (as Althusser (1971) describes such uneasy articulations) stems from a tendency to view entertainment and politics (broadly conceived as the relationship of straightforward leisurely diversion to a more complex and self-consciously critical response to culture and society) in essentially binary terms. In much the same way, but within academic discourse, the Left Leavisite position regards the consumption and use of commercially available cultural items as entirely commoditized and its users and their symbols wholly coopted and incorporated within dominant ideology. On the other side of the binary divide is the quite 'shameless' embrace of the pleasures (variably commoditized) of the body through the agency of rock. So thoroughgoing is this split within rock discourse that cultural producers, especially in the politically-charged independent sphere, feel compelled to 'heal' it in a variety of ways. For example, the lyricist quoted above who sought to fuse seriousness and fun, or cerebral quality with physicality, attempted to resolve this 'problematic' by resorting to the notion of personal politics:

> W: We don't want to baffle people. We want to get, have immediate impact. The kind of things we want them to think about, and I suppose that is exclusively to do with the words, I suppose, but which I find difficult to talk about actually, basically, we're talking about broadening people's outlook. Sort of, I mean, pseudo . . . not really on a political level, but personal politics sort of thing, not party politics.

The difficulty experienced by the speaker is, fundamentally, of adjudicating between the need for 'immediate impact' (which roughly corresponds here to entertainment) and the ideal of 'broadening people's outlook', which entails some notion of political intervention, 'enlightenment', and which is not seen as intrinsically entertaining. The concept of 'personal politics' is invoked as a strategic alternative to a 'party politics' distanced both from the kind of intellectualism which is baffling rather than entertaining and from the kind of broad, social critique that is seen to alienate audiences through its affective remoteness. This tendency to emphasize what another interviewee described as 'politics with a small "p"' is common among those involved in independently-produced rock, principally because it operates, ideologically, as a concept which mediates between overt political address and what one musician described as music that was 'non-political . . . just singing about the girl next door and having a good time'. Politics is often admitted to the domain of 'indie' rock at the 'micro' level of interpersonal relations essentially to differentiate it from the chart-oriented pop previously described as 'pretty appalling', and also in response to the politics of punk which, while emphasizing social realism and alienation, also revealed an overall hostility to orthodox political practice.

In the previous chapter the pivotal role of punk in providing the cultural impetus for the development of new independent organizational forms was stressed. Punk's contribution to political discourse within rock in the period under review (and, indeed, to the present day) is similarly critical. One significant independent group, which later went on, after some personnel changes, to find international success in the pop charts, described punk's disruptive impact on their experience of art college in the mid-seventies:

> G: Just talking in academic terms to academics just seemed like a dead loss, and at that time the Pistols and The Clash had just been to the Poly, and The Clash album just released, and just the whole simplicity, positivism, vibrancy and aggression and all things that were anathema to academia but were still very deconstructive, aggressive and questioning were going on.

The group, having been stimulated by punk in the first instance, decided to make an independent record for the following reasons:

> G: It was a kind of classically political action, in that it suited our interests and needs to make a record, it also suited our idealism, you know, which we did have a kind of political idealism, and it suited our abilities and the means of production we had access to.

The 'classically political action' involved in making an independent record (including record sleeve advice for other groups about how to make records) stemmed from the group's involvement in 'traditional Left politics . . . we saw things in terms of Uppity Young Marxists'. While members of the Young Communist League, the members of the group saw the world as:

> G: a very cut and dried place. You've got your classes, your contradictions, you've got your ideologies, you've got your projectivity and you've got, you know, scientific truth about history and here you go, you know, just get stuck in there and begin to sort it out, you know, and that's how we saw it, in those very simple classical political terms.
> Q: And it's different now?
> N: Yes, it is different now. Markedly different now.

Thus, the initial political, oppositional orientation of the group which led them to view independent rock production in fairly orthodox political terms was modified to the extent that 'we don't think we're Marxists at all anymore', because 'you can only revise things so far. The paradigm bursts after a while. You keep finding things that don't work'. The group's disillusionment with a 'big "P" political dimension . . . in the mass sphere' stemmed from the problems of coping with the immediate, strategic problems of what 'local councils are up to, or what Thatcher's doing' and also with what was seen to be an undue emphasis on economic determinism, which was associated with the 'ghost of traditional politics, classical politics'. As the group became more involved in independent rock production, their conception and practice of politics changed:

> G: Politics kind of shifted to those who were informed a lot less by idealism, although it never ever seemed a particularly idealistic politics to us, I don't think. It always seemed a very harsh and realistic politics, I think, in the pursuit of a harsh and realistic politics for ourselves and of ourselves, as working subjects, you know, our politics now are born of interests, they're a lot more micro-politics and a lot more pragmatic.

Thus, while the members of the group saw themselves (from, it should be recognized, an uncommonly theoretically-sophisticated and self-consciously reflexive position) as still politically engaged, it was through a commitment to an 'under-formed, new politics' which reflected the emerging concern with personal politics at the expense of its programmatic form. At the same time, the acute awareness of the place of politics in rock discourse, which had been given particular prominence by punk, meant that:

> N: I'd still see, if someone were to ask me, you know . . . are you a political group? Or does politics inform your work? I would still see the work as political in the sense that I don't believe the political can be escaped or transcended, but not traditionally political, i.e. not big "P" political, institutionalized politics.
> Q: So what do you see are the political possibilities of independent record production?
> G: That's an interesting question. I think the answer to that is that, how you conceive of the future and the possibilities for independent record production depend on the conditions for your calculation, i.e. depends on your political bias at the outset.

This group became, after several years of pioneering involvement in the independent sector, distanced from the position of those who see 'independent record production as striking a blow for the revolution . . . as we did once'. The rejection of a Marxist-inspired 'agit-pop' orientation precipitated a simultaneous repudiation of the ideology of rock independence. Not only had it departed from revolutionary politics, but it had also moved away from:

> G: that D-I-Y aesthetic [that] has kind of suffered from overkill. And so the aesthetics of independent production . . . I think they've just blown it to pieces, I think it's fairly died. I don't think it's any longer anything to be celebrated, I think. It's been stated, it's been celebrated, at the moment it's out-wearing its usefulness. We were actively involved in stating and celebrating it and I'm quite interested in moving on.

Steve Redhead (1990: 72), at the start of the following decade, notes a similar pattern of celebration of a 'new underground – a new bohemia . . . [f]ollowing on from the 1960s counter-culture and 1970s punk', which in turn is questioned because '"independence" no longer signifies "deviance" in the way that rock theory claims'. The concepts of marginality and independence can, therefore, be seen as re-constituted in a series of 'natural histories' of involvement in the rock music industry. The acknowledged concern with small-scale, independent production had, in the specific case of the rock group quoted immediately above, given way to a desire to escape from what was described as the 'independent ghetto'. This shift did not necessarily entail a complete departure from the independent network to the major sphere, but rather required a move into larger-scale production, dissemination and consumption – a professionalization and extension of the independents which would give them:

> N: a significant and interesting place, if that place were to gain chart potential. I mean, in terms of the ghetto, they're overplaying, they're overkill, they're well smoked, but in terms of the charts, I think that's a different proposition.

This interest in 'chart potential' clearly signals a major break with the

anti-commercial, small-scale independent ideology which had once distinguished the rock independents. The shift from a position favouring classical
politics and marginal rock production to a new, personal politics and an
aspiration to make the mainstream charts (which necessarily requires larger-
scale production) stems from a pronounced re-integration of the concept of
mass entertainment. This development occurs through the exploration of the
contours of a range of dualities – rock/pop; marginal/central; minority/pop-
ular; and so on – which are constantly thrown up in rock practice, as is
evidenced in the following statement:

> G: Rock music seems to me to have, at its kind of peripheral margins, on the one
> hand pop music and on the other hand really marginal music, unprecedented
> music . . . I'm interested in the kind of interface between excessively marginal
> music and ultra-popular music, more than I would be in just peddling more
> rock music.

The 'interface' between 'marginal' (small independent) and 'ultra-popular'
music is seen to be compelling because it represents, substantially, a site at
which politics and entertainment potentially converge in rock discourse. Rock
ideology, which is heavily infused with the politics of the sixties, is contrasted
with unselfconscious, entertainment-oriented pop consumption. Whereas
rock audiences interpret music within 'an almost manufactured and distributed rock ideology ... peddled by the press', pop music is felt to be interesting
because:

> G: Before the rock press ever got to be very pseudo-theoretical . . . they were mak-
> ing music that was in some sense music that was sexual, violent and
> nonsensical – I mean it really did challenge the kind of circumscription of sense
> versus nonsense, which is important I think in psychologistical terms and sex-
> ual terms . . . it, you know, transgressed all these immediately but in a very
> particular way without recourse to an overblown and ill-informed and manu-
> factured rock ideology.

The stress on immediacy and the unmediated reception of pop through its
direct appeal to emotions recalls Frith's (1981: 35) statement that 'pop songs
celebrate not the articulate but the inarticulate', while the sixties' legacy of
rock was its self-conscious intellectualism and, frequently, its oppositionality.
Punk, as we have seen, sought to re-instate the direct address of pop and par-
alleled its basic temporal form (the three-minute single as opposed to what
another independent musician called 'hippy waffling'), but at the same time
drew upon those elements of rock ideology which emphasized resistance to
corporate cultural capitalism in a manner that aligned it with some of the
more avowedly political interventions (such as Rock against Racism) of 'classical big "P" politics'. It is as part of the rejection of classical politics that the
antinomy between 'sense versus nonsense' is invoked and that the rationalist
discourse of programmatic politics is supplanted by an irrationalist injunction
to, in the title of a well-known record by the American 'new wave' band
Talking Heads, 'stop making sense'. This is a mutation of the ideological
antinomy between the self-conscious politics of independent rock and the
unconscious, unmediated subversion of pop, so that it is the 'nonsense' of

reflexive, postmodern pop (Redhead, 1990) which is believed to be more challenging to the social order than the 'commonsense' messages of orthodox, revolutionary politics communicated by some 'engaged' rock bands (such as, from the punk period, Gang of Four and The Clash).

It is important to recognize, however, that this ideological and cultural journey from the more orthodox politics of the independent 'ghetto' to the unconventional, strategic politics of 'ultra-popular' music is also a significant economic initiative. The 'swamping' of the independent market by the 'nouveau hippy cottage industry', as described by the drummer of one seminal independent band, made it even more difficult for independent cultural producers to survive on their principal sources of musical income – the sale of records and tapes, and the receipt of fees for performances. These problems of extreme economic marginality meant that the resources of a major record company had obvious appeal:

Q: Do you think you'd ever accept an offer from a major if you got one?
N: That's a possibility, I wouldn't rule it out.
M: In spite of the colour telly!
G: In spite of the colour telly, which is actually a lot cheaper than you think! Our one luxury apart from the drink. Our lifestyle is extremely marginal, supported by the Social Security, that sort of business, and which means that if they should turn nasty on us and a number of other things should occur, then economically the group might be in crisis and we might have to pack it in.

The material problem of survival in the independent sphere, then, of itself prompts an ideological reconciliation with the mass leisure of pop. At the same time, this realignment is also presented as a political shift, albeit towards pragmatic, micro-politics. It is apparent, therefore, that the difficult conditions which obtain for independent personnel as cultural workers encourages a shift from idealism to pragmatism (see also Redhead, 1990: 74). In this sense, the account I have provided of one group's movement from being pioneers of independent rock production to viewing it as 'out-wearing its usefulness' may be regarded as the product of the obvious vulnerability of rock producers on the margins of the industry and of the difficulty of maintaining a balance between two elements within independent rock ideology which are held in perpetual tension – classically oppositional politics and unconventional, unselfconscious entertainment. The nature of the political as it is conceived in the rock independent sphere is diverse and often inconsistent. This is an unsurprising phenomenon given the chaotic and often contradictory nature of the production and consumption processes. One (unpaid) worker for a regional label and retail outlet, for example, connected socialism to communitarianism:

B: I suppose it touches on socialism, the small label thing is concentrated on socialist beliefs . . . We're not concerned, at least not at Attack [pseudonym], with anarchy or with anything like that. We don't want to know anything about that. The basic means of Attack is bring Brighton music from our own label into the ears of a lot more people, millions or thousands, anything, as many as we can reach and just hope it appeals to people. We haven't got really a political stance at all, maybe just the only thing is just from a socialist point of view.

> We're a very small company, when I say small, I mean small. It's very ... I don't
> get paid for working in the shop, none of us do, the shop runs at a loss all the
> time, that's another sad fact. It's, it's just a love of music, really, and the label I
> believe, it's the community sense, that's all it is. Politics doesn't enter into it with
> us. I think I can safely say that ... not to any major degree, anyway.

Here music and politics are perceived as radically separate, with the enterprise identified as socialistic on account of its size, its communal use of
facilities (such as practice halls and equipment), and 'personal political'
sense of locality. However, a more recognizable (albeit resigned) political
hostility to the majors was also displayed in a discussion of the label's licensing and distribution association with a larger record company and the
signing of the independent label's most successful act by a multinational
record company:

> B: It's a shame majors are capitalists, and are in it for the money. I don't believe for
> a minute that any of them have any real belief in the music, just is it mar-
> ketable? . . . It's a sad fact. They are capitalists, we hate them but they're doing
> it for us. We're making bread out of it, they're making much, much more bread
> out of it, and we're getting through to a lot more people. That's the only reason
> they do it, really.

This uneasiness concerning such alliances between majors and independents was exhibited in a variety of expressions of antagonism and acceptance.
One independent label owner, for example, conceived majors and independents as being in peaceful co-existence, with the independents providing a
non-oppositional alternative:

> Q: Do you see yourself at all in opposition to the majors?
> S: No, I think we should be an alternative, not in opposition. We can't afford to be
> an opposition.
> Q: Some people say they'd like to destroy CBS, Polydor, etc.
> S: Why? Maybe when I'm fifty I'll enjoy listening to Abba records. Um, there are
> a lot of shitty people in that side of the business I would like to see personally
> fall down a manhole, but the service they actually do is OK for their market . . .
> I wouldn't be able to get hold of some of the music I like. I like Vangelis, now
> Vangelis needs a big company behind him to pay him tens of thousands of
> pounds in the studio to be able to get that music. If there weren't big companies
> all that would be gone.

Evident here is some of the familiar hostility to the majors (in terms of a
dislike for some individuals who work within them), but it is accepted that the
interests of both majors and independents can be accommodated. This attitude contrasts markedly with the musician who declared that 'independents
hate major labels!' and another who believed that the major companies were
'trying to knock the independents on the head'. As noted in the previous
chapter, there was also disagreement on the 'synergistic' arrangement of the
independents operating as 'nurseries' for the majors, these cooperative ventures being variously regarded as benign and inevitable or as malign and
resistible. The independent label owner quoted immediately above adopted
the former position, having put out a regional 'sampler' album as a showcase
for acts who could thereby come to the notice of major record companies.

This was particularly the case for the group he managed, which he believed to be in a position to sign up with a major:

> S: I just try and guide them. If a record out on my label will help them, we put it out on my label, but if it won't I'll do the best I can to try and get them on another label. With one band, we've had two singles out by them and they've got to the stage where they need more money behind them that only a major record company can give and there are two or three other record companies now interested in the band. But they needed the couple of independent singles first, to be able to get gigs in London, reviewed in papers and things like that. It was a stepping stone only, but it was always known to be just a stepping stone and a very good one.

This function of the independents as a 'stepping stone' for the majors tended to be viewed with equanimity by those pragmatist independent operators whose major criticism of the majors was on the grounds of conservative or faulty taste rather than political economic control. For such people, establishing an independent company and/or label was seen to be a necessity resulting from their failure to gain a major recording contract. Involvement in independent rock production was treated as a method of building up an audience and of coming to the attention of cultural gatekeepers (such as radio and the music press). In this way rock acts would be more likely to be noticed by the majors' A and R persons and would also be in a stronger bargaining position to insert 'artistic control' clauses in their contracts. From such a perspective, the 'nursery' system is not only inevitable but also desirable, an effect of the market with little bearing on any conception of the politics of cultural access and control. This attitude contrasted markedly with that held by the more self-consciously politicized independent activists who saw in the passage of artists from independents to majors a quintessential exemplification of the subordination of the former to the latter:

> P: The independents are serving like the apprenticeship makers and the majors are just coming along, waving the big cheques and, like, pinching the best, they cream off all the independent stuff, which is totally wrong. The only bands they don't get are the bands that are strong enough to hold on until they get what they want, eventually. There are not many bands who are morally strong enough to do that.

Concrete criticisms of this kind about the industrial structures and practices of majors and independents are often freely and forcefully expressed, but more abstract conceptions of politics and cultural production are, even in an independent sector putatively sensitized to such concerns, often resisted. As Stratton (1983b: 305) has argued, 'Music, that is "pop music", is known to be this thing because of the way in which it is experienced. It is however experienced non-analytically, magically.' The conceptualization of musical practice as 'ideally' separated from politics and simultaneously resistant to critical analysis both sustains and obscures the politics/entertainment antinomy. Politics is viewed by some operating in the independent sphere as unproblematically constituting a set of practices external to their own, an attitude which in turn prompts an idealized evacuation of the political by construing it in only the narrowest and most unpromising of terms:

S: So my policy is I don't like politics in music. There wasn't any until recently, comparatively speaking, in music history.

Q: Not in the sixties?

S: We managed in the sixties. There were slight protest songs in the sixties, but that was true, everybody didn't want the bomb. So there were protest bands and songs, a few protest songs about not being in Vietnam or something. They were noble sentiments but that wasn't, um, that was more philosophy than politics. Politics came into it at the very end of the sixties, and yet we lived quite well before without it. The Beatles never brought politics into it, neither did the Stones or any of those groups.

Here the concern to expel politics from rock occurs through an emphasis on a de-politicized cultural expressiveness, although it is also recognized that at certain moments there will be an articulation of the musical and the political. The disjunction is resolved in this instance by separating politics from philosophy (or action from 'noble sentiment') in spite of the acknowledgement of instances (Vietnam, anti-nuclear protest) in which political activity clearly was a pivotal element of rock discourse. This problem is elided by suggesting that the value orientation was so generalized as not to be political at all, while politics is viewed largely in terms of its fragmenting rather than unifying capacity ('Let's kick the fuck out of blacks, or wogs, or the SWP or whatever'). From such perspectives, musical entertainment is something 'to enjoy, to relax to, to escape with' and where, if politics is admitted at all, it is at the level of personal ethics or politics, or as the expression of a philosophy which is felt to be fundamentally apolitical. The members of one independent group distanced themselves from overt politics in the following way:

Q: Do you deal explicitly with political issues at all in your music?

Z: Um, not in terms of injecting our own views into politics, or whatever. It's like a voyeur thing.

W: It's more a case of making observations and sort of commenting on those, rather than delivering a manifesto, we sort of make suggestions more than statements. Because, I mean, we're influenced a lot, as everybody is, by the media in general. I think a lot of it is just sort of observations on that and the way that we see it, you know, it's not political in the sense of making statements.

Z: These are my views, I will now sing about them, sort of thing. I mean we, people aren't quite sure what ... I think they know now that we don't overtly make political statements.

The treatment of political issues in music is viewed in this case as occurring by means of 'observations' and 'suggestions' in song lyrics rather than in 'manifestos' or 'statements'. Politics is associated with (and almost reduced to) the latter, and is viewed as being somehow outside music and so requiring to be injected into music rather than as an integral dimension of it. The 'voyeurism' of observation is offered as an alternative to 'delivering a manifesto', which is how political activity and ideas are represented and positioned within the discourse. It is this restricted view of politics which is required to be explained.

Politics in independent rock music (and in most other forms) are primarily associated with lyrical content, which is seen to comprise, almost in caricature fashion, political manifestos or statements on the one hand, or to be substantially outside or above politics on the other. In the case of the latter approach, the politics which were admitted were restricted to personal observation viewed in largely apolitical terms. This is in part an aesthetic problem. While politics may be located or identified in lyrics without great difficulty, the politics of sound (music) are more difficult to establish and, for most respondents, are denied altogether. Thus, not only are politics in rock often positioned within a binary structure of manifesto/entertainment, but they are also confined to the lyrics of songs rather than to musical form. Some members of the independent network did, however, take a wider view of the relationship between politics and musical aesthetics. As one independent musician remarked about an avowedly Marxist group (then signed to the major EMI):

> M: Really, the only radical thing about the Gang of Four, apart from their political lyrics, which isn't really radical anyway, it's just putting, I think, old clichés into a rock format . . . but the only radical thing about it is Andy Gill's guitar playing, I suppose, because he's dared to, well really, you could say, play badly in a way. He's dared to put on record the sort of things that most people do when they're pissing about – but put it in a way that sounds good. But they're still very traditional rock songs really, the structures of the songs are still a very traditional rock kind of thing.

In this statement, the radical political dimension of rock is not seen to lie in its lyrics, however 'revolutionary' they might be, but in the way that an instrument is played and in musical structure. The guitar which is played deliberately badly brings music which is inexpert or normally confined to spaces outside recorded music into a cultural arena from which it has been previously excluded. It is in this sense that rock is seen to be potentially radical, by subverting understandings of what constitutes 'good music' and by linking the subversion of cultural forms with an implied transformation of social forms (Wicke, 1990: 182-3). In examining the conventional relations between music and lyrics, one independent lyricist noted that:

> W: The group accept my lyrics without question, more or less, nobody ever asks me what they're about, which I find . . . I find, that's just the way it works and they seem to be quite happy, because . . . I listen very strongly to the words, whereas a lot of musicians and a lot of people don't actually listen to the words very much, but I do. So maybe we're just happy to have them as they are, but it's surprising that they never ask me what they're about.
>
> Q: But if they don't know what they're about how can the music fit the lyrics?
>
> W: Well, they don't necessarily have to, that's one thing we quite like the idea of.
>
> Q: Well what happens if you have like a romantic song, for example, and a particularly frivolous backing?
>
> W: Well, that's quite an interesting idea, I don't see why they should fit together.
>
> Q: Yes, but then they might make your lyrics ridiculous, and you might have meant them seriously, or vice versa.
>
> W: Yeah, yeah. I suppose we quite like that dislocation.

Such 'dislocations' are emphasized as permitting open and multi-faceted textual possibilities which are contrasted with the (fore)closed discourse of overtly political rock. 'Good' lyrics and music are seen to be produced only under conditions which permit a high degree of freedom from the ideological constraint of political manifestos and statements. This openness is frequently accompanied by an unashamedly subjectivist regime of taste:

> S: . . . I've got 3,000 records sitting around this room and every one I like. There's everything there from Stockhausen to Marianne Faithfull to Kraftwerk. It's just something that I hear. I can either dance to it or it's got memories asociated with it, or whatever.

This repudiation of any conscious consistent aesthetic is expressed schematically and teleologically, as in this independent group member's description of its sound:

> P: It's pop music in a broad sense. I mean, one thing, probably all our songs have lyrics, they've nearly all got tunes and verses and choruses, not all of them, most of them, but I don't think you can be any more specific than that really.

This unspecific orientation to music echoes the responses elicited by Stratton (1983b: 296) in his analysis of attitudes to music in the mainstream rock industry – 'Good records are records that are liked.' Stratton noted the routine separation of an 'ineffable' music essentially resistant to analysis from the 'rational', predictable economic operation of the popular music industry. A similar gulf exists between the domain of politics, which is normally delineated as lyrically-enunciated statements/manifestos, and the sphere of 'good music'/entertainment, which, while it is separated from politics, cannot often be defined in any but the most subjectivist and vague manner by those who operationalize it. The dichotomous structure of politics and entertainment, therefore, tends to treat the former as closed and the latter as open, thereby hampering any effective exploration of their relationship. The independent network, which is conscious of its stylistic foundation in the resistive gestures of punk, is constantly confronted with this disabling duality. It reveals the extent to which rock, for all its oppositional mythology (especially among the independents), is still subject to the de-politicizing pressures exerted against any and all cultural producers jostling for space in the marketplace of musical commodities.

Conclusion

In this chapter I have examined the operation of the concepts of politics and entertainment in rock, especially in relation to inter-cultural musical exchange, electoral intervention and populist charitable mobilization. The British independent moment was presented as an historically important instance in which the politics of musical production – not merely of musical content – were given specific priority. Although a commitment to politics (principally, socialist) by some musicians, label owners and so on was evident, rather more common was a suspicion and rejection of politics viewed as either overly restrictive or merely gestural – as one musician dismissively observed (of the fans of the avowedly anarchist band Crass), '[they] feel like they're doing something political by buying something with an "A" on it, with a circle round it, you know.' Only occasionally are politics in rock conceived as being more than clichés or slogans. The predominant view of cultural practice is individuated and arises out of the substantially petty bourgeois position and orientation of most independents, coupled with a common concern not to appear hypocritical by trading political commitment as simply one more marketing device. As one musician put it:

> G: But there's always that danger of pushing yourself into too much of a dilemma and making yourself look a real hypocrite because you're in the marketplace just as anyone else, you know. Your job, not your job, but your preoccupation, is to sell records, you know, and by doing that you're involved in like capitalist processes as much as anyone else. It's the degree of autonomy you can do whilst achieving that end that's important, really retaining your integrity.

This statement reveals the dilemma of the independent cultural producer who is not principally commercially motivated but is nonetheless inevitably commercially involved, and has a 'job' that is a 'preoccupation', because, while it is analogous to conventional labour, 'creative' cultural production is differentiated from those other forms of labour viewed as routine and mundane. The symbolic importance of 'integrity' is that it represents resistance to the standardized and professionalized processes of commerce. While this tension between creativity and professionalism is felt most keenly in the independent rock sector, it also runs through the entire apparatus of rock culture. The rock/pop distinction was, after all, constructed from its inception out of the contradictions of disorderly expressivism and increasingly rationalized production systems. It might, of course, be objected that in the nineties many of these concerns have been rendered obsolete by the emergence or development of 'post-political pop' (Redhead, 1990), 'world music' (Frith, 1989b), niche markets (Reynolds, 1989), flexible corporations (Negus, 1992) and digital technologies which pose substantial challenges to orthodox relations of production and consumption (Durant, 1990; Goodwin, 1990; Hayward, 1992b), especially when in the hands of 'hard rappers' (Costello and Wallace, 1990). Yet, in spite of these undoubtedly important changes, popular music's conditions and relations of production display considerable continuity. This is because digital samplers and licensing deals cannot in themselves overcome perennial questions of how popular music is generated, mediated, organized and experienced. If there are 'many "Underground" rappers who are each month, now, captured and contracted by the big white-run recording corps' (Costello and Wallace, 1990: 23) and constant reconfigurations of musical styles and organizational relations, then it is even more imperative to understand how rock and pop cultures seem at once to be subject to dramatic change and yet appear eerily familiar. If 'Pop might be eating itself, but the old ideologies and aesthetics remain on the menu' (Goodwin, 1990: 272), the conditions of its production and consumption as culture must be further interrogated.

4

Rock Culture: Getting Away with It

Contemporary rock, like any other post-folk cultural form, constructs relationships between producers, texts and audiences across the many divides of society, space and time. As popular culture, rock has drawn much of its power from the mutual identification of artist and fan under conditions of structural, industrialized separation between producer and consumer. On occasions, as in the case of punk, rock has claimed to obliterate the distinction between performer and spectator altogether by proposing their ready interchangeability. The meanings of rock as culture lie, therefore, among and between cultural producers, mediators, consumers, texts and practices. In this chapter I will examine these social relations of rock production, once again using the 'punk independents' as a key reference point. Specific emphasis is placed on the idea of cultural labour and its relevance for questions of affinity and authenticity in rock, and also on the related question of the construction of local and global rock 'constituencies'. First, however, it is necessary to recognize that rock's cultural labour is performed in the pursuit of pleasure, and that this pleasure takes many forms, not least those addressed to the body. The various potential sources of rock's pleasures and meanings are briefly explored as a prelude to a more detailed discussion of the social and institutional framework within which they are expressed and fashioned. As was noted in the previous chapter, the body's position in rock culture is problematized when its celebration is felt by some musicians and critics to be at variance with lyrical and musical form, rationalist ideological critique and 'anti-corporeal' sub-cultural resistance. In addition, the figure of the body is positioned in relation to its 'other', the machine, as competing technologies of rock production. It is this ambivalent nexus of the corporeal and the technological which, it is concluded, is constitutive of rock culture.

The pleasures of the riff

In the foregoing coverage of the economics and politics of rock, the discussion returned, periodically, to its pleasures. If it were not pleasurable on a grand scale, rock would be of little interest to cultural corporations or political parties. The sources and forms of pleasure in rock are manifold, and, like the phenomenon itself, exist in varying degrees of proximity to the strictly musical. Enjoyment of the poetry of rock lyrics, the visual inventiveness of rock video and fashion, the camaraderie of fandom and the resistive assertion of style all constitute important elements of rock culture which have no necessary connection to rock *qua* music. If it is technically possible to embrace the constituents of rock culture without actually liking any rock music, it is unlikely that such a position is widely adopted. For, while there is considerable disagreement about what constitutes rock music – and, even more keenly contested, what is good and bad in it – an appreciation of sound is of central importance. As Lawrence Grossberg (1990: 113) notes, this enjoyment may in part be an automatic physical response to loud noise:

> Rock and roll is corporeal and 'invasive'. For example, without the mediation of meaning, the sheer volume and repetitive rhythms of rock and roll produce a real material pleasure for its fans (at many live concerts, the vibration actually might be compared to the use of a vibrator, often focused on the genital organs) and restructure familial relations (by producing immediate outrage and rejection from its nonfans, e.g., parents).

Whatever the sonic resemblance rock may sometimes have to jackhammers and jumbo jets, it is apparent, however, that such sensory experience always occurs in the cultural context of the 'gig', disco, domestic lounge/bedroom and so on. Rock, in all its manifestations, is closely connected to the body and its pleasures, from 'the grain of the voice' (Barthes, 1977) to the sensuality of dance and the spectacle of the street. It was noted in the previous chapter that the history of rock is closely connected to its status as 'body music' (Middleton, 1990: 258). Yet, whatever its proximity to the material body, it is at the confluence of the corporeal and the cultural that rock's pleasure is made and re-made. Through various dispositions of the body, rock stars and fans alike 'materialize' and articulate rock culture. Hence, Susan McClary and Robert Walser (1990: 289) argue from a musicological perspective that to:

> acknowledge the 'groove' is not to reduce music to some essentialist notion of 'the body' or to seek explanations in biological urges. The rhythmic impulses of rock music are as socially constructed as are the contrapuntal intricacies of the Baroque fugue.

An encounter, therefore, with discordant electronic feedback – which in the first instance is a physiological experience – is interpreted as the hearing of music or of noise only through a cultural process of classifying sound. This activity is often productive of fine distinctions of musical form and genre, with sounds being sorted according to logics of taste and function. As Allan Moore (1993: 24) asserts:

> Indeed, in order to give a musical work existence, the conjunction of the sound and the listening mind is required: as listeners, we need to internalize the music. This means that the act of listening is actually a creative act. What the ears register are only vibrations. The brain has to interpret these vibrations as sounds, and then bring into play prior (learnt) experience in order to perceive relationships between these sounds.

This social mediation of corporeal processes is also (re)productive of ideologies of the body and of culture. For example, the emphasis on corporeality in rock (and also in sport) takes on a racialized dimension in mirroring the white racist association of 'blackness' with nature/primordiality and 'white-ness' with culture/civilization. Just as Ellis Cashmore (1990: 89) has criticized 'the view that blacks have natural qualities suited to sport' (see Chapter 5), Paul Oliver (1990b: 5), in addressing the problem of how to define black music, has challenged the:

> 'all Blacks have rhythm' stereotype, which in the past has justified the imposition of inferior status on the grounds that the skills and qualities that they may have are based on 'primitive' intuitions, rather than on intellect or sensibility.

The ascription of particular (positive or negative) mental and manual characteristics to categories of person is inevitably linked to prevailing ideologies of domination and subordination. It is necessary, then, to recognize that the 'pleasured' body so central to the experience of rock is also always the mediated body in its cultural milieu (Falk, 1994: 10).

In the previous chapter reference was made to the independent rock band which, operating according to the maxim of 'serious fun', discovered that its music largely failed to engage with the body through dance. Harvie Ferguson (1990: 68) describes this combination of the cognitive and the corporeal thus:

> The body as a concretion of signs is a thinking mechanism, the first and most fundamental site of reason's architectonics. In the differentiation of bodily feelings we feel the impulse of reason. The categorical opposition[s] with which we began – mind/body, subject/object, theory/fact – begin to disintegrate. Each term is recognizable in the other. Metamorphosis is reborn. And just for a moment we believe that the primordial world is once again within our reach.

For those who are either appreciative (Pattison, 1987; Tumas-Serna, 1987) or critical (Conway, 1983; Stove, 1983; and most recently, the Parents Music Resource Centre – see, for example, Redhead, 1990: 18) of rock's 'primordiality', the primary emphasis is on its overpowering physiological impact. While, as Grossberg pointed out above, there may be instances where the level of rock's sensory attack is formidable, to conceive of it as a return to the primal is a position beset with contradictions. Not only does rock often fit comfortably with some of the more orderly routines of everyday life (driving, leisure-time listening, factory labour), but also the industrialized organization of rock production, exchange, circulation and consumption is clearly reliant on rather more deeply rationalized processes than the 'primal scream'. Indeed, Grossberg (1988: 56) argues that New Right attacks on rock are paradoxically 'taking place at just the moment when rock music seems to have been so totally and successfully integrated into every aspect of everyday life that it poses little opportunity for resistance of any sort', while Cooper (1991: 54), similarly, sees rock's expressions of 'youthful disenchantment' as a largely de-politicized 'beguiling nihilism'. As we have seen, this commercialized and professionalized dimension runs counter to romantic images of creation, spontaneity, authenticity and unalienated communication pervading rock ideology. Alan Durant (1984: 196–7) captures this 'broad historical outlook' which sees rock 'as "direct" declaration or confession of life and experience, in an address unmediated by conventions of representation', in pointing to the importance of such 'emphases within punk and New Wave Music on DIY ('do-it-yourself') during the mid 1970s'. The working through of relationships between musicians and fans, professionals and amateurs, and cultural workers and consumers was a conspicuous feature of independent rock culture in the late seventies and early eighties. These concerns remain central to any conception of rock as a community or series of 'taste publics' in which exists an 'organic' relationship between artist and audience according to some measure of authenticity (rather than its simulation). One immediate obstacle to this notion is the idea that rock music-making is usually more than a labour of love.

Technology and the labour of culture

Rock literature is, as we have seen, replete with accounts of struggles between artists and record companies for artistic and other forms of control under the social relations of rock production. Within rock ideology (Harron, 1988), this contest is represented in romantic terms as one between creative musical expression and commodification. As Herman and Hoare (1979: 52) put it:

> Captured on record, the song becomes a commodity to be transformed into profit for the industry. The singer who works for a record company (or the singer dependent on publishers for income) becomes a productive labourer, exploited and expropriated – notwithstanding the rare attainment of rich rewards.

Such assessments of the position of the artist draw on Marx's distinction between writers like Milton who 'produced *Paradise Lost* for the same reason that a silk worm produces silk. It was an activity of *his* nature' and 'literary proletarians' who were 'subsumed under capital' and controlled by publishers. Particularly relevant to this discussion is the theoretical proposition that:

> A singer who sells her song for her own account is an *unproductive labourer*. But the same singer commissioned by an entrepreneur to sing in order to make money for him is a *productive labourer*; for she produces capital. (quoted in Solomon, 1979: 75)

There are three conceptions of cultural labour here. The first is engagement in artistic practice for its own sake because of a need to make symbols, engage in the auto-pleasure of cultural expression, and to communicate ideas and beliefs. The second is that of a petty bourgeois activity in which an agent who owns and controls no large-scale means of production sells a skill or a service. Both of these pursuits are regarded as unproductive labour because they do not produce capital, and may be contrasted with the third conception of cultural labour – the sale of cultural creations to a capitalist agent or organization, which will transform the item (and, indeed, the creator) into a commodity, thereby extracting and generating value. Marx tends to treat these forms of labour as mutually exclusive in order to draw out the distinction between productive and unproductive labour, and it is assumed that once exchange value is produced, commodity logic must prevail. Yet, as

Herman and Hoare (1979: 52) point out, a rather more complex set of relationships exists between cultural practice and its exploitation, with producers and products moving both towards and away from direct economic exchange:

> [Thus] singer and song straddle two worlds uncomfortably – on the one hand there are vast conglomerates like EMI, Philips and CBS; on the other there are ceilidhs, folk clubs, friendly jam sessions or even bath-tub soloists.

Cultural producers cannot always easily be assigned to one or other sphere of labour, and it cannot simply (*a priori*) be assumed that because a cultural item is transformed into a commodity, it is therefore essentially commercial in nature, or that the motivation of the creator is qualitatively different if the creation is not 'circulated' for exchange. In any case, a pristine domain of free cultural practice seems even more implausible from the standpoint of the colonized lifeworld of late-twentieth-century capitalism (Habermas, 1987) than it must have appeared to the proletarians and peasants during the more 'primitive' phase of capitalist accumulation in the mid-nineteenth century. Not only is an increasing number of workers operating within the cultural sphere (Lash and Urry, 1994), but also much contemporary cultural production is only made possible by direct or indirect economic exchange. It is only where cultural activity is determinedly amateur, occasional and at the level of what we recognize as a 'hobby' that it can be partially insulated from commerce. Even here, however, culture is clearly 'consumptive', a target for the leisure providers who, for example, promote the purchase of traditional or hi-tech musical instruments so that hobbyists can imitate in private the musical styles already made commercially available to them through the music industry.

Rock culture is, then, heavily reliant on the commercially-produced technology so consistently abhorred by some of the more vigorous anti-modernists who have criticized it (Frith, 1986). For the 'Left Romantics' (like Harker, 1980), it is the intrusion of high technology which facilitates the capitalist appropriation of rock and pop. Raymond Williams (1981: 53) traces the integral relationship between the technological development of the means of cultural reproduction and the ascendancy of the cultural corporation in the following passage:

> There is then a qualitative change from earlier socio-cultural relations, even within the earlier market phases. For the effective (if of course never absolute) origin of cultural production is now centrally sited within the corporate market. The scale of capital involved, and the dependence on more complex and specialized means of production and distribution, have to an important extent blocked access to these media in older artisanal, post-artisanal and even market professional terms, and imposed predominant conditions of corporate employment.
>
> This does not mean, of course, that older forms of relation have not survived elsewhere. In the older arts of painting and sculpture, orchestral music and, as we have seen, some writing, the complex relations of the individual producer (and originator) have persisted. But in music, for example, these older relations have become minor by comparison with the new corporate institutions of popular music, based on the new technologies of disc and cassette, where the corporate capitalist mode is decisive.

The critique of the involvement of big capital and high technology in music sometimes, as we have seen, is advanced as an 'organicist' opposition to developments in the forces of cultural production and an advocacy of a return to the folk form. Rosselson (1979: 48), for example, wishes to resist such developments by reviving 'The folk-club circuit and the folk idiom [which] have to be taken seriously as possibilities to build on, because they have exactly those strengths lacking in the commercial world'. These strengths of folk include an essentially local and communal orientation, the absence or marginalization of business interests and profit motives, the breakdown of barriers between performers and audiences and, crucially, the absence of any technology other than the acoustic:

> There is generally no amplification. Communication is based on the spoken word rather than the shouted sound. Glamour and image play little part. Floor singers and audience participation are encouraged. (p. 48)

Such rejections of the development of the forces of cultural production and of the involvement of corporate capitalism in rock propose a withdrawal from modern, technologically manufactured and transmitted culture by those who wish to resist capitalist hegemony. The 'non-auratic', popular democratic possibilities created by developments in technology and form (Benjamin, 1973; Enzensberger, 1976) are denied in this acoustic 'folk' tradition of ballads and work songs performed in the non- or pre-capitalist spaces where authentically oppositional popular culture can be articulated. Intriguingly, echoes of this position can be found in the current vogue of the 'Unplugged', where established 'electric' rock artists (like Eric Clapton) return temporarily to the acoustic form in the hi-tech environment of the TV/audio studio, often producing worldwide hits which are played principally on digital home audio equipment. The return to previous technological forms is accompanied at other sites by the deployment of new technologies in performance and recording which seem to obliterate the distinction between musician and machine (Hayward, 1992b). The normative level of 'the human' within musical labour is, therefore, a function of the constant disturbance of the conditions of musical production by the emergence, mobilization and appropriation of new audio technologies, from the electric guitar to the synthesizer and on to the digital sampler (Durant, 1990).

Rock music and technology exist in a necessary and difficult relation. Rock is a musical form which from its inception was involved in high levels of technological intervention. This is not to argue that rock is uniquely technological – an acoustic guitar or piano is also a form of technology – but rock's pioneering combination of amplification in performance (which was regarded as traitorous by folk apologists) and transmutation through studio recording has given a peculiarly apposite twist to the sixties' adage that 'The Rock Machine Turns You On'. Yet rock's contradictory alliance of romanticism and modernism produces considerable ambivalence in regard to technology (Frith, 1986). The machines that are produced by industrial capitalism are also the means by which rock critiques of commercialism and alienation are disseminated, while the humanism of 'rebel rock' often collides with the machine aesthetics of a disengaged avant-garde (Goodwin, 1990: 269). Control over technology has been central to the cultural politics of rock. As the discussion of the rock independents demonstrated, it was in gaining access to the means of musical (re)production that their anti-corporate radicalism was widely held to inhere (Laing, 1985). The politics of technology have also been manifest in various other ways – for example, in the idea of technical perfection in progressive rock (Street, 1986: 192) or in the practice of 'home taping' by consumers who, through the advent of audio tape, have broken the producers' monopoly of electronic musical reproduction (Jones, 1992: 138). The technological questions which I will concentrate on here concern, however, authorship and authenticity. These are particularly pressing issues in an era of the rapid supersession of the analogue technology on which rock has been founded.

As Goodwin asserts (1990: 264), the widespread use of computing technology in rock and pop (such as the digital sampling of other musical recordings) has produced a new and 'increasing problem of distinguishing between originals and copies on the one hand, and between human and automated performance on the other'. Postmodernist theory, with its emphasis on pastiche, quotation, unauthenticity and inter-textuality, seeks to render these problems as outmoded and irrelevant, as reflecting former, theoretically naive 'phases of the image' (Baudrillard, 1983a: 11). It is apparent, however, that notions of originality and human creativity still retain significance. Whether or not a group played or sang on its record remains important for fans. Perhaps the most prominent recent case of musical 'fraud' concerned the pop group Milli Vanilli, who in 1990 were discovered to have 'lip-synced' in performance and not to have sung on their records. The ensuing outrage involved the ritual destruction of their records, the stripping of their Grammy Award, the return of purchased material to their record company, the collapse of the group's career, and a subsequent recording by 'session singers' calling themselves The Real Milli Vanilli.

Similarly, the confusion of human and machine is often disturbing for rock fans – as Jones (1992: 192) notes, at a '1990 concert by the group New Order, fans were occasionally displeased when song introductions or breaks emanated from the PA speakers without the group's performance on an instrument'. The maintenance of a necessary illusion of nominated and imaged human subjects playing specified roles and exercising continuing command over technology appears to be paramount in rock and pop consumption (see Struthers, 1987). This self-delusion is prompted partially by the persistent aura of the star(s), whose genius cannot be diffused by suggestions of industrialized and rationalized simulation. It is also, crucially, created out of the compact between musical producer and consumer, in which the content of a 'brand' must correspond to that displayed on its label (Lash and Urry, 1994: 137). The consumer is not the only party with an interest in affixing the author to the product. The producer, who is reliant on income from legally binding copyright material, also has an incentive to assert the rights of intellectual property. The securing of those rights, which, perhaps paradoxically, are dependent on the very rationalization and commodification of music that is antipathetic to the romantic strain in rock ideology, is made problematic by the deployment of technology in a manner that repudiates unique claims to artistic creativity (Costello and Wallace, 1990: 86). The extent to which practices of imitation, borrowing and sampling are regarded as democratization, re-appropriation, exploitation, intellectual theft or aesthetic 'disfigurement' is keenly contested according to structural location in the process of musical production, circulation and consumption.

The increasing use of digital technologies such as Musical Instrument Digital Interface (MIDI) and techniques like sampling (reproducing sounds, including other recorded music, on 'new' musical recordings) have exerted considerable influence on conceptions of creativity and independence. The earlier discussion of the 'British independent moment' demonstrated that the traditional romantic rock ethic was still present – indeed, the punk independents might be seen in retrospect as a spectacular assertion of rock as dissident, organic and humanistic. Seizing the means of musical production by gaining access to rudimentary studio technology was a necessary activity in matching new 'authors' with alienated audiences. These new productive arrangements also produced novel musical styles and technological applications. As Alan Durant (1990: 186), for example, has noted:

> House records, such as Steve Silk Hurley's *Jack your Body*, Bomb the Bass's *Beat This*, or Lil Louis's *French Kiss*, bring together current digital music technologies with a DIY (do-it-yourself) attitude to music production, and with a specific urban aesthetic and cultural politics based on mixing and rapping – with little concern to respect intellectual property.

Whereas many in the rock independent and major sectors were and are attached to promoting images of the musician as celebrity and ideologies of music as 'serious' and subversive, the comparative anonymity of House and techno acts, their emphasis on dancing rather than listening, and their free deployment of other people's sounds have challenged prevailing notions of stardom, music and creativity. It is not surprising that, as with home taping and piracy, the digital sampling of snatches or elements of music over which intellectual property rights are claimed should result in litigation. Philip Hayward (1992b; see also White, 1987) discusses a number of legal cases from the eighties and nineties, such as those involving M/A/R/R/S, Black Box, Vanilla Ice, David Bowie and Queen, in which sampling was held to infringe copyright and royalties and fees were sought. Whatever critical stability may have been achieved in fixing a normative relationship between musicians, machines and texts has been seriously disturbed by these technologically-enhanced practices and their ensuing conflicts over creativity, authorship, control and remuneration. The technophobia that Negus (1992: 28) notes in critiques of technology 'seen to be replacing musicians with machines, enabling charlatans to create music by stealing other people's ideas and in the process leading to a decline in musical skills' is pitted against the celebration of new forms, sounds and social relations of musical production prompted by the new technology's downward adjustment of 'skill levels'

(Durant, 1990). Once again, hope is held out of the bridging of the modernist cleavage between producer and consumer.

The enduring preoccupation in rock and pop culture with ideas of community, competence and creativity again recurs in addressing the relationship between technological development and commodification. The concern that the machine can first over-ride the humanity of the producer and then 'program' the consumer's stimulus response counterposes technology and the body. Yet, as we have seen, rock and pop constitute 'metal machine music' (as Lou Reed described an album of 'industrial' noise) born out of the development of the forces of musical production which, far from submerging the body beneath the machine, has deployed the machine to produce new disciplines of the body. As Andrew Murphie and Edward Scheer (1992: 181) observe:

> Adorno saw the groove of the record as an indexical hieroglyphic of pure sound. At the dance party, that groove transforms itself into a writing on bodies, not only a semaphore between bodies, but a hieroglyphics between record and bodies. In dance there is an immediate and accepted connection between nature and technology.

Rock and pop culture, in a broader sense, is a technology of the body or, more accurately, a fluctuating system of technologies which work over and produce the body, here as corporeal object in movement and repose, there as iconic sign of materiality and sensuality. Once again, these questions are particularly pressing within the independent rock sector, with its heavy ideological investment in humanism and grass-roots authenticity. They have not, on the whole, been resolved in favour of a return to the folk milieu. Instead, (re)productive musical (especially recording) technologies have been appropriated and adapted rather than repudiated in the contacting and fashioning of new taste groupings. The shift away from mass cultural production and the resuscitation of seemingly 'residual' forms and methods of cultural labour by the rock independents may display some aspects of a folk ideal, but the dispersal of audiences, the technologies of contemporary sound, and the economics of all but the most 'hobbyist' of independent enterprises make it impossible to realize. Furthermore, this technology, because of its capacity for reproduction and multi-point distribution, also involves the kind of atomized communication (in its lack of the simultaneity and spontaneity of performance) and cultural division of labour (between the producer and vendor of items and the 'consuming' audience) which substantially parallel cultural processes operating within large, formal organizations. The paradoxical concept of the labour of culture, with its various permutations of the human and the mechanical, can be examined fruitfully as it applies to the independent sphere, that domain of musical production in which it is often claimed that the problem of the alienation of cultural labour can be resolved.

Independent work

The most pressing problems for the majority of people involved in making independent rock and pop music are economic rather than aesthetic. The idea that a minimal condition of material wellbeing is a prerequisite for engaging in any but the most spontaneous and fleeting forms of musical expression is banal, but it is frequently submerged in the rhetoric of autonomy and freedom. It is necessary, in the absence of alternative sources of income, for independent activity to be supported by fees for services or by sales of recorded music, irrespective of whether producers are of an idealist/alternativist or pragmatist/professionalist persuasion. 'Amateur' status (as in sport) can only be maintained through a limited 'hobbyist' orientation or by means of patronage. In fact, the career ethic is strong in the independent sector, with many if not most participants wishing to make their involvement in independent rock production their exclusive activity and source of income. This aspiration is no less compelling for those musicians and label owners who of necessity do other, unrelated jobs (such as clerk, petrol pump attendant and freelance journalist) in order to support themselves. Indeed, in spite of the amateurist ethos of independent rock ideology, many of the more established independent acts and companies are contemptuous of what they regard as the self-indulgent, uncommitted, 'cottage industry' end of the independent spectrum. As two members of a group which had issued several independent records stated:

> G: How many independent records are being released a week now?
> N: Oh, twenty, dozens, come out every week.
> G: An awful lot, a hell of a lot, and a lot of them are made by people who do see it, it seems to me, as a very kind of nouveau hippy, you know, they all live in outbacks, they've all got silly names, and they all make their C90 cassettes and their independent singles for their own amusement almost, or for, you know, there seems to be little ...
> N: [Interrupts] They're very willing to accept the limitations that they start out with, have set themselves.
> G: They're very willing to deal in kind of cottage industry terms.

Another musician expressed his disapproval of 'cottage' independent production thus:

> P: I have certain reservations when people use the independent medium, not into creating an alternative pop music or an alternative pop culture, but end up sounding like faulty air conditioning, you know, they're just wanking in the closet. Although it's alternative and it's nicely packaged and there's only 1,013 copies which are all individually numbered and have you got the latest whatever record? . . . It's like having a secret with your mates, but I don't find it very exciting at all.

These perhaps surprisingly judgemental comments reveal a good deal of hostility towards those producers of independent rock who do not seek to disseminate their music widely, but who rather make music 'for their own amusement'. Thus, although many of those involved in the independent network on a regular basis are favourable in the abstract to an amateurist ethic, their support is predominantly for a limited kind of amateurism which can be differentiated from 'wanking in the closet', and thereby reflects at least an ambition to become skilled and to reach an audience larger than a small circle of friends. This attitude, which appears to run counter to the openness and tolerance of independent ideology stems, in large measure, from economic competition. There is an acute awareness of the limitations of a market which may become saturated with items for sale, with 'serious' producers competing not only with rival 'serious' artists but also with those who are seen to be playing at music-making rather than playing music with proto-professional conviction. As one musician put it:

> C: I think one problem is it would be all very well if a limited number of people were musicians, but because it's an over-subscribed activity I don't think you can apply the same sort of standards. Like a certain number of bricklayers, a certain number of market forces acting on you can work out profitably. But when there are so many people trying to do it . . .

Similarly, a label manager stated:

> K: I mean, the Zig Zag Catalogue that came out last year had lists and lists of record labels like 'Funny Farm Records with FFI by the Funny Farm Band'. They never got past one, did they? They were just a bunch of blokes who thought, 'Let's get out a single.' Which is great in a way, because that's what we're about to some extent – saying to people, 'Do it! Do it! Do it!' The snag is that it does swamp the market and it's difficult for people to decide what's good, what's bad, whether you're going to have time to hear it. And that is one of the problems that those sort of things create. But they're not independent labels, are they? They're just, just people making records.

This negative view of 'just people making records' at the most rudimentary and informal of levels stems from the problem of 'swamping the market', yet it also creates ambivalence because casually making a single is 'what we're about to some extent'. In order to distinguish this label's production from such casual activities the concept of the 'label' was invoked, with its connotation of regular, systematic production and widespread dissemination, thereby ironically paralleling the often-drawn distinction between majors and independents. The independent network is thereby polarized into those who are 'nouveau hippies' indulgently making records for their own amusement, and those dedicated, serious independent enterprises seeking to produce music consistently and to communicate with (and sell to) much larger audiences. The above-quoted independent record label owner made a similar point about the most rudimentary level of record music production of all – the home-produced cassette:

> K: One or two I sent off for and they really were dire. It was quite a con, the idea of cassette albums I don't think is very viable, because anyone can just sit down and reel off however many you've asked for. I can never see people actually distributing enough to bring into shops for people to buy.

These adverse quality judgements run counter to the anti-professionalism which gave punk and the independents their impetus, particularly in differentiating themselves from the majors. The idea that anyone could and should be a musician and put out records which would challenge the majors' control of the means of cultural production militated against a modernist, professionalized system in which a clear specificity and separation of function exists between creation and organization. The rhetoric of punk independence demanded that hierarchical divisions of talent or skill between artists and audiences be overcome, just as the technological and organizational domination of large musical producers could be disrupted by appealing to the culture of 'Do-It-Yourself' (Laing, 1985). This egalitarian impulse is made clear in the following statement:

> R: The independent network started in 1976 when there wasn't really a recession . . . That came about, true punk started with kids being out of work – real true punk spirit as it started in west London. But the independent network was there basically as a rebellion against the majors, not because of the recession. People just wanted to stick two fingers up and say, 'We're young, we want to do it our way.'

It was this culture of amateurism that encouraged many 'non-musicians' and inexperienced entrepreneurs to become involved in the rock independent network, seeing their lack of specialized skill as an advantage rather than as a shortcoming, as liberatory rather than constricting. As one member of an independent band declared:

> P: I've been liberated from this thing that I am not a musician, I am not in this little club and can actually make something that's pleasing, or maybe interesting, you know, to the ear and put a rhythm to it and bring it out on a single and 3–4,000 people think, 'Great, let's go out and buy it!'

Similarly, a member of another group stressed that:

> M: Anyone can play a drum machine and learn what order to do things . . . I'm not pretending it's any wonderful artistic achievement to play a drum machine, because it's obviously not . . . I'm a sort of *idiot savant*, in a way.

This musician, in operating an electronic device which synthetically reproduces the sound of a conventional instrument, saw himself squarely in the role of '*idiot savant*' and also as a 'dilettante', rather than as a 'serious musician'. Although this was often a matter of necessity rather than choice, it was nonetheless the case that the aesthetic possibilities of such amateurism had also been explored in a self-conscious, intentioned manner. As a musician (who had pioneered and championed independent rock) stated:

> G: I was interested for a while in the aesthetic of do-it-yourself production, in an accidental aesthetic, in an aesthetic that was born by the fact that people were using cheap studios, they couldn't play very well, they were ignorant of studio technology, they had no producers, their ideology of production was markedly different from any historical precedents. And that gave rise to a music that had developed an aesthetic all of its own. A kind of shambolic, chaotic aesthetic that I actively was very interested in.

However, the unintended outcome of this conscious democratization of cultural production was that when it had passed from a strategic, ideological intervention in rock discourse to a widespread practice, it was seen to have undermined the economic position of those who had pioneered independent rock production itself. Having helped to popularize 'the aesthetic of do-it-yourself production', this musician found a market 'swamped' with 'product'. Not only was the greatly expanded level of independent production seen to affect the economic viability of individual record releases, but it was also felt by those less committed to the concept of sustained independent status to make it much more difficult to be 'spotted' by a major company. Small-batch commercial releases are viewed by many acts seeking a major record contract as more sophisticated and widely circulated forms of the traditional 'demo' tapes, which were delivered directly to record companies in the hope of stimulating interest in an artist or band. As two musicians put it:

> B: In the old days we used to make demo discs, now they make their own label.
> C: It's another way of making a respectable demo for a lot of bands. Whereas a band used to make a demo and send it out to record companies, now they will put their own single out, hoping full well that CBS hear a copy, or whatever, and treat it as a demo. In the meantime they've got a record out and I should think a majority of labels never get past that, because they either fold or get signed, or whatever.

The proliferation of 'respectable demos' (now often in compact disc or digital audio tape format) has caused a greater over-supply of recorded music for sale, and the intense competition for music buyers and record contracts means that 'So many bands want to make it that a lot of bands will sign anything, just to get a contract'. The struggle for a major recording contract and the history of exploitation it has produced is well documented (see, for example, Simpson and Stevens, 1986). It was noted in Chapter 2 that the development of new relationships between music corporations and independent enterprises has weakened the established pattern of the long-term signing of rock acts by the majors in favour of more short-term, limited contractual arrangements with independents (Negus, 1992; Lash and Urry, 1994). Under these circumstances, organizational flexibility and speedy response to new styles – not to mention a certain independent kudos – are the foundations on which market success is intended to be built. It is by no means certain that these arrangements make competition for 'tie-ups' with the majors any less intense within the music industry or that they necessarily empower musicians by allowing them to remain formally outside the corporate sphere. It could instead be argued that, in reducing their exposure to failure, the majors have exported risk and 'product development' to the more economically marginal organizations within the rock and pop music industry (and, according to Buckingham, 1994, also in television). Whatever the outcome of such 'post-Fordist' industrial trends, the problem remains of how those involved in the expanding independent sphere can secure an adequate and regular return for their cultural labour.

Whereas those of a more pragmatic disposition tend to take the unpredictability and exploitation of the rock music industry as given, other more politically committed individuals and groups canvass ways of overcoming what is sometimes perceived in classical Marxist terms as the expropriation of the surplus value of the musician's labour power. This alienation of the musician from his/her product encourages attempts at establishing some kind of 'theory of value' for the musician's labour. One independent label owner expressed his opposition to the majors thus:

> K: . . . in this sort of record business either somebody's got a lot of money or you've got no money. And just to be able to do it on a musical, in purely musical terms, it's, I mean, like stocking, recording or making records, then I'm all for that, but you've still got to make money and if you're down at the bottom scale, then you don't get any whatsoever. There's no fair distribution of wealth, really, it's the ultimate capitalist industry.

It is in order to overcome this maldistribution of wealth and resources – which, it should be noted, does not seem to have been substantially countered by the spread of post-Fordism in the music industry – that some individuals and groups attempted to establish new social relations of rock production:

> G: . . . we were interested for a while in attempting to go to Hard Times [pseudonym for leading independent record company] to present them with something like a new theory of the value of our labour. Which I think is fairly interesting, I mean, that you should go to someone like Hard Times and say, look if you're interested in working with us then let's attempt to get some purchase on how much money the labour the group puts into its product is worth. Because it's obviously a lot more than can be sorted by when you produce a record and at the end of the day it sells 200 copies, tough luck! And if it sells 2,000, fair enough and if it sells 20,000 a pat on the back. I mean, that hasn't taken into account in any way any labour theory of value.

This tentative attempt to counter the vagaries of the rock marketplace is an expression of discontent with an economic order based on record sales alone. Although the group 'neglected really, to sort that out', they nonetheless felt that it was important to discover, in an unusually self-conscious and intellectually sophisticated way, how much 'within cultural production . . . cultural labour is worth'. What was achieved in some instances was the establishment of a new relationship between artists and their record company. Of course, where the label is set up by a group of musicians, the label and the group are coterminous, and any outlays, profits or losses emanate from, and are returned to, the group/label. In the case of labels with only one act (but often also in larger, multi-act independent operations) a great deal of the labour is performed without payment, as in the case of the specialist independent record shop employee who also assisted with an independent label:

> B: We're a small company, I don't get paid for working in the shop. None of us do. The shop runs at a loss all the time. It's another sad fact. It's just a love of the music and the label.

A studio engineer using an independent, community-based facility also often did 'sessions for nothing'. Voluntary unpaid labour or self-exploitation of this kind facilitates independent rock production at its most small-scale and marginal. It represents musical activity which is still not penetrated by the commodity ethic, an 'amative' as well as amateur relationship with the

making and distribution of music. It is important in the face of the deepening industrialization of music and culture to remain aware of this level of
practice. Punk, with its simultaneously romantic and pragmatist ideology of
anti-cultural corporatism and do-it-yourself survivalism, has bequeathed to
rock a legacy of innovative independent production which exceeds its significance as musical, visual and gestural style. As one musician stated:

> O: I think you got a lot of backyard studios out, that's the good thing. Punk got
> people playing in garages with cheap equipment and the next thing that seems
> to have happened is a lot of home studios.

Another independent musician was stimulated by punk to establish a group
and a record label because 'now more than ever it seems like anyone can
start one'. This notion of 'self-help' carried over into what is now widely
regarded as a post-Fordist production regime (which could alternatively be
regarded as pre-Fordist in nature) fostering much rock activity outside the
metropolis. The metropolitan domination of popular music, signified by the
pilgrimage of provincial acts to the 'big smoke' in search of the big break, is
at least questioned by the re-assertion of the possibility of materially viable
musical practice at the local level.

Rock culture and the local

The courting of the majors in an attempt to gain a record contract and
thereby national and international recognition, while still common, was challenged during the British independent moment by the notion of local or
regional rock. It is represented in the range of city and regional 'samplers'
(with names like *Vaultage* and *Bouquet of Steel*) which emerged in Britain
once independents in particular areas outside London had become established in the 'post-punk' period. In contrast to the national and international
emphasis of the marketing of the majors' music, the provincial independents
in Britain prompted discussion of the Brighton, Sheffield, Liverpool,
Manchester, Glasgow or Edinburgh sounds (just as, then and since in the
USA, cities like Akron, Athens and Seattle have figured in the musical geog-
raphy of independent and major contemporary rock). This interest in
regionalism was supported strongly by one independent label/distributor
manager:

> R: The whole thing of kind of low overheads and high ideals and all that kind of
> thing means that people can earn a lot more by selling a lot fewer on a regional
> basis. I mean, it's my belief that somebody, you know, for instance in York
> who's got something sincere to say about York and he can say it kind of adeptly
> and using both music and record as a medium, that there's absolutely no reason
> why he should sign a deal with EMI and release a record in London. I would be
> far happier to see him earn his living as a local musician.

This attachment to place in musical representation was also expressed by
the assistant in an independent record shop and label who was motivated by

an identification with the 'Brighton Beat', while one musician favoured arrangements like a:

> P: local record label servicing the needs of kids in that area, say South Yorkshire or something, limiting its objectives, small overheads, four-track studio. I think that's tremendously exciting and worthwhile, you know. Just because it's not changing the world, I don't think people should slag it off.

Another independent musician felt that locally (provincially) based labels were:

> T: good focal points for groups who maybe a few years ago would have thought the only contact they can have with music or ever getting anything out is London, you know, which isn't the case anymore . . . It's nice that because of the way that the independent records have developed, there can be a certain devolution and local labels can cater for local people, yeah, you know, they can do it.

This emphasis on localism can sometimes tip over into parochialism (one respondent, for example, referred constantly to the nefarious influence of 'outsiders') and what Stubbs (1989: 272) calls the 'grubby end of Indie culture', a locally chauvinist suggestion that 'a conspiracy is at large – inspired by terror – to overlook the scurry of grassroots activity, with the praises sung of ever more hopeless and generic bands (Stoke's finest!)'. In other instances the local is seen simply as the springboard for the projection of the 'sound', as one independent label owner in a provincial British industrial city put it, 'across the UK, the world, and that's important'. Nonetheless, the idea of conducting a viable rock career in which, from a non-metropolitan base, recordings can be widely circulated and performances staged in distant locations, proposes a rather different pattern of practice to that of the semi-professional local musician (Bennett, 1980) and a departure from the familiar narratives of provincial-rags-to-metropolitan-riches which are the stuff of corporate rock superstar-oriented legend. Recent ethnographic studies of local music 'scenes' in Britain (such as Cohen, 1991; Finnegan, 1989) reveal that while the siren call of metropolitan, national and international success is still strong among musicians, rich and diverse local musical cultures with quite powerful identities of place are of continuing significance. Not only is a local orientation in music-making accompanied by the idea of symbolically expressing the unique dimensions of locality, but it also often lends itself to the construction of 'real' as well as 'imagined' local rock communities. A practical degree of cooperation between local rock acts may result, which contrasts markedly with the naked competition associated with professionalist rock organizations. One independent regional sampler, for example, emerged from 'a small friendly community' of bands who shared equipment and practice space, while a group's manager described the rise of:

> K: collectives which we don't really have much contact with directly, but you hear about collectives being set up where a lot of that kind of isolated competitiveness of groups is broken down quite a lot. I think to some extent that is part of the new wave, where there's meant to be a lot of gear sharing and that.

This kind of cooperation and communalism is reinforced by a sense of dis-

distance from the operation of the majors, whose lack of 'ear for the street', inflexibility and corporate inertia is for determinedly local acts symbolized by the commercial failure of many bands who had made the transition from independent to major labels. It is often felt by people involved in provincial rock production that when a rock act leaves the independent network to sign with a major, it not only cedes some of its artistic control, but also becomes detached from the local, independent milieu in which it had prospered. As one musician/co-owner of an independent label stated, this market can be quite 'disciplined' and exclusive:

> T: There are people that never buy a major record . . . they don't buy records off majors. I don't buy records by majors unless they're old!

Another independent record company owner, in discussing the fate of local independent bands who signed with majors in the early eighties, proposed the existence of an independent rock taste culture whose constituency was defined not so much by locality as by the ideology of independence:

> S: I've found that all the kids that I know that, for want of a better word, were the independent market, will buy records from the independent market almost exclusively and occasionally dip into the major market to buy something. There does seem to be a very distinct stratum of record-buying public . . .

Hence, some groups 'who sell 60,000 of one single and do incredibly well with all their releases and have never been out of the independent charts' sign up with majors and 'they've flopped ever since, they don't sell'. It is even suggested that they would sell 'ten times more' on an independent than on a major label. The existence of an audience (commonly represented as a 'community') which buys almost exclusively independent records is often asserted, thereby suggesting a greater degree of cohesion and contact between producers and consumers in the independent sphere. As Negus (1992: 16, 18) has pointed out, a preference for 'romantically' independent music may be readily translated simply as a market niche which can be exploited by the majors in the setting up of '"bogus" independents' or of cooperative licensing deals with established independents (Lash and Urry, 1994: 130). The need for such subterfuge is testimony to the resilience of anti-corporate cultural capitalism in rock. It is evident in the oft-repeated, apocryphal stories concerning corporate boardroom anger at the innovative superiority of independent 'packaging' and content. The continued healthy sales of an act's independent recordings long after it has left to join a major, and the frequent failure of the majors to 'handle' acts from an independent label whose previous audience felt that they had 'sold out', are also frequently stressed (although, of course, not the numerous market 'failures' of the independents).

One notable example of this phenomenon is The Smiths, a group from Manchester signed to the significant British independent Rough Trade, a label which in its chequered history has been involved in the retail, manufacture and distribution of independent rock (and, later, dance) music. As Mick Middles (1988: 123) has documented, The Smiths, 'one of Britain's most successful rock bands', achieved considerable national and international commercial success with Rough Trade in the early and mid-eighties but ended up 'Broke, bitter, confused, wary' (a description that applies equally to the condition of another prominent Manchester independent band, New Order, after the collapse of the style-leading independent Factory Records) by the end of the decade. In seeking to overcome the problem of 'evolving into a seriously huge beast' yet lacking 'the push of a major record company' (Middles, 1988: 113), The Smiths had signed a reputed million pound contract with EMI. The 'move from right-on indie label Rough Trade to massive and massively square major EMI' (Reynolds, 1989: 254) did not prevent the group from breaking up within a year. While it is not possible to deal in any detail with the case of The Smiths here, their history – of independence, provincial (Mancunian) and regional (northern British) identity, chart success, ambivalent involvement in (pro-Labour Party, anti-apartheid) politics, iconic 'indie' status, intense fan identification, transition to a major label and eventual disintegration – encompasses and crystallizes the manifold tensions out of which rock culture is made. The narrativized rise-and-fall of an independent band which 'sells out' is not so much an empirical phenomenon (independent status no more guarantees success than a major contract secures inevitable failure) as a resilient feature of rock discourse. Rock is a popular cultural form in which the concept of creative control is particularly central. From the perspective of the independent sphere, the modernist division of labour of large, formal cultural organizations is regarded as a systematic mechanism for the relinquishment of control to those who have no 'organic' link with the creation and presentation of rock. Some successful bands remained with an independent label and in a provincial setting as a means of evading the aesthetic and organizational subordination endemic to the metropolitan majors. One member of an internationally successful independent band explained this choice on grounds of artistic freedom:

> X: Because it's a question of control, you know, we feel we have more control over our own product . . . I know it's an appallingly over-used phrase, but it is the case. I mean we're not sort of, we can do our own artwork, it's not written into the contract that somebody says, you know, 'We've been to the sort of graphic designers and this is your artwork', you know.

The intimacy of working relationships, especially among those involved in locally-based independent production, was well captured by the musician who didn't 'like working for people I don't know'. Being on an independent label is also seen to guard against the corporate drive to rationalize creativity and to insert 'product' into the marketplace for economic rather than artistic reasons, and so be forced to:

> X: have an album out each year and four singles. The fact that we've got at the moment two albums and two singles ready to come out and we can bring them out when we want, and after that if we don't want to do another record for two years, we can do. There's no contractual obligations, so that's the only way we could really work because we don't want the pressure of having to keep to deadlines.

The product over which control is maintained is, however, not typically regarded as 'a piece of high art or something' and, indeed, there is often contempt for what is seen as artistic posturing, by means of which 'a lot of people cover up their own shortcomings by looking for the big, faceless record company destroyed me, I'm a meaningful artist sort of shit'. The naivety and unpretentiousness of amateurist self-expression is, therefore, held to be a virtue, a humanist spoke in the corporate cultural capitalist wheel. The independent emphasis on untutored, unfettered creativity can, of course, be exaggerated. As Glyn (1979: 78) has argued with regard to the independent film industry:

> Production in the independent sphere does not take place outside the dominant sys-
> tem of capitalist relations. The subjective placing of themselves outside the industry
> derives from the independents' different methods of work and different relationship
> to capital – differences which include reduction in the degree of division of labour,
> flexible crewing standards and different forms of payment. Some of the differ-
> ences are merely the result of the economic and political weakness of the
> independent film-maker, while others, such as the departure from industrial forms
> of division of labour, have a justification in terms of film-makers' objectives.

Not only is the existence of a space of motivational/processual purity outside capitalist social relations implausible, but also, as Macherey (1978: 67) argues (in respect of literature), an unbounded notion of artistic creativity fails to appreciate that cultural items are 'a product (and the producer is not a subject centred in his [*sic*] creation, he is an element in a situation or system)'. Thus, the 'labour of production' is performed under 'determinate conditions', and, in the case of independent rock, those conditions normally constitute economic disadvantage and technical inferiority, as well as the unavoidable necessity of being in some way materially sustainable. This point is made in the closing exchange from the interview with the independent rock group which has been given prominence in this chapter, in which the question of material survival and economic marginality recurs:

> G: That's what makes the whole area of cultural production in capitalist society
>   really quite fascinating.
> N: It's very frightening given we are where we are.
> A and C: (Together) Yeah, it is.
> Q: How to produce without being exploited or exploiting?
> N: Well, it's not really a case of how to produce and not be exploited, more of how
>   to produce and get away with it!

It is the hope of 'getting away with it' (the title, it might be recorded, of an Electronic song by ex- and current members of the aforementioned The Smiths and New Order) – economically, politically and artistically – that sustains so much rock practice in the independent (and, of course, the major) sphere. The culture of rock independence cannot be separated, then, from its material conditions and ideologies of production, anymore than it can be said to be 'over-determined' by any primary cause. Its emphasis on the local and the specific is reliant on the conception of communities of production and consumption which, in their appeal to the concrete and the authentic, can be rhetorically separated from the abstract and synthetic properties of the globally-oriented structures of the corporate mainstream. As Redhead (1990: 72, 74) argues (noted earlier), this separation is now (and to some degree always was) both ideologically and empirically dubious, because '"independence" no longer signifies "deviance" in the way that rock history claims', while since the early eighties 'independent records have usually reflected the market differentiation and massive pluralism of pop taste available from the major record companies'. It is, nonetheless, in this 'rediscovery' of bounded communities of culture, with their peculiar combination of pre-capitalist organicism and late capitalist mediatization, that some of the most enduring contradictions and sites of contestation in rock culture can be divined. The return of the local, in pre- or postmodern guise, is a development which accompanies and interrupts established trends conventionally held to run in the opposite direction. The local in contemporary rock culture inevitably invokes the concept of the global, in regard both to cultural imperialism (the export of rock commodities from the capitalist economic core to the periphery – see Robinson et al., 1991; Wallis and Malm, 1984) and, perhaps more surprisingly, to the 'contra-flow' of so-called 'world music' from the non-western to the western world (Manuel, 1988).

Rock culture and the global

The discussion of local independent rock's construction of community and its claim to authenticity is particularly significant in considering 'world music' (the politics of which were briefly discussed in the previous chapter), the broad marketing category which has come to be applied to those musics which have reached the dominant capitalist western music markets from the 'Third World'. It is apparent from the foregoing discussion that rock can be simultaneously conceived as local, national and global, as synthetic and authentic, as organically real and as technologically simulated. These are crucial considerations in any assessment of rock culture in that contacted audiences, potential audiences and audience-critics are constantly working with and through the received value frameworks according to which taste judgements and identifications are made (Crook et al., 1992: 59). We have noted how a particular conception of the local-representational has coalesced around sounds and scenes in certain geographical and socio-cultural spaces. What, then, is the cultural status of music that is emanating not from the sphere of the subordinated provincial or the hegemonic metropolitan, but from the (post)colonial periphery? The idea of world music, however empirically imperfect, represents a reversal of global cultural flows (Appadurai, 1990), as the western rock and popular music that is widely held to have threatened to obliterate cultural diversity (see, for example, Mattelart, 1979) is at least partially turned back by 'traditional' musical forms and new syntheses of the old and the new, the indigenous and the imported.

The various models of international musical exchange reflect, in different degrees, the ways in which popular music may be exportable in finished units, adaptable to local conditions, resistant to external influences or amenable to unpredictable and innovative syntheses. Robinson et al. (1991: 262) organize these variations into stages of production, according to which periphery/core relations move from cultural domination and imperialism (involving 'invasion' of cultural commodities and the repatriation of profits) to a second adaptive stage of cultural imperialism involving imitation of western cultural forms by local producers who are, nonetheless, still working at the behest of transnational cultural corporations. Their third stage involves 'transculturation', in which the 'indigenization/modernization' of musical production in the periphery is accompanied by the strategic use of non-western 'ethnic' music to invigorate an increasingly derivative and exhausted western popular music industry. Subsequently, the now developed 'eclecticism' in the periphery, by the fourth (and, presumably, final) stage, feeds into a 'transeconomism' which is 'exemplified by increasing fragmentation in internationalized musical genres and smaller production units within the core industry', thereby reflecting, as noted in Chapter 2 above, a post-Fordist/flexibly specialized 'worldwide shift from industrialized/mass market economics to informatized/customized economies' (Robinson et al., 1991: 262).

Whatever the theoretical and empirical validity of such mega-narratives of the international development of the pop music industry, they are justifiable attempts to understand the nature of cultural processes of contact and transmission which are, at the same time, industrial processes of musical production and ideologically-loaded articulations of meaning. In such analyses, concepts of cultural imperialism, indigenous cultural resistance, 'folk' authenticity and postmodern hybridity are regularly invoked in attempting to interpret complex and confusingly inconsistent trends towards both localization and globalization, both a defensive aesthetic purity and a riotous stylistic promiscuity. The celebration of musical diversity across the globe, as in Marre and Charlton's (1985) *Beats of the Heart: Popular Music of the World* or Peter Manuel's (1988) *Popular Musics of the Non-Western World*, is a necessary corrective to the crude and totalizing assertions of international musical homogenization. It is also often accompanied, as Middleton (1990: 140) points out, by a tendency to formulate a notion of musical authenticity, so that 'Critics, fans and musicians have joined in these attempts to construct their own preferred music as a "pure" alternative to the "commercial manipulations" of the mainstream, and almost every variety of Afro-American and Country music, jazz, rock, and now "roots" or "world" music styles have been construed as a new "folk" genre'. Each new assertion of authenticity, implicitly or explicitly, is advanced through the identification and often stigmatization of what is conceived as unauthentic.

The possibility of such musical 'purity' and 'authenticity', in terms both of form and of precise matching with specific social groups, is increasingly unlikely in an age of rapid cultural, communicative and technological exchange. As Frith (1989b: 2–3) argues, no people or country can now be fully insulated from 'the electronic means of musical production, reproduction and transmission' and its consequent 'universal pop aesthetic'. Costello and Wallace (1990: 89) note, similarly, that even 'hard rap', 'black supremacist' bands like Public Enemy 'cannot locate even one pure black source'. While the intermeshing of the local, regional, national and global dimensions of musical culture is today inescapable, it is possible to exaggerate the impact of 'Westernization' and to underplay the importance of 'changing local tastes deriving from socio-economic developments within the culture itself' (Manuel, 1988: 23). Furthermore, in advanced capitalist nations with significant non-western immigrant populations, some most surprising cultural adaptations, syntheses and innovations may be evident. Banerji and Baumann (1990: 137), for example, note the politico-aesthetic complexities of musical form in their discussion of Bhangra, the South Asian 'dance and song genre' that in Britain fuses 'rural Punjabi dance and its songs with sounds, social forms, and production strategies associated with disco music and pop' and, more adventurously, 'influences from hip-hop and house, as well as dance techniques such as spinning, body-popping and breaking'. The contradictory cultural position of Bhangra is apparent in the varying responses it elicits from different social and cultural groups:

> Its aesthetic tenets, as well as virtually all of its texts, are Punjabi, and not easily accessible to non-Asian listeners; in circles devoted to world music, on the other hand, we have heard it called 'too British', 'too westernized' or 'too much like disco pop' to be acceptable as 'authentic world music', such as, for instance, *qawwali*. (pp. 137–8)

Banerji and Baumann's discussion of Bhangra displays some clear parallels with independent rock in its consideration of the dilemma of professionalization which confronts an ethnic genre music which engages with the white-dominated mainstream music industry. Similar dilemmas confront those cultural producers who, having commenced activities in highly-localized settings and addressed them to very specific audiences, may wish to go beyond amateurism or semi-professionalism and construct careers in which their music (now required to be technologically sophisticated) reaches into a commercial market where its uses and interpretations cannot be anticipated or controlled:

> The Bhangra market in Britain still comprises productions made by musicians themselves and recorded in a converted front room at home. The cost of such home productions could, in some circumstances, be as low as £3,000. Such amateur production remains a tempting, if in the end often self-defeating, strategy especially for the proliferation of new groups formed since the 'Bhangra boom' of 1986–7. (p. 148)

The problems caused by this move from the local to the national/global hinge on a familiar conception of cultural control. The pressures exerted on cultural producers to be more accommodating towards new commercially significant audiences (by 'diluting' exotic form and esoteric content) are exacerbated by the various appropriations of musical culture once it has been released into a (potential) crossover market. Ambivalence towards the wider recognition of 'minority' cultural forms is, as Paul Oliver (1990b: 172) notes, endemic on the 'musical margins':

The subculture protagonists of many kinds of specialized popular music genres have insisted on wider acknowledgement for 'their' music when it has been the province of a minority interest – and subliminally regretted the loss of its exclusive nature when it had achieved greater popularity.

The shifting relations between white and black musical subcultures, both with each other and with the mainstream music industry, produce difficult and dynamic interdependencies. As Anthony Marks (1990: 112), for example, points out in the British context, intercultural organizations like Rock against Racism 'made admirable political advances, bringing together black and white youths for the purpose of peaceful protest' (see also Widgery, 1986), but white appropriations of reggae and the 'decline of the punk ideal was as sudden as it was total, and it left black groups with a diminished audience'. However tolerant and mutually accepting different musical taste cultures may be, they cannot magically escape wider structures of racism and economic exploitation, but nor are they doomed simply to reproduce them. Instability, ambiguity and uncertainty are built into contemporary cultural production, not least because the structural requirement to generate new forms and sources of profit creates opportunities for some unlikely cultural fusions. In this process, the refusal of subordinate groups to play their prescribed passive role is important. A reliance on non-commercial, traditional 'roots' music may be culturally affirmative for peoples who feel beleaguered and alienated in a hostile, Anglo-dominated cultural environment, but it may also leave the existing order of cultural power largely undisturbed. An alternative and less defensive strategy is to seize and deploy whatever resources are at hand in expressing, through music, the specific experiences of peoples whose lives are marked by a series of complex negotiations between their inherited culture and the hegemonic cultural formation that surrounds and threatens to obliterate it.

These issues are particularly pressing for indigenous peoples who, having suffered invasion, physical coercion and cultural assimilationism, are seeking to preserve their identity and difference. In Australia, for example, the difficulty of plotting a pathway between cultural protection/preservation/separation and cultural innovation/development/engagement has been great for Aboriginal people still struggling for social justice and cultural respect (Breen, 1989; Castles, 1992; Ellis, 1985; Lawe Davies, 1993; Shoemaker, 1994). The recent instance of the worldwide hit 'Treaty' by the Aboriginal rock group Yothu Yindi is instructive in considering questions of cultural maintenance, affirmation, synthesis and adaptation. The song, an impassioned plea for land rights sung partially in an Aboriginal language, became successful as a dance hit in the early nineties when it was re-mixed into a 'techno' form. Its use of traditional instruments like the didgeridoo in combination with conventional rock instruments (such as the electric guitar) and the full panoply of digital studio devices produced a song and image (through its striking video) that can be described neither as authentically 'tribal' nor as a commercial capitulation to white culture. As John Castles (1992: 38-9) argues:

Yothu Yindi seem to symbolise more clearly the possibilty of avoiding the constrictive tendency of always locating Aboriginal music in a collective past or an ideal future. Perhaps their current success signals the emergence of an aesthetic which allows the maintenance of cultural identity as fusion, thus appealing to both local and broader audiences. In this context 'appropriation' may become a metaphor for affirmative action.

It is in the strategic use of diverse cultural forms and new technologies that the musics of non-western peoples seek to avoid 'ghettoization' (a condition also often deplored among the 'white rock' independents). The continuous process of re-combination, re-contextualization and pastiche commonly associated with postmodernism is here combined with a traditionalist 'folk' concern with ethnic heritage and discrete cultural identity. As Marks (1990: 117) concludes in his survey of the impact of Afro-American and Afro-Caribbean popular music in Britain:

> [Moreover] the barriers of race and style seem to be disintegrating rapidly. In 1988 African, Yemenite, Bulgarian, Israeli and Cajun music all reached the charts in some form, often remixed in hip-hop or house style fashion. Technology has made digital sampling available very cheaply, enabling musicians to borrow music from other countries, cultures, or periods of history, and give it a new context. This surge of activity, coupled with the continued buoyancy of the club scene, makes it impossible to define the state of the art; indeed, styles change so rapidly that it is difficult to keep track of them all. Such a mix-and-match approach may offend purists, but British dance music, black and white, Afro-Caribbean and Afro-American alike, seems set to remain vital and vibrant into the 1990s.

Dick Hebdige (1987: 10), similarly, in his examination of 'the relationship between Caribbean music and cultural identity', tries to 'show how the roots themselves are in a constant state of flux and change. The roots don't stay in one place. They change shape. They change culture. And they grow. There is no such thing as a pure point of origin, least of all in something as slippery as music, but that doesn't mean there isn't history.' This vitality, pragmatism and eclecticism, abhorred by some and celebrated by others, prevents the comfortable settlement and closure of popular music discourse. It is not indicative of the transcendence of social relations of power by playful signification in the cultural sphere, but rather reflects how culture always and everywhere is produced out of the clash of social histories, structures and agencies. Thus, such abstractions as 'world', 'roots', 'fusion', 'ethnic' or 'folk' music only acquire meaning by relating symbolic practices to their contexts. Contest over conceptions of the global, local, cultural, commercial, authentic, synthetic, oppositional and collusive is the very stuff out of which rock culture is shaped and interpreted. As Frith (1989b: 6) points out, 'diverse sounds from the margins' appear especially significant 'as the music of the multimedia, multinational centre of the entertainment industry becomes ever more uniform (Whitney Houston and Phil Collins providing a world-wide commercial soundtrack)'. Middleton (1990: 293), likewise, argues that:

> As the transnational corporations plunder the musical assets of the Third World, 'world music' can hardly be a neutral term. But it is not a settled, univocal one either. Struggles over the ownership, meanings and uses of these assets will have a

growing importance, given wider ramifications within the 'global economy' by capital's ransacking of the *physical* assets of 'underdevelopment' as well.

The flow of units of music and capital across national boundaries and between social groups is an unavoidable (and not inherently undesirable) consequence of the highly-developed stage of the global cultural economy under late- and/or postmodernity. The dynamic and contradictory nature of this change makes any authoritative summation of the condition of rock culture impossible. It is, however, certain that if the rock era is indeed over and the historical circumstances that produced it superseded, the concerns with the relationships between the making of music, money, identity and ideology so central to rock discourse have proliferated rather than disappeared. They have been taken up with increasing vigour by new groups of musicians with very different origins and styles.

Conclusion

This chapter has explored various aspects of rock and pop culture, seeking to demonstrate how it is produced out of the interplay of cultural labour and institutions. It concluded by demonstrating that it is no longer feasible to confine cultural forms and practices to specific locations and groups, although the claiming of cultural territory remains a pivotal means through which culture is (re)made and (re)defined. In this respect, contemporary rock music is not alone. There are other popular cultural disciplines of the body, other means and forms by which the body is shaped, draped, trained, surveyed, displayed, stimulated and sold. These are serviced by other organizations and technologies devoted to the task of diffusing new texts, images and practices across the globe. One such popular cultural form, rivalling rock in popular cultural significance, is the subject of the following chapters – sport.

5

The Sports Industry: Playing for Pay

The twentieth century has seen an enormous expansion of the global sports industry, shadowing and in many ways exceeding the commercial development of the popular music industry. This is not to argue that the nature and extent of their industrial histories can be characterized as parallel stories of capital accumulation. There has been considerable variation in the levels of acceptance, rejection and commitment of capital both between and within popular music and sports forms. On the other hand, there have also been periods where the onward march of commerce into sporting and musical camps has seemed to signal a wholesale transformation in the economics, organization and socio-cultural character of the making of regulated movements (sport) and structured noises (music) in the name of pleasure. The seventies was one such period. As Frank Stilwell noted (1977: 83) in a short political–economic commentary of the time, the simultaneous expansion of the pop (as represented by the internationally successful Swedish ensemble, Abba) and sports (in the shape of a seminal, entrepreneurially-funded 'rebel' cricket tour; see Barnett, 1990: 144–7) industries produced some curious patterns and comparisons:

> What do 'Kerry Packer's Pirates' and Abba have in common? One answer (albeit not the only possible one!) is that they are both examples of the increasing penetration of capital into our social fabric. Packer's recent venture into sports promotion and the development of groups like Abba which bring younger and younger consumers into the music industry can both be usefully interpreted in this context. Capitalism is a dynamic system: no stone is left unturned in the quest for profits and the restless process of accumulation causes continual assaults on conventional social mores.

If Stilwell revisited this passage from the vantage point of the mid-nineties, he could not fail to be struck by the dramatic changes that have since been wrought in sport and popular music. The *fin de siècle* successors of 'Packer's Pirates' now make an estimable living by traversing the world playing numerous one-day games tailored to the requirements of television schedules, sponsors and advertisers, while Abba's tentative and hit-or-miss appeal to the younger consumer has been supplanted by the carefully planned and executed – if often exceedingly transitory – campaigns to secure the (pre)pubescent dollar for the likes of New Kids on the Block and Take That. More confusingly, however, we have also seen over the last two decades such less easily classifiable popular cultural phenomena as Live Aid, Sport Aid, 'indie' pop, Sport for All, militant rap, the Gay Games, Artists United against Apartheid, the (British) Football Supporters Association, rave, fun runs,

ragga, digital sampling, pop and sports fanzines – and the simulatory Abba
cover band, Fabba. The (hyper)commodification of much of the sports and
popular music industries should not, therefore, be seen as producing uniform outcomes according to a singular cultural capitalist logic.

Implicit in this recognition is a simultaneous awareness of the points of
convergence and divergence for different cultural forms. There are many
resemblances between sport and rock as popular culture – for example, in
their mutual reliance on the studied yet apparently 'spontaneous' assertion of
the body. Just as music-making has increasingly shifted over the last century
from largely uncommodified 'noise' production to the systematic dissemination of sounds, lyrics and images for profit, so predominantly unremunerated,
loosely rule-governed physical play has transmuted into professional, commercial sport. This does not mean that playing music or sport can no longer
be inherently pleasurable, but that, first, the aspiration to specialize and professionalize in a given area of popular cultural practice is in the late twentieth
century much more widespread, and that, second, even the most tentative
involvement in the cultural sphere requires the purchase of substantial leisure
goods and services, ranging from equipment (such as hi-tech running shoes or
musical instruments) to instruction (such as fitness consultants and music
teachers).

For all these similarities in the development of sport and rock as culture
industries, they also retain distinct histories and institutional structures. The
corporate economics of rock, for example, are not organized as dependently
around periodic global spectacles of international competition like the
Olympic Games and the World Cup. Sport, as an institutional formation, is
also much more closely connected to the formal apparatus of the
liberal–democratic state in its function as 'moral' educator and amplifier of
citizenship and national identity. It is necessary, then, to interrogate the field
of sport both as a 'unique' domain and as a phenomenon whose particular
properties are subject to erosion. In critical sports analysis there is a frequent
tendency to romanticize a golden age of pre-capitalist sport (akin to that of
uncommodified folk music). This trait is evident among the Left, for whom
the modern manifestations of commercial sport are but another sign of growing capitalist hegemony in the sphere of civil society, and also on the Right,
for whom sport once mystically transcended the prosaic demands of everyday
life until corrupted by bourgeois and proletarian acquisitiveness. Stoddart
(1986: 118; see also Sissons, 1988), however, has noted that, while the rate of
commercialization and professionalization has varied between sports, and
the pace of change since the early seventies has dramatically quickened, the
relationship between sport and commerce is long established:

> Before the middle of the nineteenth century and the full flowering of the British
> public school sports spirit, to make money from sport was not uncommon. Boxing
> and wrestling were most prominent but had no monopoly on the practice.

The idea of a purely expressive sport can be seen from this perspective as
colluding with the fantasies of Empire and aristocracy. Whatever the

shortcomings of a nostalgic longing for pure, uncommodified village games, however, it is unquestionable not only that sport is now a major industry in its own right, but also that it is crucial to the health and operation of other major industries, notably media and advertising. In this chapter there will be an examination of key elements of the 'sportsbiz' in addressing the vexed question of who owns and controls sport in the (post)modern world. First, however, we must briefly ascertain what constitutes the deceptively universalist concept of sport.

What is sport?

Elias and Dunning (1986b) have described the emergence of sport as an integral part of the 'civilizing process' of modernism, by which the regulation of games spread out from its British core as part of a growing regulation of violent confrontation. This explanation of the proliferation of what we have come to recognize as 'sport' stems from what they call 'figurational sociology'. The figurational approach, which bears some resemblance to the explanatory framework of Giddens (1984), conceives sport as a set of practices which symbolically resolves certain tensions within modernizing societies experiencing 'state formation' (Jary and Horne, 1993). England, the first capitalist and industrial power, is also seen to be the point from which the institutions and practices that we call sport emanated. Elias (1986: 126), in advancing this argument, quotes the German author Stiven's 1936 comment that:

> As is well known, England was the cradle and the loving 'mother' of sport . . . It appears that English technical terms referring to this field might become the common possession of all nations in the same way as Italian technical terms in the field of music. It is probably rare that a piece of culture has migrated with so few changes from one country to another.

Through a series of transformations, ancient (and 'imported') 'game-contests' and folk pastimes such as 'rough play' became what we recognize today as organized, competitive, professional sport. The distinctive (if inherently unstable) nineteenth-century English/British combination of binding rules of competition, heroic mythology, rationalized deployment of the body, edificatory values, scientific measurement, communal identification and commodified leisure activity was crucial to the emergence of international competitive sport. As Goldlust (1987: 53) argues, while other forms of organized physical exercise have been promoted (for example, in the former Eastern Bloc), they have not prevailed. The outcome is that:

> the sports model constructed in Britain in the nineteenth century has swept all before it and emerged as a truly universal modern cultural form . . .
> . . . One consistent theme that emerges [from this survey of] the birth and growth of modern competitive sport is the increasing shift away from the Victorian ideals of individual participation and self-cultivation towards the public exhibition of high-achievement sport as both a universal vehicle of mass entertainment and a symbolic representation of international political/ideological struggle.

While the figurational perspective provides some significant insights, it fails to deal with two key problems. The first is the nature of sport itself. Instead of conceiving sport and its associated social relations as part of a continuum in the manner proposed by figurational sociology, a more fruitful approach would be to seek to understand its social constitution. In other words, following Bourdieu (1988), we might ask how a set of practices is located within 'the space of sports'. Such an approach, rather than following the taxonomies of Caillois (1961) and Caldwell (1976) in defining the ideal typical sports and games, would seek to understand how an activity (say, chess or darts) comes to be regarded as a sport, how it is compared and contrasted with other sports, and how it operates within the network of institutions – educational, communicative, regulatory and so on – that mould our experience and understanding of the phenomenon of sport.

The second shortcoming of the figurational perspective concerns its handling of the power relations driving the global dissemination of sports. Clearly, the concept of imperialism is important here, while, within as well as between nations, gender relations are given little consideration. Most obviously, the alternative proposition that the drive for capital accumulation propelled the global diffusion and expansion of sport is given insufficient weight. Chris Rojek (1985: 171), in his review of critiques of figurational sociology (such as Buck-Morss, 1978), notes the assessment that its pluralistic stress on the multiple sources of change leads to a:

> relative neglect of the important categories of bourgeois repression and the capitalist ethic in the development of human figurations. Meanings under capitalism are not constructed by the individual's position in the dynamic web of interdependencies, but by the general power dialectics which give capitalism its distinctive shape and form. The figurational approach in general is therefore condemned for underestimating the significance of struggles of class, race, and sex, in the integration and dynamics of capitalist society.

While it is apparent that sport cannot be reduced to a mere effect of the spread of capitalism across the world, it cannot be plausibly denied that professional sport and capitalism are closely connected. This articulation of sport and capitalism may be demonstrated at a number of levels. Sports clubs and associations, professional sportspeople, sports equipment manufacturers, the stagers and promoters of sports events, the sports media, advertisers, sponsors, agents and governments are all deeply implicated in the material maintenance and exploitation of sport. It is for this reason that the term 'sportsbiz' has emerged to describe the complex of institutions which constructs and surrounds the regulated expression of physical culture.

The sportsbiz

In the late twentieth century, the 'industrialization' of sport has been very rapid. This is not to argue that sport and commerce are historically-opposed institutions. Sports such as boxing, horse racing and soccer have for over a century operated with a developed commercial arm. Several sports, however, embraced industrial practices (such as substantial player payments and the extraction of large fees for television rights) only after considerable delay and resistance. The uneven professional and commercial development of sport reveals the extent to which pre-capitalist ideologies of amateurism and free play have persisted within forms of popular culture. These ideologies are by no means self-evidently politically progressive – a patrician distaste for the grubby realities of class-bound life and a favoured feudal regime of control over players by 'voluntary' administrators have at least partially succeeded in keeping both capitalism and egalitarianism at bay in sports such as rugby union. Once a breach is made in the amateurist defence, however, rapid capitulation has usually followed. Tennis, for example, which only went 'open' in the 1960s, is now one of the most overtly commercialized sports, having achieved a relatively comfortable accommodation between the traditional control of conservative associations (such as Britain's Wimbledon Lawn Tennis Club) and the entrepreneurial cluster of agents, promoters, sponsors and advertisers. Indeed, as Ellis Cashmore (1990: 133) has argued, 'Nowadays, "amateur" is virtually a pejorative word implying unskilful and lack of refinement – the opposite of professional.' The term 'shamateurism' has increasingly been used to characterize the remunerative arrangements for athletes in the Olympic Games and, especially, in rugby union, the major sport most officially opposed to paying players for play (although not to charging spectators, television companies and the manufacturers of endorsed products).

When the commercialization of sport is bemoaned, several 'stock' counter-arguments are mounted. The right of any citizen to exploit their particular skill for profit and reward is asserted, alongside the general right of spectators and fans to derive entertainment from the expert sporting labour performed on their behalf in a contractual relationship freely entered into by both parties to their apparent mutual advantage. Sport, it is argued, provides opportunities for social mobility, especially for those social groups (such as African-Americans) whose alternative options are negligible. An 'emulation effect' is proposed, by which grass-roots participation in sport is encouraged through spectacular feats of professional success (for example, tennis in Sweden and Germany following the successes of Bjorn Borg, Mats Wilander, Boris Becker, Steffi Graf, Michael Stich and so on). Finally, it is claimed that commercialized sport does not prevent – and may actually assist – the simultaneous development of uncommodified, popular sport such as fun running and touch football. These arguments are often initially persuasive, leaving critics of the sportsbiz appearing to be conservative, out-of-time and fun-denying. The demise of orthodox Left critiques of culture and the associated rise of postmodernism have produced something of a critical vacuum. While, as noted in Chapter 1, there has been a powerful strain of 'puritanic rationalism' (Docker, 1989: 6) on the Left, a penchant for gestural oppositionalism (Cunningham, 1992), and a tendency to treat popular pleasures with disdain

(Fiske, 1989), the need for sustained scepticism and critique of capitalism and culture remains. Even if, as Toby Miller (1993) argues, this (often moralizing) critical urge is symptomatic of an 'ethical incompleteness' under the condition of postmodernity, it is an impulse that cannot be lightly discarded. The traces of functionalism in the figurational sociology of sport (Jary and Horne, 1993) and of liberal pluralism in postmodernism (Curran, 1990) undermine their critical potential. Considerable analytical value, if qualified, still inheres within orthodox political economic critique of the social relations of sports production.

The sports labour market

Stoddart (1986) has characterized as 'conservative' those critiques of modern sport which have objected to the continuing and deepening involvement of commerce. He argues that it is ironic that Left thinkers should line up with the reactionary, aristocratic/bourgeois forces within sports organizations against an exploited player 'proletariat' who are in competition, like any other subordinate group under capitalism, for the means of life. While it is conceded that critical theorists have often seemed to be strangely at odds with those athletes whom they have sought to protect from their own exploitation, it can also be suggested that such 'contradictions' are produced by very obvious differences in motivation, interest and experience between the researcher and the researched. Researchers in fields which lend themselves to ethnographic study, such as youth subcultural studies (Hebdige, 1979; Willis, 1978) and youth gender studies (Nava, 1992), are only too painfully aware of the problems of bridging this gap. Critiques of the structures and practices of sport, similarly, are likely to encounter the 'ideological' resistance of those agents whose concrete interests are reliant on direct or indirect commodity exchange. The individualist ethic of capitalist enterprise has a particularly strong (elective) affinity with professionalized, competitive sport (McKay and Kirk, 1992), and so is powerfully resistant to the abstractions of class and other forms of domination. The drive to extend commodity relations is, once admitted to new social spheres, both blind and remorseless. In the case of sport, the introduction of a profit regime is rapidly transformative of its organization, form and social relations in most instances. The involvement of individuals within any social sphere is never simply a matter of individual choice and voluntary determination. Professional athletes occupy a particular position within the structure of sports, simultaneously producing and reproducing a sharply hierarchical structure of the distribution of rewards (McKay, 1991). As was pointed out in the above discussion of the economics of popular music, capitalist culture industries are distinguished by reward structures which concentrate most benefits in the hands of a few individuals. Elite sportspeople, along with owners of clubs and sponsor, media and advertising organizations, are, therefore, in receipt of rewards which vastly outweigh those gained by the great mass of non-elite performers and would-be performers.

For these reasons, it is important not to allow the success of highly selected and visible athletes to obscure persistent (and often growing) inequalities within sport. When, for example, in 1993 a single race in Britain between sprinters Linford Christie and Carl Lewis provided as much prize money (£200,000) as the rest of the athletic meeting combined, the inequalities between athletes, rather than simply between athletes and other individuals and organizations (such as promoters and television companies), were starkly evident. To discount the significance of hierarchies and inequities of sport as a demonstration of support for some of its more privileged practitioners would be, ultimately, to endorse these structures of power and reward. This point is illuminated if sport is viewed as a cultural resource with associated cultural rights (Murdock, 1993) rather than as the preserve of professional practitioners and those entrepreneurial organizations which maintain themselves by means of selling it. The 'stake-holders' (as social and cultural planners increasingly describe them) of sport also include casual players and spectators, neither of whom derive income from it. In Britain, for example, the Football Supporters Association has been an important force in the recent re-evaluation of soccer. It has been particularly vocal on the question of the treatment of soccer fans as consumers and their safety as spectators, thereby reflecting the contemporary upsurge in consumer rights advocacy among the many disparate and overlapping groups which claim an interest in sport. While much of it was substantially industrialized by the late twentieth century, the space of sports is not reducible to the space of industry, the space of labour and the space of spectacle.

Assertions of the seamless web of compatible interests in the sports industry – the elusive 'win–win situation' – fail to engage with the deep inequalities within sport itself. One way of rejecting evidence of inequality in sport is to argue that for many disadvantaged athletes it is, literally, the 'only game in town'. Hence, while it may be acknowledged that the sports world is ruthless, competitive and unfair, it is argued that it is one of the few industries where access is relatively easy for those who are excluded from other areas of business. Sport (along with popular music), it is contended, provides one of the few roads out of the ghetto. The social mobility justification is advanced most strongly where well-rewarded sports stars are from racial and ethnic minority groups in which there are deep problems of poverty, alienation and crime. The black American basketballer, in particular, has in recent years come to symbolize the capacity of sport to transform the individual circumstances of poor, talented and motivated people. In the face of such positive role models, critics of the material success of black sportspeople are likely to be accused of giving succour to those racist elements which resent any modest improvements in the condition of non-Anglo peoples. The sports industry, however, like most institutions shaped by the discipline of capital accumulation, is by no means a heartening instance of ready social and material improvement. McKay (1991: 11, 13), for example, in examining Australian data on sporting participation, concludes that 'sport is participated in by predominantly young, affluent and relatively well-educated male Australians', while also taking note of American statistics (Leonard and Reyman, 1988) that the chances of upward social mobility through sport were in the early eighties .004 per cent for females and .007 per cent for males. Cashmore (1990: 91) has similarly observed that, while many young black people are driven by the experience of social deprivation to achieve considerable success in at least some sports (such as athletics, boxing and basketball), handsome rewards are thinly distributed:

> Few attain the heights they wanted to conquer and even fewer surpass them. An unstoppable motivation and unbreakable commitment are valuable, perhaps essential, assets to success in sport and this is why so many possessors of these achieve some level of distinction. But titles are, by definition, reserved for only a very small elite and, while blacks are always well-represented among the elite of all sports in which they compete, there are never enough championships to go round. The majority inevitably fail. Blacks' success in sport may look impressive, but, compared to the number of youths entering sport, their interest primed, their success is not so great, even when their chances are affected by 'stacking' and other racialist manoeuvres.

The practice of 'stacking' to which Cashmore refers largely confines members of racial and ethnic minorities to certain 'appropriate' sports or to specified positions within a sports team. Physical and psychological stereotypes underline these distributional patterns – for example, that black footballers may be athletically gifted but lack leadership qualities and resilience. Edwards (1969) and Cashmore (1982; 1990) have both argued that apparently benign stereotypes of black sportspeople's innate sporting ability – as with the claim in music that black people have 'got rhythm' – confirm widespread racist separations of the natural/animal/manual from the civilized/human/cerebral. Indeed, they have argued that success in sport is a negative indicator of black progress, so that the greater the resort to sporting careers, the lesser the overall degree of progress in more powerful and prestigious 'vocations' such as education, law, medicine and high finance. Racialism, Cashmore (1990: 92, 93) argues, ensures a ready supply of black sports stars, as well as a much larger number on 'a route to nowhere'.

The conspicuous exploits of black athletes can be likened, in class terms, to proletarian labour. The control functions of coaching and proprietorship are virtually inaccessible to a player whose security of tenure is weak and whose ability to exert power over the sporting 'labour process' is highly limited. Dean Anderson (1993: 61), in examining cultural diversity among American intercollegiate football coaches, notes that the 'overrepresentation of blacks as athletes in intercollegiate sport', both as scholarship holders and as players, suggests initially that 'equal opportunity' and 'a meritocracy based on skill and achievement' exists in American university sport. However, a survey of 88 colleges revealed that 96 per cent of athletic directors and head coaches were white. Further analysis of positions played and coached by race revealed that the key 'central' positions of quarterback and offensive line were associated principally with senior white directors, coaches and coordinators, while the 'peripheral' positions of wide receiver, running back and defensive line were the major domain of black assistant coaches. As a result, black players and coaches rarely entered 'the pool from which head coaches and offensive coordinators are traditionally selected' (Anderson, 1993: 64). This conscious/unconscious, direct/indirect and intentional/unintentional pattern of racialized organizational allocation of function and position maintains a framework of discrimination. Anderson (1993: 66) thus concludes that:

Access to the playing field has been gained. At the same time the vertical movement of blacks in intercollegiate football up the career ladder from the subordinate position of student-athlete to a position of dominance, remains constricted. This suggests that relations of dominance and subordination in intercollegiate football may be structured along racial lines with a focus on 'inherent' physicality as the key to the construction of dominant images of whites and blacks.

Norman Yetman and Forrest Berghorn (1993: 308), in their longitudinal study of racial participation and integration in women's intercollegiate basketball, similarly demonstrate that despite 'feverish efforts to increase black representation on their coaching staffs' in the early seventies by many US colleges in responding to the protests of black athletes, the data reveal that in 1990 'white females dominate the head coaching ranks of women's teams, with white males a distant second. Black females and black males are only slightly represented.' This racist conception of black muscle and white brain resonates with the allocation of manual and mental labour on which class-based ideologies of dominance are founded. It gives the lie to naive propositions of ready social mobility for the disadvantaged in and through sport. It also reveals the racialized and gendered nature of power (including position in the labour market), through which the subordinate position of women in sport (Cohen, 1993; Hargreaves, 1994) is compounded by prejudice and discrimination on the grounds of race and ethnicity (Williams, 1994).

While it is undoubtedly the case that black sportspeople have not generally reached the pinnacles of sporting power, some have been materially successful by any standard. Conspicuous success in sport, especially of ethnic/racial minorities, is frequently placed in the framework of role-model emulation. In ideological terms this usually means that the sports superstar symbolizes what can be achieved by disadvantaged young people if properly motivated and led, helping also to raise their esteem in the general population through the unifying function of local, regional and national representative sport. Yet, as McKay (1994) points out in his political–economic critique of the use of positive representations of black sportsmen in the promotion of leisure corporations like Reebok and Nike, almost infinitesimally small opportunities for black social mobility through sport are imaginatively transformed into prospects of ready advance for African-Americans. Simultaneously, white guilt about structural racial inequality is 'comforted' while non-unionized (often female) workers in countries like Indonesia make these 'glamorous' products for South Korean subsidiaries on wages of around 80 US cents per day (INGI Labour Working Group, 1991). Hence, 'It is a perversely post-modern "irony" that a first world company uses a second world nation to

exploit workers in the third world, while deploying images of internally colonized black men to promote the alleged fairness of the system' (McKay,
1994: 10-11).

Such uncomfortable realities are rarely acknowledged in the heroic iconography of sport, but are nonetheless central to its political economy. The use
of sport as a model of ambition, diligence and enterprise is frequently applied
to whole populations, so that successful sportspeople also become national
symbols who straddle and symbolically unite the disparate social groups of
the nation. One of the primary justifications for the establishment in the
early eighties of the Australian Institute of Sport, for example, was that an
elite institution producing world sporting champions would inspire young
people across the country to take up healthy sporting activity and would
also boost the national morale. Similar arguments have been used to support
state investment in sports infrastructure in Europe and America (Gruneau,
1982). It would be unwise to discount entirely the positive role-model argument. Cashmore (1990: 90) recalls the deep offence caused to some black
athletes by his critique of black involvement of sport. More recently, the
success in the 1994 Commonwealth Games of the Aboriginal athlete Cathy
Freeman was enthusiastically celebrated by her people – and by many non-
Aborigines. In material terms, however, the emulation thesis can be likened to
the anti-egalitarian trickle-down thesis of neo-classical economics. That is, to
propose simply that the advancement of some sportspeople must lead, indirectly, to the benefit of all is to legitimize the very deep inequalities of reward
in the sporting arena. It is by no means clear how, either within or across
sports, the success of one athlete contributes to that of another. Indeed, the
concentration of rewards and resources among an elite few is likely to reproduce rather than overcome sporting inequality. Even the apparently plausible
argument that the total level of sporting participation increases with local,
regional, national and international success must be seriously questioned. It
is just as likely that there will be a movement of participants towards those
sports which, through massive media publicity, can be shown to be the most
individually lucrative rather than the most successful in terms of, for example,
performances against other countries. To put it crudely, one (seemingly highly
improbable) Wimbledon win by a British male tennis professional is almost
certain to recruit more tyro tennis players than a string of World Cup netball
victories will induce British girls to take up netball as a profession. The cir-
cularity of the commercial–media logic in promoting certain sports over
others ensures that the sports labour market is heavily skewed towards mostly
male, action-packed and often violent sport.

Against the claim that contemporary 'Sport for All' and 'Life. Be In It'
health campaigns have produced legions of uncommodified sportspeople, it
needs to be pointed out that the justification for such state-initiated and com-
mercially-sponsored campaigns is substantially economic (see Chapter 6). The
aim to produce a healthy workforce and a more self-sufficient aging population may be laudable, but it has little to do with any conception of the intrinsic
value of sport and sports-related pleasures. Similarly, the health-and-fitness

boom of the last decade or so has been commercially stimulated as an adjunct to the fitness, leisure, fashion, cosmetic, advertising and dietary industries (Fitzclarence, 1990; Gruneau, 1993). These points are made not to repudiate in their entirety contemporary trends in sports participation and body maintenance, but to rebut the atomistic proposition that developments in sport are based on conscious, voluntary and individual 'contracts' between professional athletes and spectators; elite, aspirant and grass-roots athletes; consumers, the state and business enterprises; and so on. The operation of the sports industry is complex because it is a dynamic constellation of actors, organizations and industrial and social sectors. To argue that today's sport is a business is commonplace. It is, in any case, not only a business, but the spread of commercial practice through the most resistant sports (such as rugby union) and the newest and most apparently 'fun-based' games (such as beach volleyball) is having a profound effect on what we now call sport. By examining key aspects of this burgeoning business of the body in competition and motion, the 'free play' element in contemporary sport is put in perspective.

Agents of sports commerce

In his journalistic overview of *The Sports Business*, Neil Wilson (1988: 8) covers several of the key actors, organizations and activities comprising sport 'at the highest level . . . not recreation for the elite but a division of the entertainment industry'. Among the array of promoters, sponsors, competitors and others who make up the industry of sport, one group of operatives is particularly representative of the triumphal entrepreneurial spirit in the sports game. These are the agents, who, since their flowering in the USA in the early sixties, have risen to the status of a:

> new professional class within sport that transformed the lot of the muddied oafs and flannelled fools of this world, and caused the pendulum to swing so far the other way that there are players in US basketball earning more than $2,000,000 from their clubs for a season's work and in Britain soccer players earning £2,000 a week. (Wilson, 1988: 75)

These upper limits of athletic reward have been greatly exceeded since Wilson presented them. Shaquille O'Neal, for example, who rapidly replaced Michael Jordan as basketball's global hero after the latter's (short-lived) retirement in 1993, reputedly signed a contract worth US$24,000,000 in that year. Agents moved into the sports arena in large numbers in the early seventies to perform the functions long embraced by their counterparts in the more established entertainment disciplines. In representing sportsmen and women who had, in the main, received little of the income that organized sport was generating in the age of television, they could habitually represent themselves as 'sports attorneys', the champions of the sporting underdog. In the United States, agents have been instrumental in mounting challenges to the attempts of the owners of sports franchises to regulate the sports labour market, most notably in the 1992 successful anti-trust case of *Freeman McNeill et al. v. National Football League* (Staudohar, 1992). In spite of several instances of agents engaging in unethical practices (Miller et al., 1992), players and agents have presented a largely united front in seeking to extract financial concessions from team owners (as well as media companies and sponsors). In most cases these arguments have taken the form of straightforward free labour market advocacy, with players demanding 'their basic economic rights' (Meggyesy, 1992: 112) and agents positioning themselves as the champions of their clients in demanding that 'league and team executives will have to adjust their perception of players and treat them as business partners rather than chattels or pieces on a gameboard' (Steinberg, 1992: 115). Sports agents, whose interests lie in generating maximum income from the activities of their clients, conventionally present their involvement with sportspeople as altruistic. The prominent American agent Robert G. Woolf, for example, in providing players with a three-fold package entailing 'making money, managing it and, crucially, protecting the client from the dangers of having it', states that 'In the end, our aim, the whole purpose of our work, is to set a player up for life, or at least as far as his talent makes it possible for us to' (quoted in Wilson, 1988: 81).

The sports agent and the large management agencies to which they belong, however, often do rather more than take a percentage of earnings for 'placing' and protecting their charges. Organizations like Mark McCormack's International Marketing Group (IMG), the world's largest sports agency, perform so many functions and derive income from so many activities that the simple task of player representation is overshadowed by multifarious and potentially conflicting commercial commitments. The agency has a crucial role in acting as a 'middle man' (the gender of whom is used advisedly) in handling 'economic relations between individual sport stars, sport organisations, promoters, sponsors, advertisers and television companies' (Whannel, 1992: 75).

By simultaneously staging, promoting, marketing, televising, and arranging sponsorship and advertising for an event, agents may find that vigorous player representation is not necessarily in their best interests, or, alternatively, can exert undue pressure on their clients to appear in the many made-for-TV sporting events for which they are responsible. Steven Barnett (1990: 188), for example, records how IMG was instrumental in allowing the Japanese whisky company, Sun Tory, to:

> circumvent domestic television restrictions on whisky commercials; golf was an ideal vehicle, given its wide exposure on Japanese television. IMG arranged the tournament and the television deal, as well as representing the sponsors. As a bonus, McCormack himself provided some of the television commentary.

The financial power of the agents also represents considerable cultural power. Peter Ueberroth – who, having delivered a US$150,000,000 profit to the 1984 Los Angeles Olympic Organizing Committee (Lawrence, 1986a: 207), can hardly be described as anti-entrepreneurial – has judged that agents 'are now lords of the game' (Wilson, 1988: 75). Whannel (1992: 77), similarly, has pointed to the way in which 'McCormack's organisations have acquired a significant power to define the cultural nature of sports such as tennis and golf', not least through its television subsidiary, Trans World International (TWI), which claims to be 'the world's largest independent producer of sports programming and the world's largest representative of television rights to international sporting events'. The economic influence of agencies like IMG and West Nally does not, however, go uncontested. Wilson (1988), for example, in tracing the history of the broken relationship between IMG and the successful British middle-distance runner of the seventies and eighties (now Conservative Member of Parliament) Sebastian Coe, records the following statement from Coe:

> To be honest, IMG singularly failed to appreciate the nature of athletics and in part perhaps that was my fault. All their other clients were in tennis or golf, or professional sports. They could not understand that there were things you could not buy. Perhaps that's the American mentality. But European track and field could not be approached that way. You could not take a cheque book to them and buy them. They had been around too long, doing it their own way and doing it pretty well. (quoted in Wilson, 1988: 64)

While this statement may seem questionable in view of the rapid commercialization of athletics over the last decade, it reveals at least one instance where high-pressure American sales techniques – in this case an early eighties' proposal for a lucrative three-race series between Coe and close rival Steve Ovett – did not succeed. Even in the heartland of American commercialized sport there may also be obstructions to the personal profit imperative, as exemplified by the refusal of golfer Jack Nicklaus in the mid-seventies to take part in a challenge which could have earned him a million dollars for one round of golf on the grounds that 'It would not be in the interests of the game' (quoted in Tatz, 1986: 58). Such resistance, however scattered or uneven, indicates that, contrary to some assessments, professional sportspeople are not merely accessories to the wholesale commodification of sport. Sportspeople are commonly attached to their sports in an all-consuming manner, having made great sacrifices of time and effort as child and adult in the refinement of their skills. They may, like Coe quoted above, be critical of the business elements operating within sport, but it is very difficult for athletes to match the power of the commercial machinery of sport. Players' unions are essentially 'defensive' industrial organizations which struggle over the distribution of rewards rather than the manner in which they are generated, while individual athletes have strong incentives to maximize their returns from an often short and uncertain sports career.

Sportspeople are, then, both celebrated and exploited by the industry of sport. It is their labour and performance that is minutely scrutinized and whose skills are bought and sold in the sporting marketplace, their bodies which are punished, manipulated and invaded in the quest for greater efficiency, and their images moulded and displayed to sell and promote goods and services. As McKay (1991) has pointed out, this industrialized emphasis on 'performativity' encourages an ever more 'scientized' and 'medicalized' view of the body of the professional athlete and of the non-professional who has responded positively to state and business injunctions to 'tone up' and 'get in shape'. This increasingly efficient sporting body is:

> seldom portrayed as a pleasurable site for ecstatic, intrinsic, aesthetic, sensuous and holistic experiences. It is depicted as a mechanical object which must be managed, maintained, conditioned, tuned and repaired for instrumental reasons such as improving linear performance or increasing one's physical attractiveness. (p. 141)

Such remarks are reminiscent of Adorno's (1967) critique of professional sport as essentially alienating because of its repetitive and rule-bound nature. Certainly, professional athletes often express disillusionment with the highly routinized nature of their lives. It should be acknowledged, however, that there is nothing automatic and preordained about the rationalization and regimentation of sport. It is clear that, as with any industry (but particularly in the culture industries), careful 'risk-management' is necessary for its survival. As Hirsch (1970) noted in regard to popular music (see Chapter 2 above), the 'task environment' must be carefully controlled in order to minimize the chances of market failure. In the case of sport, the success of a 'product' is reliant on a number of interlocking institutions and activities. First, a sport must have a popular base within communities, and, if it does not have one, then interest and support must be stimulated through high-pressure promotion, sustained (if not saturation) media coverage and spectacle. Soccer may be taken to be an example of the former, while the 12-metre yacht racing in the America's Cup (particularly in eighties' Australia) is an instance of the latter (James, 1986). Second, a sport must have a reliable governing body, preferably one that is receptive to the blandishments and material inducements of the commercial sector, and which can exert due influence on the network of clubs, teams and regional associations which form the organizational infrastructure of sport. Such bodies may be national or international, with, for example, the Australian Rugby League (supported by media magnate, Kerry Packer) exhibiting a determination (now matched by Rupert Murdoch's pay television-inspired Super League) over the last decade to discipline the commercial practices of its member clubs (Wilson, 1990), and the International Olympic Committee developing over the same period into the very model of a commercially 'accommodating' organization of governance (Simson and Jennings, 1992; Whannel, 1992). Third, a sport must demonstrate itself to be attractive to the commercial trinity of sponsors, advertisers and television companies, which, separately and in consort, profoundly influence the destinies of most sports. Sponsors such as tobacco and liquor companies have been vital to the economic development of contemporary sport, with so-called 'incidental' television coverage (Harris, 1988; Martin, 1990) a vital means of circumventing the state regulation of the advertising and promotion of unhealthy products.

'Mega' sponsors such as Coca Cola and McDonalds have similarly been integral to the development of global sports spectacles such as the Olympics and the World Cup. Sponsors are also often direct advertisers, and the successful attraction of an array of advertisers anxious to secure prime spots in major sporting events is a major source of income for television companies, who can in turn pass on some of the material benefits of television rights to individual sports. Coverage by free-to-air television and, increasingly, 'pay' (that is satellite and cable) TV is crucial to the financial health of professional sport in the late twentieth century. It is virtually impossible to imagine how a sport could achieve real prominence without a major presence on the small screen (Cunningham and Miller, 1994: 89). Finally, a sport must transcend the confines of sport itself, insinuating itself into the worlds of youth fashion, video imagery, celebrity gossip and consumer merchandising and paraphernelia. Here, sport and pop begin to converge, with the style of the sporting superstar increasingly resembling that of the traditional pop star figurehead. Nowhere has this fusion been more complete than in the American form of basketball culture, with its heavy emphasis on the stylized marketing of African-American street cool (McKay, 1994). In this way, the sports industry is imbricated with a series of interdependent economic and cultural institutions, and so is further cemented into a leisure complex in which the constituent parts appear increasingly naturalized and indispensable. The complex industrial processes and relations identified above together produce sport as one of the world's largest economic enterprises. The reliance on relatively orderly and predictable relations – for example, between popular sports, the television companies who purchase rights to them, and the sponsors and advertisers who seek to capitalize on their mass exposure and emotional power – favours the stability and routine of geographically-limited 'league' competitions (like British soccer and American baseball), travelling world circuits (such as those in tennis and motor-racing), and a rolling schedule of global sports spectacles (like the Olympics and the Athletics World Cup). There is also a corresponding drive to produce novelty, controversy and a sense of vitality. The development of new rules, events, prizes and media technologies can only partially meet this demand for demonstrable change in the organization and presentation of sport. Each brings closer scrutiny of the paid performer by the paying public.

Making and unmaking sports celebrity

Sports stars, who are simultaneously the objects of attention and the currency of exchange, are called upon to display a range of context-specific personae. They are expected to excel in the sports arena, but they are also pressured to function as role models for young people, as embodiments of corporate endorsement values and, in some instances, as provocateurs and controversialists. This tension between on-field efficiency and off-field accountability is manifest in the requirement for there to be both idiosyncratic sporting 'characters' (such as John McEnroe in tennis) and more conventional 'ornaments to the game' (like Pete Sampras in the same sport). While to some extent this problem is handled (most outrageously in professional wrestling) by the invention of cast lists of heroes and villains, there are often severe difficulties in getting those sportspeople in prescribed roles to follow the script, or, in more orthodox industrial sociological terms, to function as disciplined, cooperative and compliant workers.

Two conspicuous examples in recent years of elite sportspeople who have rapidly suffered the devaluation of their stocks in the sports labour market are world champion boxer Mike Tyson and runner Ben Johnson. Tyson's trial and jailing for rape in 1992 severely truncated his sports career, although a well-hyped, pre-release 'comeback' was underway by 1994 and in full swing post-release in 1995. Johnson tested positive for performance enhancing drugs at the Seoul Olympics in 1988 after winning the hundred metres in world record time, but returned to the track after being disqualified and banned. Although he never recovered his pre-Seoul form, Johnson received handsome appearance money, especially in staged 'head-to-head' races with his rival Carl Lewis, until again being detected in the use of steroids and incurring a life ban. While both Tyson and Johnson were widely condemned for their crimes and misdemeanours, few critiques acknowledged the sports market's contribution to them. In the case of Tyson, it may be argued that the violence, arrogance and contempt for women that he displayed was consonant with a sycophantic culture of celebrity in masculine sport, where women are routinely regarded as 'groupies' and 'hangers-on' with nothing to 'trade' but their sexuality. Johnson, more generally, was the product of an elite sports culture in which the drive to win and to gain the extravagant material rewards offered by international sporting success over-rode seemingly naive and outmoded notions of fair play and bodily health (Lueschen, 1993; McKay et al., 1994). Such attitudes and behaviour cannot be rationalized as aberrations attributable to individual pathologies. Rather, they demonstrate the ways in which the economic structure and cultural complexion of professional sport interact in a manner that produces problematic forms of (especially masculine) sports celebrity.

Another more complicated story of crisis in the sports celebrity labour market concerns the American basketballer Magic Johnson, who in 1991 declared himself to be HIV positive. Johnson, who at the time endorsed such everyday mass-marketed products as Pepsi, Converse, KFC and Nintendo, experienced some corporate uncertainty about his new association with a still stigmatized condition which was believed first to threaten his marketability (King, 1993) and then to enhance it (Wenner, 1994). Selection for the 1992 Barcelona Olympics and subsequent (if somewhat predictable) gold medal success further restored Magic's sports labour market position, until it was again undermined by the reluctance of several fellow basketballers to engage in vigorous body contact with him on the court (Rowe, 1994a). Johnson subsequently embraced and then abandoned a coaching role, his general public standing and related utility as endorser of corporate commodities made fragile by the malign articulation of metaphors of disease and sexuality (Treichler, 1987). Michael Jordan, Johnson's successor as premier international icon for American basketball, subsequently retired from basketball in 1993 after allegations of a gambling habit and the violent death of his father, only to re-surface the following year as an aspiring (and, it must be acknowledged, struggling) professional baseball player of somewhat diminished visibility. By 1995, Jordan was back on the basketball court. Finally, the arraignment on charges of murder in 1994 of the very prominent sporting identity O.J. Simpson, with the bizarre precursor of a 'live' televised police chase leading to the relay of the trial itself on the small screen, provided an unprecedentedly 'public' variation on the mythicized narrative of the fallen sports hero (McKay and Smith, 1995). These biographical examples of the tribulations of some of the world's most saleable human sports commodities demonstrate more than the fragility of sports celebrity as a career option. It will not have escaped attention that each instance cited is that of a black male, and in each instance racialist discourses concerning the 'flaws' of black masculinity were invoked. Commercial sport, for all its self-celebration as a prime mechanism for the social mobility of 'people of colour', provides only limited immunity from prevailing power structures and ideologies.

The volatile nature of the sports labour market can, however, produce responses to 'deviancy' that appear to be perverse rather than punitive. For example, when in early 1994 the American figure skater Nancy Kerrigan was physically assaulted by an associate of her major rival Tonya Harding (who claimed to have no prior knowledge of the 'plot'), the incident stimulated unprecedented media interest in both winter sports and the sportswomen concerned. When a few weeks later Kerrigan and Harding competed in the Winter Olympic Games at Lillehammer in Norway, the CBS television network achieved its largest ever audience and the tenth largest in American broadcasting history. Both skaters were the subject of instant books, proposals for television and film drama, and, particularly in the case of Kerrigan, numerous inflated offers to endorse products. For Harding, a musical career as a punk singer was canvassed at the same time as the 'home' movie of her wedding night went on sale. The twists and turns in these recent sports narratives of the Johnsons, Tyson, Simpson, Kerrigan, Harding and others indicate that, while sport can hardly be said to function as an orderly and predictable business, its commercial apparatus – as well as that of its ancillary industries – is effectively geared to capitalize on quite sudden and dramatic changes in the fortunes of its star personnel. For most professional sportspeople, a career in sport provides neither exemption from the need to seek later employment nor adequate preparation for labour in another field. The passage into obscurity and/or penury can, therefore, be dramatic and traumatic, as the recent suicides and jailings of some retired British soccer professionals have demonstrated. The sports superstar, however, has sufficient prominence (that is, exchangeable currency) to spin off into the wider realm of popular entertainment, while on some occasions the peculiarities of individual sporting and extra-sporting biographies may (as in the case of Kerrigan and Harding) confer a degree of fame (or infamy) out of all proportion to any sporting performance record. Viewed in this way, sport takes on a specifically postmodern character as the pretext for the chaotic interplay of surface imagery. This phenomenon is termed 'panic sport' by Kroker et al. (1989: 172), but the confusion of signs of sport is not necessarily accompanied by organizational disturbance. Here, assessments of the corporatization, growth and stability of the sports industry inevitably draw it into current debates about the decline of Fordism, the disorganization of capitalism and the process of postmodernization.

Fordist, post-Fordist and grass-roots sport

The commercialization of sport in the twentieth century appears to have accompanied (albeit often reluctantly) the full flowering of Fordism, loosely defined as that industrial and social system which, by means of the mechanization and fragmentation of work tasks in spatially concentrated sites of production, fostered the standardization of mass-produced, advertised and consumed commodities (Murray, 1989). There are certainly elements of the sports industry, both within and between nation states, that are in accord with the Fordist ethos. For example, the mass communication of sporting contests and the mass advertising and consumption of branded sportswear reflect the Fordist attachment to scale and standardization. Furthermore, the emphasis on the nation state and symbolic nation-building in earlier phases of Fordist modernization (at the end of the nineteenth and beginning of the twentieth centuries) is strongly connected to the use of sport in 'the establishment of national symbols and ceremonies and the reinvention of traditions', only later emerging as 'spectacles which have become commodified and promoted to wider audiences' (Featherstone, 1993: 178; see also Whannel, 1992: 16). Yet the association of sport with Fordism is incomplete, not least because of sport's deep reliance on rapidly shifting images and symbols rather than on the production of use-valuable commodities *per se*, and also because of the incongruous co-existence of the sports–media complex in the shape of the likes of CBS and Adidas on the one hand and many 'feudalistic' sports organizations and idiosyncratic local sports on the other.

At a more general level the historical stability and global domination of Fordism itself can be questioned. While it is clear that the rate of economic and cultural change has accelerated, the boom–bust cycles of capitalism and the deep political conflicts of the inter- and post-war eras counter exaggerated assertions of the temporal, regional, civic and governmental stability of Fordism (Harvey, 1989). It is similarly tempting to over-emphasize the difference between the culture industries, which are figured as transient and prone to widespread market failure, and those more solid manufacturers of consumer durables with a more limited but successful product range. Rates of product failure are, it should be noted, historically high in the 'non-cultural' industries (Schumpeter, 1954), while Lash and Urry (1994: 123), in their survey of current trends in industry and culture, argue, as noted in Chapter 2 above, that the culture industries are now the model for the manufacturing sector (rather than the other way round). Such discussions are addressed to the more commonly recognized culture industries of publishing, television and recorded music rather than to sport. Yet, as I have argued above, sport may be classified as a significant culture industry in its own right. The inter-meshing of sport as a social institution with a growing range of economic and cultural organizations and functions renders increasingly problematic the analytical and empirical delineation of sport as a distinct sphere of social and cultural practice. Instead, the industrialization of sport has seen it move beyond straightforward payment for play in front of spectators to a complex series of transactions in which it supports (and, in turn, is supported by) a wide range of secondary and tertiary industries. Whatever the status of sport *qua* culture industry, it has clearly flourished in those post-Fordist sectors in which the closely targeted, image-conscious niche-marketing of sport/leisure practices and identities have combined with more fluid and dispersed meth-ods and sites of production. A variety of 'water' pursuits, including sailing, deep-sea fishing and diving, exemplifies this move towards 'tailored' sport, while even some mass spectator sports, such as British soccer, have felt the impact of post-Fordist consumption regimes in the form of its substantial capture by subscription satellite television. At the same time, there is evi-dence of an inconsistent and sometimes resistive response to the global diffusion of mass American sports and Americanized sports promotion and marketing strategies in their classically Fordist modes in countries like Britain and Australia (Maguire, 1990; McKay and Miller, 1991). Yet the sheer scale of major global media sports spectacles (like the Olympic Games and the World Cup) and the highly rationalized exploitation of profitable opportu-nities surrounding them suggest that pronouncements of the demise of the Fordist sporting moment are somewhat premature.

It would also be misleading to propose that the involvement of commerce is inevitably destructive of grass-roots sport. The pleasures of participation and spectatorship still apply in spheres of sport governed by no more com-plex an economic infrastructure than small raffles and club takings. In this form sport is tied much more closely to specific communities as an expression of everyday social relations. As such it is by no means free of the politics of everyday life – the gender order, for example, of community sporting organi-zations is often grossly unequal – but nor is it enslaved by the logic of commercial sports expansionism. Local and regional sporting affiliations have stubbornly persisted into the late twentieth century, in spite of the attempts by sports administrators to generate greater television revenue by creating more national and international competitions (Stewart, 1990). In Australia, for example, with its highly regionalized history of commitment to different football codes, there has been considerable resistance to the 'export' of rugby league to Victoria and Australian rules to New South Wales and Queensland. In soccer, which in Australia has a history of low-capitalization and intense localism, a national competition has struggled for several years, while in the United States the staging of the 1994 World Cup finals represents the latest, somewhat desperate attempt to establish the commercial future of the 'world game' in the New World's most important sports market (Rowe et al., 1994). The history of rugby league in Britain is a similar cautionary tale of regional affiliation and national economic ambition. To take another example of a less-than-smooth integration of sports commerce and culture, the sports industry has been very slow to challenge the culturally-conditioned gender segregation of much sporting participation and spectatorship. The discovery of the economic power of the female sports viewer, recognition of the substantial grass-roots foundation of female sports (such as netball and hockey), and the movement of more women into traditionally masculine 'contact' sports have all demanded more supple and flexible ways of constructing and conceiving sports markets. Many women's sports, it appears, will bypass the Fordist moment altogether and be targeted for niche marketing, while women as television spectators are viewed as integral to the maintenance and growth of Fordist mega sports spectacles. That these questions have only recently become pressing is testimony to a powerfully patriarchal alignment of sporting and masculine ideologies which has to some degree impeded the commercial logic of sports market exploitation.

The industrial development of the sports industry is, therefore, by no means a textbook model of unfettered commercial expansion. For those who are attached to sport, this development itself provokes ambivalence. Nostalgia for former times when sporting contests were clashes between fiercely loyal 'urban tribes' (or edifying contests between sporting rivals) and criticism of the commercial corruption of sport is seemingly contradicted by a willingness to consume in vast numbers sports mega spectacles in which the participants have been bought and sold on the sports labour market. This 'psychic stratification' of sports following is, itself, symptomatic of the persistent and deep split within sports discourse between sport as a transcendent and as a mundane activity. In this respect, it reflects a still uneasy accommodation of commerce and popular culture. The affective (often profoundly romantic) investment that 'sportslovers' have made in sport contrasts with the continuous process, intensive production and sales techniques of the sportsbiz. As was shown to be the case with popular music, this combination of high romanticism and high finance is the contradictory resolution of the antagonism beteen commerce and culture. Fordist and post-Fordist regimes represent, in this regard, different models for delivering sport profitably without 'turning off' its participants and audiences.

Conclusion

This review of some of the current features of the sports industry reveals markedly uneven development. In particular, there are simultaneous trends towards a predominantly Fordist national and 'globalizing' sport as well as towards more diffuse sporting forms which exhibit both pre- and post-Fordist features. Instead of asserting the final triumph of Fordist or post-Fordist sport, it is more defensible to acknowledge the co-existence, with Williams (1977), of dominant, residual and emergent forms, the balance of which is determined by both macro and micro forces. It would be surprising if sport could avoid the kind of close and disruptive contact with capitalist values and practices experienced by other domains of popular culture. Indeed, in many ways it functions as an ideal vehicle for generating audiences, transmitting brand names and establishing 'label loyalties'. Once safely installed within sport's structures of governance, commercial assumptions become increasingly indistinguishable from those pertaining to the interests of sport. Individual sports are enjoined to expand, to compete with other sports and codes, and to establish modes of operation paralleling those of the boardroom. Deliberations concerning sporting rule changes now often resemble the preoccupation with 'product development' familiar to any commercial enterprise. The movement towards the advanced commercialization of individual sports has occurred at different speeds and with varying degrees of turbulence. Nonetheless, the rapid phase of development experienced by the 'sportsbiz' in the late twentieth century stands as a notable instance of the (hyper)rationalization and (hyper)commodification of culture (Crook et al., 1992). Irrespective of particular summations of the state of the sports industry, the significance of the proliferation and circulation of images as integral to the increasing alignment of culture and economics in capitalist production cannot be ignored (Hall, 1989). This trend does not presuppose the evacuation of politics from popular cultural forms like sport, but marks their insinuation into an expanding range of sites in which the material and the symbolic intertwine in increasingly complex and contradictory configurations. For this reason, a reflexive analysis is required of sport's ideologies and their associated modes of politics.

6

Ideologies in Competition

The previous chapter concluded with a discussion of the ways in which the sports industry is implicated in the global–local dialectics of economics and culture. These are necessarily political concerns – the flow of sporting culture across the boundaries of nation states and into their institutions and meaning systems inevitably provokes questions about national, regional and local cultural sovereignty. The inter-governmental and civic institutional cooperation necessary for the conduct of international sporting competition is itself a significant manifestation of world geo-politics, as is the ideological significance ascribed to sport by states and civil societies. The politics of sport, like those of rock music and other forms of popular culture, are generally manifest in the ways in which they are deployed, often unconsciously, to support or undermine structures of power that are deeply imbedded in our practical consciousness. While there are often overtly political deployments of sport (most notoriously the Nazi exploitation of the Berlin Olympics in 1936 and, conspicuously in recent decades, the sporting isolation of South Africa under apartheid), its politics are more significant in the everyday construction of ideologies whereby, for example, gender and racial politics, articulated in terms of inherent male or white sporting supremacy, become important means by which dominant groups seek to symbolize and naturalize their power. The history of politics in and of sport can, therefore, be rendered as a series of spectacular 'collisions' and collaborations between sporting and political institutions, and also as a set of seemingly unremarkable but ideologically-loaded articulations of political and sporting languages.

The relationship between sport and orthodox politics is marked by a contradiction between the denial of politics in sport (as encapsulated in the oft-repeated adage that 'sport and politics don't mix') and the political mobilization of sport (when used, for example, as an index of national or ethnic progress). In this chapter the politics of sport will be discussed first in relation to formal politics (such as the Gleneagles Agreement and associated 'bans' on international sporting contact with South Africa) and then in the context of state intervention in the organization and resourcing of sports and sports promotion campaigns. The analysis will then be broadened to address the manner in which sport may be said to reproduce inequalities of class, gender and race/ethnicity, enlisted in support of nationalism, and deployed in ideologically-inflected fashion as metaphor and image in politics, business and advertising. Sport is simultaneously heavily politicized yet widely regarded as beyond or above politics (Hoberman, 1984). The ethos of pleasure and entertainment that surrounds it discourages overt associations between sport and political values and institutions, while rich and deep politics of sport operate in the context of widespread incomprehension and denial. Black sportspeople may be subjected to racist abuse, the abilities of sportswomen denigrated, and both often excluded by private sports (such as golf) clubs, but many sports lovers will claim that sport is – or at least ought to be – apolitical. On occasions this overt separation cannot be sustained, as in the case of the 1993 Christchurch by-election in Britain, when a candidate opposed to the then manager of the English national soccer team stood on behalf of the Sack Graham Taylor Party. The election platform was not successful, but Taylor, having failed to take England to the 1994 World Cup finals in the USA, resigned a few months later, taking 'his' eponymous political party with him. More seriously, the Thatcher government's attempts in the eighties to introduce identity card schemes for British soccer fans prompted a good deal of political activity and lobbying, with the opposition Labour party re-asserting its class-based origins as the champion of the 'people's game'.

While it is rare for political parties and sporting issues to be quite so closely associated, all major political parties and tiers of government in liberal democracies have sports policies and ministries. Indeed, the distribution of grants to sporting bodies has become a major means by which governments can seek popularity and prestige (McKay, 1986; 1990), not least through the politics of the pork barrel. For example, in Australia in 1993 the Labor government distributed A$30 million in grants to community sporting groups shortly before a federal election. After the election had been won and the allocation process demonstrated to be poorly documented and justified, a political scandal popularly named the 'Sports Rorts Affair' precipitated the resignation of the appropriate Minister, Ros Kelly. Sport itself may seem to be secondary to electioneering in such instances, but the denial of the sports–politics nexus is much more difficult to maintain where nation states formally agree actively to discourage individuals and associations from engaging in sporting competition with another nation over a lengthy period. The sports boycott of South Africa (only recently lifted) is the most prominent example of such supra-state political cooperation in the sports arena, but the threat and conduct of sporting boycotts is now an established weapon in the armoury of international diplomacy.

Sport and the politics of the boycott

South Africa is always mentioned in discussions of sport and politics because it is such a vivid instance of the politicization of sport – or, as we might construe it, the sporticization of politics. The gradual dismantlement of apartheid and the agonized movement towards a multi-racial, democratic state mean that the choice of appropriate tense is difficult, for while apartheid may officially be dead, its legacy is everywhere evident. As a thoroughgoing system of political exclusion, apartheid contained at its very heart the means and will to connect politics and sport. The formal exclusion of black and coloured 'sections' of the population from involvement in representative sport was supported by the material deprivation which ensured that resources (such as training facilities, coaching and equipment) were grossly unevenly distributed between whites and other peoples (Jarvie, 1993). The enormous material inequality produced by apartheid will, as a consequence, sustain sporting inequality long after its politico-legal apparatus has been destroyed. Sport under the regime of apartheid necessitated political intervention at national and international level. The refusal of National Party governments (and their appointees and fellow travellers in sporting associations) to admit Maori rugby players and non-white cricketers to South Africa in the sixties and seventies involved more than simply sporting relationships (Cashmore, 1990). The denial of passage to the citizens of other countries necessarily involved national governments in the politics of sporting exclusion. In the liberal democratic states of the west, this racist obstructionism caused a political dilemma. African and Asian countries, in which the state often took a much more active and official role in the operations of sporting bodies, demanded sporting and other sanctions against the racially discriminatory state of South Africa. The act and threat of the sporting boycott constituted a particularly potent tactic employed by black African nations, particularly when applied to the Olympic Games (which rely so heavily on the image of peaceful international competition). At the same time, the establishment power of organizations like England's Rugby Football Union and the Marylebone Cricket Club was mobilized effectively to resist state intervention in sporting contacts.

The outcry against South Africa gathered such worldwide momentum in the late sixties and seventies (not least amongst radicals and liberals in countries like Australia and Britain) that several states did cooperate in the sporting isolation of South Africa. Ironically, perhaps, a major vehicle for running the boycott was the legacy of the brand of imperialism that brought whites to the African continent in the first place. The British Commonwealth, the last formal organizational remnant of a once 'glorious' Empire, functioned in 1977 to attack a key symbol of imperialism by framing the Gleneagles Agreement (Jarvie, 1993). The Gleneagles Protocols called on member states to apply the maximum legal pressure to dissuade organizations, teams and individuals from sporting contact with South Africa. Apart from procedural obstruction in diplomatic relations, liberal–democratic states could exert financial pressure by threatening to withdraw the public funds that were increasingly being directed to sport as part of an expanded state role in sports provision. Nation states also 'encouraged' international sporting organizations like the International Olympic Committee to expel South Africa from Olympic competition (in 1970, following suspension in 1964) under threat of a mass boycott.

The Olympics boycott has been a continuing feature of political expression in sport since the mid-fifties. The boycott has provoked often fierce struggles between liberal–democratic governments wishing to make significant symbolic statements of political protest (as in the American boycott of the 1980 Moscow Games over military intervention in Afghanistan by the (then) Soviet Union) and formally autonomous sporting organizations (usually with impeccable establishment credentials) seeking to assert their independence of government and commitment to sporting business as usual. Such conflicts have had wide ramifications in their testing of the relative powers of the executive arm of the state, the judiciary and various combinations of the citizenry engaged in sporting pursuits. The 1980 Moscow Olympics is a particularly instructive case where the state and sporting apparatuses were involved in complex, contradictory struggles. In Britain, the USA and Australia, the conservative governments then installed were dedicated, at least officially, to a New Right agenda of small government, *laissez-faire* politics and economics, and opposition to 'socialistic' intervention in the operation of civil society. These values were challenged from within conservatism itself by more patrician and interventionist concerns with the maintenance of order and public morality. Thus, while each government wished strongly to punish the Soviet Union by means of a mass boycott of its 'showpiece' Games, it was necessary to avoid the appearance of totalitarianism entailed in coercing groups and individuals not to participate in the Games and so infringe civil liberties. Ironically, it was the USA of the Carter Presidency, with its stronger libertarian tradition and constitution, which acceded to the triumph of Cold War rhetoric – the decision was made by the American Olympic Committee for the USA team to remain at home (before the swearing in of Ronald Reagan). In Britain, the Thatcher government could not carry the day, in spite of the furious protestations of a prime minister whose form of 'authoritarian populism' (S. Hall, 1985) sought uncomfortably to combine the advocacy of freedom with a reactionary intolerance of dissent. The British Olympic Association did take its team to Moscow, earning in the process the undying animus of the Thatcher government (Hill, 1992). In Australia, the Fraser government narrowly failed to persuade the Australian Olympic Federation to boycott the Games *in toto*. It resorted to offering financial 'compensation' totalling over A$500,000 to 6 athletes and 7 sporting organizations not competing in Moscow, although this was less than one sixth of the financial adjustment made on behalf of business organizations (such as the Seven commercial television network) which claimed to have lost revenue on account of the conservative coalition government's stand on the Moscow Boycott (Stoddart, 1986: 77).

The direct articulation of sport and politics is, as noted above, fostered by heightened state involvement in the funding and organization of sport. This 'rationalization' of sporting activities and structures is an important aspect of the sports–politics nexus. While it is clear that politics in and of sports cannot simply be reduced to the functioning of the formal state apparatus, it is equally apparent that it is difficult to conceive of any feature of sporting practice which does not engage deeply with the broader notion of 'governmentality' (Bennett, 1992; Cunningham, 1992). Sport is rarely given prominence in discussions of the cultural policies applied to those public and private institutions which produce and relay contemporary symbols and ideologies, yet it has had a long and developing association with those agencies charged with various modes of regulation of the body.

Sports and states

Sport has an established and important role in the politics of different state formations, particularly in regard to what we might call, in Foucauldian terms, 'institutional regimes of bodily discipline and control' (Loy et al., 1993: 76). Several writers (Hoberman, 1984; Mandell, 1971; Riordan, 1980) have noted the appeal of sport to centralist and totalitarian state regimes. Hoberman (1984: 201), for example, examines in some detail the 'sport culture' of the former German Democratic Republic (East Germany) which in the mid-eighties was in per capita terms 'by far the most successful in the world'. The GDR, with a population of only 17 million, even challenged the sporting superpowers of the USA and the former Soviet Union for supremacy in the summer Olympics of the seventies and eighties. The communist regime's massive investment in sport, fuelled in part by an assessment of the cultural needs of an unusually youthful post-war population, was aimed at heroicizing sportspeople through a corporeal ethic of 'pure performance' within a sports apparatus that had 'achieved a futuristic scientism' (Hoberman, 1984: 210). It also claimed to uphold the values of socialism by avoiding the exploitation of athletes. As one official booklet put it:

> . . . the GDR's reputation as a sporting nation is not attributable to drugs or other illicit means, but to well-planned, intensive training programmes for healthy and resilient individuals. Dr Irving Dardik, head of the USOC Sports Medicine Council, rebutted allegations by the Western media that the dominant role of the socialist countries was due to manipulation by saying: 'The true reason for their success is their organized programme of sports science.'
> The moral attitude of both competitors and society should be mentioned here. No athlete is under pressure to succeed in order to make a living or seek commercial benefit. (*Sport in the GDR*, 1984: 39)

The (former) East German critique of 'capitalist sport' advanced by an avowedly non-exploitative, collectivist sporting formation which, in performative terms, was also internationally triumphant is still echoed in the political pronouncements of socialist and communist nations like China, Cuba and Bulgaria. The international ideological struggle over the meaning of success and failure in competitive sport is, as will be discussed below, an important symbolic element in the relations between nation states and also political blocs. Stereotypes and caricatures of brainwashed, drug-ridden sporting robots on one side and commodified, falsely conscious corporate stooges on the other have abounded in the discourses of both governments and media sports commentators, at least until the emergence of the post-Cold War 'new world sporting order' in the late eighties disturbed some of the more comfortable bi-polar conceptualizations of the sporting and geopolitical worlds. In the west, the preoccupation with the idea of a sinister and malign nexus between sport, science, medicine and the Party in 'totalitarian' societies has diverted the public gaze from its own extensive history of connections between 'physical culture' and the state. Liberal–democratic states have for over a century employed sport under the rubric of physical education or physical culture in schools to prescribe appropriate dispositions of the youthful body. As John Hargreaves (1986) and Stephen Jones (1989) have argued in relation to Britain, the school (as both a state and a quasi-state institution) has been a key site in which sport and exercise have been explicitly used to meet officially-sanctioned goals of a trained, healthy and compliant citizenry (especially those of the potentially disruptive working class). The establishment and development of sport and physical education in schools were inevitably bound up in the prevailing structures of social power which led, for example, to rather different assessments of the physical capabilities and needs of boys and girls (Fletcher, 1984; Scraton, 1990).

State prescriptions for healthier bodies (and, often, it must be said, docile minds) have extended far beyond the confines of the school. The enactment of legislation over the twentieth century (for example, Britain's Physical Training and Recreation Act of 1937 – see Jones, 1989) has enjoined the adult population to engage in sport through the public provision of sporting infrastructure. With the formation of ministries of sport within executive government and of governmental and quasi-governmental sports organizations like the British Sports Council and the Australian Sports Commission, the liberal–democratic state has intervened more deeply and systematically in the conduct and promotion of sport. In particular, sport and exercise have been important features of health promotion campaigns with names like 'Sport for All' and 'Life. Be In It'. These circulate as slick and seemingly unobjectionable exhortations to the population at large (particularly those identified as possessed of 'sedentary lifestyles') to engage in physical activities facilitated by state and commercial organizations in order to enrich and extend their lives. As McKay (1991: 79) argues, however, these 'collectivist' campaigns have a highly individualist import: 'By funding relatively inexpensive media campaigns like 'Life. Be In It', the state squarely informs citizens that it is an *individual* responsibility to cultivate leisure-time appropriately. '

McKay is critical of such campaigns because of their inducement of guilt for 'unhealthy' behaviour, their concentration on the individual effects rather than the general causes of mortality and morbidity, and for their covert attempt to shift the economic burden of health care from the public to the private sector. This assiduous boosting of the 'moral economy of health' (Critcher, 1993) by the state in capitalist societies is part of a more generalized development of a 'somatic society' (Turner, 1992: 12) in which 'the body, as simultaneously constraint and resistance, is the principal field of political and cultural activity'. While Foucault (1979; 1981) has positioned the regulation of the body as central to the constitution of all societies, the emergent discursive formations which govern it are historically specific. Under the regime of 'high' capitalism, the 'consuming body' (Falk, 1994) of careless pleasure is commercially hyper-stimulated and so comes into conflict with the 'disciplined body' of denial and responsibility (Miller, 1993). The contemporary capitalist carnival of pleasure through consumption is, as Weber (1965) anticipated, a rather different socio-cultural formation to that founded on the ascetic principles (though often not the reality) of hard labour and restraint. At work, the ascendancy of mental labour in the informational economy (Harvey, 1989) has, when connected to the enormously successful electronic provision of 'privatized' pleasure represented by (both commercial and public) television in leisure time (McKay, 1990), produced anxiety about bodily passivity approaching the level of a moral panic.

The state, which has often deployed institutionalized sport as a means of inculcating values conducive to social control through sporting forms of bodily training (Shilling, 1991; 1993), has increasingly resorted to the promotion of individual body maintenance (Featherstone, 1991) in a manner that both reflects and reinforces the commodification of the body (Fitzclarence, 1990). This officially-sanctioned celebration of 'appropriate' body image and performance raises concerns about the state's involvement in the commercialization of health and fitness, as well as in the promotion of unrealistic and largely unattainable health benefits from regular exercise (Roberts et al., 1993). The ideological deployment of the image of the healthy body has also been contradicted by the 'deviant' extension of the logics of sporting competitiveness and commercialization. These have required the state to make spectacular interventions in the politics of sport and health by seeking to control the use of performance-enhancing drugs by professional and non-professional athletes alike. While sporting associations like the International Olympic Committee determine and apply their own procedures for proscribing the use of certain drugs, testing for evidence of proscribed drug use, and penalizing sportspeople in whom drug residues or 'masking' agents are detected, the cooperation of the state is crucial to their effectiveness. The most notorious example of detection and punishment in recent years is, as discussed in Chapter 5, that of Ben Johnson, who in the 1988 Seoul Olympics won the 100 metres final in record time, only to be disqualified, stripped of his gold medal, and banned from competition when he tested positive for an anabolic steroid. The Johnson case brought considerable government pressure to bear on sporting associations in several countries as part of a widespread attempt to be seen to 'clean up' the image of sporting health now made a little sickly by its association with 'dangerous' drugs.

Governments in countries like Australia and Britain have taken a high profile in the drugs in sport issue, not least by asserting their economic power in requiring sporting associations and organizations to introduce controls as a condition of funding. There were also in the eighties public inquiries into sporting drug use in the USA, Australia and Canada, with the Australian federal government joining 'the war against drugs in sport' by establishing the Australian Sports Drug Agency. In Britain, the Thatcher government in 1989 went so far as to amend the criminal law in making possession of anabolic steroids without a prescription an offence punishable by up to two years in jail (Cashmore, 1990: 109). Although this intensive state mobilization against drug use in sport was prompted largely by the inescapable media mega spectacle of the 'Johnson affair', it was by no means unprecedented. As Guenther Lueschen (1993: 96) points out, a Council of Europe meeting in Strasbourg in 1962 tried unsuccessfully to proclaim international protocols on sporting drug use, with foreshadowed French political initiatives eventually being emulated in various forms by 'all national governments or national sport organizations in Europe' in 'enacting legislation or rules against doping'. The game of detection and punishment of performance-enhancing drugs played out by the state and relevant sporting organizations is productive of new technologies of 'body invasion' and, therefore, of new relations of power between citizens and the state (McKay et al., 1994). Sport, in this way, can be seen as a significant site for the testing and contestation of contemporary politics of the body. The state's interest in sport and health is not limited to promotional campaigns, also extending to the imposition of restrictions on the use of sport – especially in the mass media – to advertise and promote 'unhealthy products', notably tobacco and alcohol. The keen interest of brewers and cigarette companies in sport as a promotional vehicle has caused the liberal–democratic state considerable problems. Free market rhetoric, consumer sovereignty and commodity excise induce the state to permit open advertising and promotion of 'beer and smokes'. Against these libertarian forces are ranged the health professionals and other moral entrepreneurs opposed to the unrestricted display and circulation of intoxicating and carcinogenic products. In between are sporting organizations, many in receipt of government funding but also particularly attracted to the often lavish support that can be provided by companies whose direct advertising of products is either regulated in the media (especially on television) or banned altogether.

The case of the 'incidental advertising' (advertising and promotional messages that do not legally constitute a direct address to the consumer) of tobacco products is instructive here. When 'spot' advertising of cigarettes was banned in several countries in the seventies and eighties, tobacco companies moved quickly to acquire naming rights of sporting events and competitions, and to situate corporate logos on everything from motor vehicles and players' clothing to the grass and perimeter fencing of sports stadiums. The result was a blatant negation of the intent of state control over the electronic media's carriage of inducements to smoke cigarettes and other tobacco products. As Critcher (1993: 226-7) has argued in the early nineties' British context, enthusiastic Conservative government prescriptions for desirable individual health attitudes and behaviour sharply contrast with their timidity in the 'one area where government might intervene to prevent attempts to encourage health damaging behaviour – a ban on tobacco advertising ...'. In Australia there have been similar anomalies despite its broadcast law's prohibition of the advertising of tobacco products. Geoffrey Lawrence (1986b), for example, demonstrated that on a single day's broadcast of a cricket match in 1982 the name of the sponsor, Benson and Hedges, was exposed 238 times on commercial television and, ironically, 195 times on the national, state-funded broadcaster. Kevin Harris (1988), in monitoring another cricket match, recorded that the Benson and Hedges name or logo appeared for 27.6 per cent of broadcast playing time, while Donald Martin's (1990: 6) study of the 1989 Adelaide Grand Prix found that the 'Marlboro name or logo appeared on screen for up to 35.7% of the sampled time, but this dropped to 7.6% after the company's sponsored cars withdrew'. Apart from instructing tobacco companies to ensure that they sponsor fast and reliable cars, these statistics indicate the extent to which governments can be persuaded to repudiate policy and law where international sporting spectaculars are deemed to be important means by which local economies can be boosted and national images positively displayed. Disagreements over the firmness with which broadcast advertising regulation of tobacco and alcohol products are applied can lead national governments – for example, the French and the Australian – into conflict over whether disputed televisual images of tobacco promotions can be captured in one country and relayed to another. More significantly, in a post-Fordist order of place-based competition for international spectacles, local states vie for the right to stage major sporting events (Whitson and Macintosh, 1993). As a result, one of the most significant bargaining tools is the degree to which individual local states will 'accommodate' and understand the needs of corporate sponsors and advertisers. In Australia, for example, the keen aspirations of the States of New South Wales, Victoria and South Australia to stage a leg of the international motor cycle and motor car competitive circuit (in or near their respective capitals of Sydney, Melbourne and Adelaide) have led to sudden and inconsistent relaxations of government attitudes to tobacco promotion on television.

The state's involvement in sport, then, can be regarded as part of a more thoroughgoing and contradictory project of re-making the embodied self as efficient and ethically complete under conditions which generate ever-more opportunities for heedless, hedonistic consumption (Miller, 1993). This task entails the formation and implementation of a range of cultural policies which require 'interpellation' (Althusser, 1971) of both individual and collective subjects. The highly individualist character of state attempts to school the embodied self is dependent also on communitarian senses of identity which in some way tie the individual to the social order. Sport is a highly efficient symbolic means to connect these two levels of identification through the collective affective investment in sport as a vehicle for partisanship of various kinds. The state is now more than ever involved in the funding, organization and promotion of local, regional, national and international sport. The different tiers of government provide and subsidize resources from municipal parks and pitches to grand stadiums and technologically advanced elite sports institutes. Just as in the case of health promotion campaigns, the politics of state involvement in sports funding and administration are at once deeply political and resistant to the idea of politics. The resilient notions that sport and politics are essentially separate spheres and that sporting values are inherently universal obstruct debate on the politics of the state's motivation and resource distribution in sport. One such issue out of which political differences emerge concerns the relative funding of elite and non-elite sport. In a sporting version of economic debates about the 'trickle-down' effects of enriching the 'best-performed' sectors of the population (discussed in the previous chapter), it is argued that the provision of the most advanced resources for sportspeople identified as the best in their chosen field will maximize the opportunity for international sporting success, which in turn will create positive national role models for aspiring athletes to emulate. This, for example, was the rationale for the establishment, maintenance and development of the Australian Institute of Sport (AIS), which was founded in 1981 as the conservative Fraser coalition government's response to Australia's poor medal-winning performance in the 1986 Montreal Olympics. McKay (1986: 122), in criticizing the establishment of the AIS, argues that there is 'no evidence that that this "emulation" thesis does anything whatsoever to democratise cultural activities', given that admiration for the sporting achievements of others cannot of itself overcome the 'structural barriers that impede access to leisure pursuits'. In calculating that, in 1982/3, 93 per cent of Australian federal government funds were devoted to elite sport and only 7 per cent to 'mass sport and recreation' (p. 131), McKay asserts that the pyramidal structure of federal sports funding confirms rather than erodes existing privilege. This position is supported by the absence of any evidence of a significant re-distribution over time. A follow-up calculation in 1989 rendered equivalent figures of 84 and 16 per cent respectively, in spite of the sustained rhetoric over the period concerning the democratization of sport and of sports funding (McKay, 1991: 77).

The pattern of distribution of central government funds for sport in countries like Australia could, perhaps, be justified if those who benefited from 'elite' funding were from disadvantaged backgrounds. At the very least, recipients of funds would have to be broadly representative of the general population if sports resources were not to be directed to the least needy. McKay (1986: 122), however, also notes that the state is rewarding the already advantaged:

> The logic of this 'spillover' theory of sporting excellence is also questionable given the fact that elite athletes in Australia generally come from affluent, Anglo-Saxon backgrounds in which they have received considerable parental and peer support for their participation in sport. Thus we have a case of an advantaged section of Australian society being explicitly provided with greater opportunities to succeed than less advantaged ones. It is situations like this that have moved Offe to describe the policies of the welfare state as 'socialism for the rich and capitalism for the poor'.

Issues of distributional equity are similarly addressed by Betsy and Stephen Wearing (1990: 165), who note that in 1982/3 the Australian federal government spent 13 times more money on the AIS than on sporting and recreational activities and facilities 'for disadvantaged groups, such as the disabled and Aborigines'. More recently, Martin Mowbray (1993), in examining expenditure by 22 Australian local governments on sports facilities, concludes that there is systematic gender and class bias in the allocation of funding to sport. The role of various fractions of the state in the provision of public sports facilities, financial support for sportspeople and organizations, and construction of health promotion programmes is somewhat at variance with rhetorically admirable slogans like 'Sport for All'. Much of what the state construes as ameliorative and mass motivational strategy can be regarded as the covert or unconscious reproduction of existing power structures within sport. In this activity the state does not act alone, because sport as a social institution is already permeated – although not entirely encompassed – by ideologies of dominance.

Sport and the reproduction of social inequality

In assessing the ideological significance of sport, the pivotal question concerns the extent to which its structures, activities and meanings have a tendency to challenge or to endorse social inequality. This is not, of course, to assert that there is a single politics of sport, anymore than there is a uniform and cohesive institution which can be conveniently labelled 'sport'. Each sporting site and its points of intersection with other nodes in the loose and constantly mutating network that we call 'society' have, no doubt, distinctive features that are resistant to sweeping typifications of sport's political character. We have seen, however, the way in which the sporting mythology of transcendent apoliticality has spread across its different sites, forms and social groupings, in the process helping to fashion the persuasive naturalization of historically-produced social conditions to which the term 'hegemony' best applies. In the previous chapter's discussion of the sport's labour market it was argued that professional sport both reflects and substantially legitimizes the 'classical' inequalities of class, gender and race/ethnicity. Sport, in common with all other social institutions under advanced (or any other stage of) capitalism, is not a freely functioning meritocracy in which individual advancement is conditioned solely by objectively determined criteria of talent and motivation. Sport's egalitarian myths, however, are routinely invoked as symbolic charms to ward off the threat of political denunciations of inherited privilege and structural inequality. They are manifestly present, for example, in John Daly's (1985: 15) summation that 'Australian sport has always catered for the masses. Community sport is available to anybody and everybody. Few sports are class oriented . . .' and in Brian Nettleton's (1985: 89) statement that sport 'acts as an avenue to social mobility; sport has often provided realistic opportunities for the common people to acquire prestige and success'. This romantic view of sport cannot simply be characterized as harmless, wishful folly. The widespread circulation of notions that sport is unhampered by the usual impediments to social mobility and equity has notable political ramifications according to which the posited existence of the 'magical space of sports' serves symbolically to repudiate radical critiques of endemic, system-wide inequalities. While this is not the place to present in detail the ways in which sport contributes to the reproduction of social inequality and its attendant ideologies, it is useful to present some instances where sport is both bound by existing inequalities and seemingly impelled to justify them.

The class-bound nature of many sports is readily apparent when the socio-economic status of professional sportspeople is considered. As was pointed out in the discussion in Chapter 5, individual sports like tennis and golf are clearly not heavily populated with the children of the manual working class or of disadvantaged racial/ethnic minorities. The cost of coaching and equipment, access to courts and courses, membership of clubs and associations – even competing class cultures of 'aesthetic' athletic expression versus aggressive displays of masculinity – all help to exclude and filter out sporting participants of modest means and marginal cultural affiliations. At the other end of the socio-economic scale, the sports of boxing and rugby league, for example, have very different typical social cohorts. Neighbourhood-based boxing gymnasiums, allied with the workaday brutality of many aspects of life in depressed urban communities, have established an 'elective affinity' between boxing and the male (especially black) underclass, just as the camaraderie and physical assertiveness of male working-class culture has been readily transferrable to the team identity and ethos of toughness that underscores the playing of professional rugby league (Lynch, 1993; Yeates, 1992). Even where aggressive masculinity is the predominant feature of contact sports, class distinctions are still readily apparent (Bourdieu, 1984). The contrast, for example, in the social class origins of the militantly professional players of rugby league with the residually (and now anomalously) 'amateurist' players of rugby union is striking, with a preponderance of labourers and tradesmen in the former and of solicitors and stockbrokers in the latter.

The above focus on male sport is itself revealing – there is a powerfully resilient association between sport and masculinity which obstructs equality of access, participation and reward for women. Sport has been one of the major means by which masculinity is constructed *against* femininity in a manner that presents a clear hierarchy of cultural power. The gender struggle around and for sport has taken two main forms. The first is essentially emulatory and re-distributive in that it demands for women equality of access, participation, resources, prize money, media coverage and public esteem (Blue, 1987; Bryson, 1985; Stell, 1991). Sport is seen here as reproducing inequality primarily because of its masculine exclusiveness in providing a comfortable focus for male identity by valorizing the physically heroic as implicitly male and so denigrating the athletic capabilities of women. Women are, therefore, exhorted from this perspective to demand their sporting rights. A second (although not entirely separate) critique of the relationship between sport and gender problematizes the masculinist conception of sport itself. Sport in its currently dominant form is seen to be shot through with hyper-masculine values of aggressiveness, ruthlessness and competitiveness (Ferrante, 1994; M.A. Hall, 1985; Hargreaves, 1994). These critiques provide various blueprints for action (or inaction where sport seems to be so irredeemably and destructively masculine that it could be discounted altogether as a desirable activity for women). They require the remaking of sport on anti-sexist lines, affirming the value of professional and non-professional sport but seeking to transform its militaristic and often exclusivist ethos. This task is increasingly proposed to be accomplished through the instruments of social and cultural policy (Hall, 1993), a reflection of the greater emphasis on social democratic reformism in contemporary cultural studies.

One area that has received particular attention is the quantity and quality of the coverage of women's sport in the mass media. In regard to the former, content analyses have regularly generated data showing women's sport to be grossly under-represented in the media. Peter Brown (1993), in his survey of empirical research studies of women's sport in the newspapers of different countries, reveals a consistent pattern of women constituting a small proportion of total sports coverage. An often-quoted figure from an Australian study (Menzies, 1980) records that in 1980 only 2 per cent of the sports pages in metropolitan newspapers were given over to the coverage of women's sport, with a follow-up study four years later revealing a fall to only 1.3 per cent (Australian Sports Commission and Office of the Status of Women, 1985: 39). A comparative measurement in 1988 demonstrated a small rise to 2.5 per cent, which by 1992 had reached the (still extremely modest) level of 4.5 per cent (Stoddart, 1994). A community-based Australian study, furthermore, found that while policies aimed at increasing coverage of girls' and women's sport may be initially effective, a constant stimulus is likely to be necessary in order to maintain hard-won improvements (Rowe and Brown, 1994). The statistics for other media, like television, are even more discouraging on equity grounds, with one Australian commercial television network's coverage of women's sport constituting only 1.2 per cent of total sports coverage in 1992, a figure, it should be noted, well below that of the 20.5 per cent revealed by one study in New Zealand (Stoddart, 1994: 9). The continuing under-representation of women's sport in the media – a phenomenon that is to some extent statistically masked by the placement of items about women in less prominent areas of the sports pages and by seasonal variations – cannot be rationalized as simply reflecting different leisure consumption patterns according to gender. The resistance to giving prominence to strong grassroots women's sports like netball and hockey suggests that a circular logic is in play which buttresses the popularity and visibility of male sports (like the football codes) through saturation media coverage.

For those critical analysts who might object that quantitative content analysis is a blunt instrument incapable of discriminating between forms of coverage, several other studies show how women are frequently represented as subordinate and sexually objectified in sports coverage (Creedon, 1994; Duncan, 1990; Jones, 1993). Jennifer Hargreaves (1993: 60) has, furthermore, noted a trend towards more overt sexualization and eroticization of the female sporting body:

Body presentation which makes more visible the form and sexuality of the female body has become increasingly noticeable in particular female sports. Those which emphasise balance, co-ordination, flexibility and grace (such as aerobics, gymnastics, ice-skating and synchronised swimming) are characterised as 'feminine appropriate' because they affirm a popular image of femininity and demonstrate their essential difference from popular images of sporting masculinity. Not surprisingly, these are the sports which have been most visibly and systematically sexualised: the performers conform to the female norm of heterosexuality; the routines contain 'ultra-feminine' postures and gestures, sensuous symbolism, sexually-suggestive movements and even sometimes poses bordering on the erotic.

While, as will be argued in Chapter 7, male sporting bodies have also come to the fore as objects of the collective, commercialized gaze, they still remain marked by the signs and codes of hegemonic masculinity, with images of masculine strength and activeness still frequently contrasting with those of feminine vulnerability and passivity. The acute discomfort caused by female bodybuilding to many individuals and sporting associations reveals the depth and power of these gendered images of the sporting body (Kuhn, 1993). The large-scale absence of women's sport from 'serious' media coverage and the presence of sporting women's bodies as objects to be sexually appraised (as man-like/unattractive or woman-like/attractive) is a significant reproduction in culture of persistent social and material inequalities in domains such as the workforce and the home. The common emphasis on women's roles as supporters of sportsmen (as girlfriends, wives and mothers) or as athletes in their own right who are prone to displays of gender-appropriate emotion and bound to their reproductive destiny as mothers (Williams et al., 1986) consolidates the gendered (and, according to Wonsek (1992), the racialized) ideological complexion of the sporting formation. While many sporting texts and discourses position men at the centre and quite explicitly exclude women, others seek to inveigle women into sports partisanship by addressing them as patriotic citizens. In this way, sport can be seen symbolically both to separate and to bind in a double ideological movement of differentiation by gender and unification by nation.

Sport and nationalism

In the above discussion it was argued that sport is often deployed simultaneously to reinforce and to reflect various forms of social inequality. This is because sport is deeply implicated in the production of various forms of 'distinction' (Bourdieu, 1984) but works ideologically as a common standard of value and performance by which underlying structures of power are erased and occluded. Nowhere is this ideological role of sport more evident than in the generation of nationalist sentiment. The conventional critique of nationalism focuses on how the image of the nation is fashioned by stitching together an imaginary unity out of the fabric of difference and division (Anderson, 1983). The nation state is above all a legal entity in that it

represents a claim (often disputed) to sovereignty over a particular space and
so to jurisdiction (also often contested) over the people within the boundaries
of that space. The bounded nation state contains within it the seeds of its own
potential destruction (or at least disruption) in the shape of class, racial/eth-
nic, religious, regional and other groupings which offer an alternative,
concrete and often more compelling means of identification. The nation must
hold itself together, as Weber (1970) noted, by rather more than physical
coercion. It is necessary to generate potent symbols of common identity and
so difference from others. The modern nation state is a comparatively recent
phenomenon (Giddens, 1985) and already appears to be in decline as an
intensified combination of global political, economic and cultural integration
points up the arbitrariness and permeability of national boundaries (Held,
1989). There are, as a result, few opportunities for many nation states, especially those which Dunning (1986b: 223) calls 'domestically pacified', to
render themselves as affectively compelling. This is not to accept, however,
that sport is a functional (or figurational) substitute for more violent means
of national assertion, but rather to argue that it constitutes a cultural apparatus that can be speedily and regularly mobilized in the symbolic
reconstruction of the nation.

The repertoire of available strategies for the aggressive assertion of nationalism is limited. Military engagements are spectacular but debilitating
exercises in demonology, xenophobia is at odds with the increasingly free
circulation of capital (including labour and tourists) around the globe, while
flag-raising and other daily patriotic rituals have decreasing appeal, especially for those who are young, urban and cosmopolitan. International
professional sport, in contrast, provides a compelling means by which the
nation can be represented as positive and dynamic. In support for national
teams and individual representatives of nations lies a sense of unity, with
'internal' structural divisions and inequalities of necessity suppressed and
local social wounds sutured by accentuating differences with other competing
nations. The success of these excursions into nation worship is, no doubt,
variable. Some sections of the population (especially women, who have only
recently been targeted by sports marketers) may be unmoved. Others – especially those with links to other nations – are likely to be alienated by sporting
hysteria and jingoism. For many of the nation's viewers of high-rating sports
broadcasts, however, the heady cocktail of sport and national chauvinism will
be seductive indeed. It is, then, through the interpellation of sports fans as cit-
izen-supporters that they are at least temporarily transformed into fans of the
nation itself. Within the framework of sport the nation has a meaning mostly
evacuated from the internationalist rhetoric of trading blocs, foreign investment and competitive cost pressures. During the Olympic Games and the
World Cup Finals, for example, it is not 'nation-less' currency and commodity markets that are to the fore, but direct (or, in the case of the Olympics, *de
facto*) competition between nations in which tangible results of victory and
defeat can be transformed mythologically into signs of progress or decline
(Hill, 1992). In the process sport and nation articulate with economic,

technological, military, demographic and other discourses of 'development'. As James Larson and Heung-Soo Park (1993: 151) argue in their study of the politics of the 1988 Seoul Olympics:

> There were three major reasons given for hosting the Olympics in Seoul. First, a turning point had been reached in Korea because of high economic growth, and the Japanese experience with the Olympics could be a model for Korea. Second, South Korea might be able to seize a very practical opportunity through the Games to terminate the state of confrontation with North Korea. And third, staging the Olympics in Seoul would provide an opportunity for Korea to join the ranks of the advanced nations.

Here it can be seen that a successful bid to host the Olympics is an economic opportunity of considerable potential benefit (as well as risk) to any nation on account of the sheer scale of the operation's contribution to gross domestic product. It is, however, the capacity of the Olympics to function as a prime vehicle for the advancement of the national image that overwhelmingly secures their appeal. For this reason, there was a particularly keen competition to host Olympics 2000, with all its connotations of new-era advancement and transcendence of the old. Hosting Olympics 2000 in Beijing would have marked a decisive moment in China's modernization programme, while for Manchester it would have signalled (somewhat despairingly; Rowe, 1994b) that the decline of the world's first industrial power had been arrested at the very place where Britain's capitalist revolution had occurred. Instead, the decision in 1993 went in favour of Sydney, which for that city (and, by extension, the Australian nation) both confirmed and stimulated many grand assessments of progress like the following:

> Nothing symbolises Sydney's rising fortunes more vividly, of course, than the fact that it was chosen to host the first Olympics of the next millennium. Even those who are reluctant to massage Sydney's sometimes brash and gloating ego concede that the Olympics denotes it as a city whose time has arrived – however fleeting that time may be. (Guilliatt and Dwyer, 1994: 1A)

If hosting a major sporting event is already interpreted as a victory, actually winning a major international sporting competition provides even greater opportunities for the celebration of a nation. Two prominent examples of the symbolic elaboration of sporting success are England's winning of the soccer World Cup (the finals of which it hosted) in 1966 and Australia's America's Cup victory in 1983. In regard to the former, John Clarke and Chas Critcher (1986: 121) argue that Britain was undergoing a post-imperial 'crisis of national identity' when its first (and, to date, only) World Cup trophy win under the rationalist tactical regime of manager Alf Ramsey became ideologically intertwined with the modernizing technologism of the Wilson Labour government:

> The 1966 victory was associated with the Harold Wilson government's desire to harness the 'white heat of technology'. Ramsey himself personified the spirit of scientific management, rational, ordered and committed to making technological innovations in the footballing labour process. (p. 122)

This emphasis on sport as exemplar of new modes of organization and of technological innovation was powerfully echoed 17 years later on the other side of the globe when Australia (also for the first and, so far, only time) defeated the USA in a 12-metre yacht race. Australia's America's Cup win took place in the context of a wave of pro-entrepreneurialist sentiment prior to the 1987 stock market crash, with its major rival the object of neo-colonial hostility towards what was commonly viewed (and orchestrated) as American arrogance and sharp practice. Once again, the sporting win was extensively interpreted by media, government and industry as a victory for faith in technology, in this case taking the form of the mysterious winged keel of 'maverick designer' Ben Lexcen. Paul James (1986: 142) draws attention to the manner in which:

> the Australian victory through international technology was generalised by advocates of the new technological push to encompass Australia's future. An *Age* editorial said:
>
>> The America's Cup was won by an effort of industrial design, as much as sailing skill, and it was a design of the most fruitful kind, coming as it did from the iconoclastic ideas of Mr Lexcen, a self-made man.
>
> Others went further to posit the winged keel as a symbol of Australia's entry into the high-tech era. It meant 'we' could cope with 'the onrush of digital culture'.

Both brief examples (and many more which could have been cited, such as the dramatic rise to current international prominence of Chinese sport) illustrate how sport's work as metaphor and its articulation with other practices and values constitute an attractive capacity to popularize sometimes obscure notions of progress (or regress) through the discourse of nation and of national destiny. It is, further, the ready harnessing of sport to the languages of advertising, politics and economics that enables it to permeate both everyday and specialist forms of speech.

The politics of the sports metaphor

Sport, as a cultural form, carries with it a bundle of myths which can be invoked in diverse circumstances. In the following chapter I will discuss the language of sport, the 'sportuguese' (Hargreaves, 1986) of commentators and fans that comprises much of sporting culture and contains its own typical messages about social relations within and outside sport. At this point the importation of sporting concepts into other domains, whereby the meanings attached to sport are employed to create new meanings in the form of sporting analogies and metaphors, will be addressed. These sporting connotations emerge out of the repetitive assertion of sporting values such as universalism, transcendence, heroism, competitiveness, individual motivation and teamship, constructing in the process commonsensical (and covertly ideological) renditions of the operations and products of business organizations and the state. These are primarily positive treatments of sport's ascribed values – sport is held to be subject to universal standards and procedures, capable of transcending the mundane divisions of everyday life and drawing out bravery and self-denial in its practitioners. It is seen to emphasize the centrality of struggle between vigorously combative opponents, celebrating the determination of individuals and the cooperation of sporting teams. Each metaphorical shift and evocation of value contain within them the potential to advance an 'interested' or politicized position beneath the guise of vernacular sports talk. Perhaps the most extensively used sports metaphor – to the point of cliché – in politics and economics over the last decade is that of the 'level playing field'. The idea of a sloping pitch advantaging one side and disadvantaging the other is widely used by a variety of 'stakeholders' to represent graphically inequities and inconsistencies in social relations. A second commonly employed sports metaphor describes regulatory changes deemed to be unfair as 'moving the goalposts after the game has started'. Contests in politics and economics are regularly construed as 'races', with 'hurdles' having to be surmounted as company and political 'teams' vie for higher positions in their respective 'leagues'. 'Captains' of industry (part-mariner, part-team skipper) are expected to 'box their weight', while an essential quality of any senior politician in England or Australia is to excel at metaphorical cricket, possessing 'a safe pair of hands' and able to let any difficult questions 'through to the keeper' (see Alomes, 1991; Rowe, 1991a). Corporate enterprises, especially banks, attempt to overcome symbolically the cleavage between profit-extractor and customer by presenting the parties as engaged in a collaborative team effort (Rowe, 1991b). Announcements of sports sponsorships are presented as if they are major charity donations, especially by multi- and transnational corporations like McDonalds and Ford anxious to assert their local credentials in individual nation states by supporting 'local' sport. Advertisements for goods and services (from oil companies to computers) employing images of sports contests and celebrity endorsers are commonplace means of capitalizing upon the engaging and stirring aspects of sport's public profile.

It could be objected that these practices represent no more than an enlivening of the dry lexicons of business and politics by means of the shrewd deployment of vivid sports imagery, and that it is only to be expected that the massive popularity of sport will result in its widespread infusion into the process of signification. In response, it must be noted that the symbolic alignment of sport and other social institutions is subject to chronically misleading and distorted comparisons between the structures and practices of sport and those of other social institutions. For example, sporting contests are highly specific forms of social encounter which are rarely replicated in other domains. They take place in specific spaces for strictly delimited periods under codified rules. Competitors are carefully matched in terms of number, standard and type, while results are rendered in an easily quantifiable form and their consequences carefully rationalized. There are very few areas of business and politics that even come close to these arrangements. Indeed, as I have argued above, sport itself generally fails to live up to its open, meritocratic and equitable image. To deploy the sporting 'imaginary' in the interpretation of the activities of other fields is, then, doubly to mislead. The playing field tends, in the realm of metaphor, to be levelled against a plausible understanding of the social world.

The politics of sport extend well beyond sporting institutions and the issues of access and equity which apply directly to them. This is not, of course, to downplay the importance of striving for equal opportunity and anti-discrimination in sport – policy interventions in areas such as non-sexist and gender-balanced media coverage or community-based sports participation programmes are worthwhile and necessary contributions to the democratization of sport (Hall, 1994; Rowe and Brown, 1994). It is, rather, to argue that a very significant facet of sport's politics lies in the monitoring, deconstruction and public critique of the uses of sporting mythologies to promote ideologies of dominance. In some cases this might take the form of interventions in public debates that have arisen within sport in the first instance but have embraced far broader public issues. In the aforementioned case of Magic Johnson, for example, 'Magic's tragedy' became the springboard for an intense and popular airing of issues relating to the body, sexuality, masculinity, femininity, celebrity, gender bias and race which took place only because of the affective power and cultural prominence of sport (Crimp, 1993; King, 1993; Rowe, 1994b). Similarly, the conviction of Mike Tyson for rape and the trial of O.J. Simpson for murder prompted widespread media consideration of appropriate male and female conduct in zones of inter-sexual contact (McKay et al., 1994; McKay and Smith, 1995). In such instances politics in and of sport combine with the use of sport's popularity as a pretext for the direction of the collective gaze onto issues of the deepest ideological importance. The two critical strategies outlined above involve intervening in the routine operations of sport (and its allied institutions) and challenging the ways in which sport's generated meanings are placed in the service of oppressive ideologies. They can be combined when confronting questions of how sport might be claimed by those who are usually excluded from its normative structures and meanings. If it is accepted, for example, that sport's ethos is overwhelmingly heterosexual to the point of heterosexism (Messner, 1992), then the advancement of a stake in sports participation, spectatorship and pleasure by gays and lesbians is disruptive to the sporting conservatism and exclusivism which are symptomatic of wider social attitudes and practices. In recognition of its importance as a social institution and as a repository of metaphoric popular ideology, sport is fertile ground for strategic interventions in cultural politics.

Sport and the politics of resistance

Sport is often placed in the service of reactionary ideologies which promote national chauvinism, racial/ethnic supremacism and gendered exclusionism. It is in the nature of power, however, that the exertion of its oppressive weight also inevitably provokes resistance and subversion (Foucault, 1980). Hence, for example, multi-racial sport has been posited against sporting apartheid and its legacy, just as women have mobilized against male control of sporting institutions, practices and representations (Bryson, 1990; Hall, 1993). One of the longest established and most resilient of sport's ensemble of ideologies of dominance revolves around the prescription and reproduction of highly restrictive sexual identities. It has frequently taken the form of openly-expressed heterosexism and homophobia in sport, with considerable sanctions brought to bear against sportsmen and women who do not flaunt – even if only for the newspapers, colour magazines and television cameras – their socially-approved heterosexuality. Michael Messner (1992: 34) observes in his study of 30 former male athletes that:

> The extent of homophobia in the sportsworld is staggering. Boys learn early that to be gay, to be suspected of being gay, or even to be unable to prove one's heterosexual status is not acceptable.

Indeed, as Brian Pronger (1990: 149) argues, heterosexuality is a system-wide and site-maintained organizing principle of social life:

> In our society, which places great importance on sex and restricts 'legitimate' sexuality to heterosexuality and the family . . . the assumption is that virtually everyone is heterosexual. This is almost universally the case in athletics, where, for example, men and women's locker rooms are always segregated. The assumption is that heterosexual desires of men and women may be stimulated if male and female athletes were to see each other naked. The fact that men may find it sexually stimulating to be in a locker room full of other naked male athletes is either ignored or sublimated through aggressive, homophobic, and sexist humor.

The close and deep association between sport and maleness means that most critical attention is paid to actual or potential male homosexuality, but there is also evidence of strong antagonism towards signs of lesbianism in sport. For example, accusations of pro-homosexual bias in Australian women's cricket in early 1994 led to an internal inquiry into the sport's organization and procedures of selection. It is hard to imagine that under prevailing conditions such widespread publicity and the ensuing course of action would have been taken if allegations of pro-heterosexual bias had been made. On an international level, the self-acknowledged lesbianism of tennis champion Martina Navratilova has provoked considerable hostility among some sports commentators, one of whom described her as 'part of the lesbianism that scares the wits out of the parents of girl tennis players' (Wells, 1991: 32). Gays and lesbians – who it should be acknowledged (with Pronger, 1990: 143) do not constitute fixed and self-evident categories of person so much as more or less 'consistent' embodiments of sexual preference – have often been obliged to submerge their sexuality within sport's aggressively dominant heterosexual culture for fear of humiliation and ostracism (Messner, 1992). Nonetheless, as with other expressions and mobilizations in diverse spheres of culture (such as in popular music and film), gay pride and gay rights in sport have been forcefully asserted. The best-known sporting manifestation of this phenomenon is the international Gay Games, which were first held in San Francisco in 1982. Less spectacular and more grass-

roots oriented activity has been evident in the establishment of non-professional gay sporting teams and of groups of gay sports fans serviced by
small-circulation 'fanzines'. One example of the former phenomenon is the
so-called 'rise of gay footy' as reported in the Australian gay magazine
Campaign, in which sport as organized by gays and lesbians (such as a touch
football team of gay men) is described as 'hard evidence of a gay community
beyond the bars' (Cuthbertson, 1992: 20; see also Rowe, 1995). Another
expression of gay sporting fan culture is the London-based sports fanzine *The
Football Pink*, which states on its cover page that it is 'The fanzine for lesbian
and gay soccer fans everywhere'. *The Football Pink* in its 'Where We Stand'
section (Issue 6, 1992: n.p.) displays its association with the Gay Football
Supporters Network, the main purpose of which is 'to put football supporters in touch with each other for correspondence, going to matches and
meeting up socially . . .'. The magazine declares its adoption of 'an anti-discrimination position and so won't publish any racist, sexist or homophobic
stuff – unless we're slagging it off'. Contents include coverage of gay black
footballer Justin Fashanu's 'coming out', a critique of the gay media's lack of
football coverage, contact information for gay and lesbian football fans, and
re-printed professional newspaper coverage of women's soccer. It should be
noted that most of the material in the issue cited is written by gay men and
about gay men's football, thereby reflecting the aforementioned male domination of 'heterosexual' sport. It is not, therefore, surprising that women
have produced their own fanzines such as *Against the Tide: the Voice of
Women Who Just Love Football*. Here admiring coverage of both men's and
women's soccer is to be found, alongside criticisms of racism in sport and of
'the amount of coverage on television and in the press' of the women's
National League, and also letters from women who 'would like to hear from
women supporters from any club, who, like myself, think we should have
greater recognition for the support we give our teams and the way the clubs
treat women fans (like better toilets!)' (*Against the Tide*, Issue 2, 1993: 4, 23,
26). Self-determining activity of this kind (there is a fuller discussion of sports
fanzine 'culture' in the following chapter) has begun, albeit modestly, to disturb the established heterosexual and/or male profile of mainstream sport. In
view of the above evidence of formal and informal sport's often reactionary
politics, it has a hard road to hoe.

Conclusion

The above-quoted instances of 'non-hegemonic' sporting activity and fandom
may be scattered and minor in comparison with the major components of the
sports–media complex, but they nevertheless represent the exercise of iden-
tity-based, positional politics within the micro-circuits of everyday life. As
was argued above, the politics of sport – and of popular culture in general –
operate most potently at the level of metaphor, the body and identity,

although the associated distribution of material resources, the control of sports organizations, and the interface with orthodox politics are by no means insignificant manifestations of its power formations. Sport's symbolic, affective and ideological weight, when harnessed effectively, represents a formidable weapon in struggles for and against equality and social justice. For many of the world's citizens, the culture of sport is compelling and absorbing. It is to this cultural dimension that attention turns in the following chapter.

Physical Culture and Armchair Exercise

Sport is both an activity requiring some degree of organized, physical exertion and a spectacle in which a disparate audience gazes on other, usually more expert performers. In the course of this century the balance has shifted heavily towards spectatorship, particularly as mediated by television, radio and print. In Chapter 5 it was argued that the pressure on sports and sportspeople to professionalize has intensified with the heightened movement of capital and its attendant social relations into sport. The more pronounced separation of elite and grass-roots sportspeople which has resulted from the accelerated rise of the 'sportsbiz' has shadowed the split between the participant as paid professional and the spectator as (directly or indirectly) paying customer. If we consider, for example, the 'folk football in medieval and early modern Britain' described by Elias and Dunning (1986b: 182–3), the transformation from the forms of 'rough play' then extant to the organized sport of today is thrown into sharp relief:

> How people actually played was dependent on local customs not on common national rules. The organization of the game was much looser than it is today. The emotional spontaneity of the struggle was much greater; traditions of physical fighting and the few restraints – imposed by custom rather than by highly elaborate formal regulations which require a high degree of training and self control – determined the manner of playing and made for a certain family likeness among all these games. The differences between games which were differently named were not necessarily as sharply drawn as they are between different sport-games today.

In contemporary Britain, folk football is now little more than a carefully-staged annual event by adjacent villages as part of the collective nostalgic fantasy of the heritage industry (Hewison, 1987). Even children's and adults' street and park games broadly follow the blueprint of codified rules as endorsed by the national Football Association and its international counterpart, FIFA. Local custom has been largely supplanted by global rationalization in the establishment of universal laws of the game, with each mode of sport carefully distinguished from all others by detailed, often arcane prescriptions for the exercise of play. While it is important, as noted in Chapter 5, not to exaggerate the degree of rationalization of sport and to recognize the persistence of casual, loosely-organized forms of play, there has been a steady imposition of structures and controls. Contests take place on purpose-built grounds of specified dimensions rather than in village streets, on commons or on the land between settlements. Participants are no longer an indeterminate number of villagers (sometimes as many as a thousand per side) of all ages drawn from both sexes, although with the especially enthusiastic involvement of young 'hooligan' men (Dunning, 1986a: 271; Elias and Dunning, 1986b: 181). Today, formally constituted soccer teams are limited to eleven-a-side or five-a-side, with a prescribed number of substitute players admitted to play only under agreed conditions. Young men, from school through amateur to semi- and full professional levels, dominate the playing of the game as well as the sideline displays of ritualized symbolic and actual violence which bear the traces of pre-industrial territorial rivalry. Soccer games are not now exclusively casual or episodic practices, but are widely organized into leagues and 'knock out' competitions, with a minority of players deriving their principal incomes by performing before commercial audiences at actual events or via television for the entertainment of viewers (supported either by subscription or by advertising). The secular and religious authorities which formerly attempted to ban folk sports today regulate and fund it, supported by a vast complex of private and public corporations and associations.

The emergence of a highly-developed division of labour between player and spectator has also fostered the development of what (in an adaptation of the influential concept of Enzensberger, 1976) we might call the sports consciousness industry, that sector of contemporary cultural production devoted to what Umberto Eco (1986) calls 'sports chatter'. The necessity to talk and write about sport – and, following Eco, to talk about others' sports talk – is a function of its industrialization, professionalization and mass mediation. Interest in sport not only must be catered for as an integral part of popular cultural pleasure, but also needs to be commercially generated as part of the promotion and advertising of a cultural commodity. The increasingly weighty presence of sports journalism in the electronic and print media is evidence of the professionalization of sports discourse as well as of sports practice. Paradoxically, it has also meant that sports discourse has become so pervasive that the claim to expert knowledge of sport can be made by a huge number of viewers, listeners and readers. It is in the interconnections and interstices of playing and interpreting for fun and profit that the culture of contemporary sport can be apprehended. In this chapter I will analyse something of the phenomenology of playing and watching sport in an attempt to grasp the significant elements of sporting 'desire'. I will then examine how this ensemble of practices, sensations and mythologies is mediated and disseminated by sports journalists, those (para)professionals charged with the responsibility of symbolically framing the institution of sport. The ways in which sports journalists negotiate the spaces between players, spectators, experts and fans help to illuminate the constituents of a constantly shifting sports culture. One such shift to be discussed is a challenge to the mainstream sports media complex from the fanzine, an informal sports publication 'inherited' from the punk independent rock scene. The consideration of sports fanzines leads to a closing discussion of the convergence and divergence of forms of popular culture.

Fixing sport

Most analyses of sport have attempted to capture and describe the experiences encountered through playing and watching it. This is a particularly problematic activity because sport is complex, dynamic and subject to contestation, a realm which 'encompasses a bewildering diversity of radically different kinds of activity, which defies a watertight definition' (Hargreaves, 1986: 10). While at the commonsensical level we believe we know a sport when we see one, what we have come to regard as sport is a diverse range of organizations, practices and judgements of value. Pierre Bourdieu (1988) prefers to conceptualize the 'space of sports' rather than the unified phenomenon of sport because it is something historically constituted through social (particularly class) relationships. In adopting a non-essentialist approach I do not mean to resort to the *reductio ad absurdum* that anything can be sport and sport can be anything. The previous discussion has traced, if only in the briefest terms, the emergence of the institutional-discursive formation of sport as it is manifest in physical practice, organizational regulation, economic exchange, communicative spectacle, social interaction and ideological articulation. Yet these regularities do not negate the requirement to see sport as always in some way ontologically provisional, as being constructed and interpreted by a complex of players, spectators, officials and other social agents in their various institutional settings, and which can be spatially fixed in such sites as the training, lounge, committee, cabinet, news and board rooms. Sport, as a cultural phenomenon, is a product of the interchange between a collection of social structures and processes with their own individual as well as converging histories. Attempts to discern the transformations of play, game-contests and rituals into something resembling the modern conception of sport simultaneously challenge ahistorical accounts of the nature of sport while also often implying continuity by tracing the socially-induced mutation of such practices into sport. Robert Sparks (1988: 359) has noted the artificiality of these constructions, seeing the analytical differentiation of leisure and sports from other 'aspects of life' as 'itself a cultural projection, part of a folklore and common sense shaped by social and historical circumstance, part of the ideological field that constitutes sports and leisure as we know them, part of our research biographies and personal lives'.

Such a problematization of the concept of sport itself, not least on the grounds of a heavy and deeply 'interested' investment on behalf of the researcher, is an important corrective to those positions which stress the timelessness and stability of sport (for example, Novak, 1976). Yet it need not induce analytic paralysis, instead productively re-emphasizing the essential (but non-essentialist) sociality of sport. Working definitions like 'sport is institutionalized competitive activity which involves two or more opponents and stresses physical exertion by serious competitors who represent or are part of formally organized associations' (Nixon, 1976: 8) may not be wholly adequate, but they help anchor the experience of sport in social institutions and so hold in check some of the more idealist/mystical treatments of the sensations of engaging in sport.

The intensity of the experience of sport is highly variable. Roger Caillois (1961), in his much quoted classificatory work on the nature of play, presents four different categories which meet different human needs, but all of which have a form of connection with what is conventionally regarded as sport. These are: the *agon* play mode, with its emphasis on the competitive disciplines of sports like basketball and golf; *alea* games of chance and risk, such as the soccer 'pools' and other sport-connected gambling pursuits; *mimicry*, as in the carnivalesque aspects of sports spectacles involving masques and intensely symbolic displays of partisanship; and *ilinx* play modes, which entail the kind of death-defying, vertiginous stunts evident in the activity of ski-jumping and motor-cycle racing. These play modes, while probably amenable to a degree of empirical verification, do not exist simply as abstract options available to potential users, but are instead adopted singularly and in combination by social groups according to their different dynamics and locations in social structures. They offer up a range of prospective involvements in different dimensions of sport (as well as in non-sports activities) which vary greatly in the nature and intensity of the experience described. Many celebratory accounts of the phenomenology of sport emphasize its capacity to induce euphoria, ego-dissolution and absolute psychic absorption. Garry Egger (1981: 15), for example, constantly compares intense sporting experiences with the taking of narcotics and the undergoing of religious ecstasy:

> From interviews with hundreds of sports men and women, Murphy and Rhea White [1978] have been able to piece together a range of 'peak experiences' that occur in sport, but that sportspeople themselves are often too embarrassed to discuss openly. These range from out-of-body sensations to feelings of euphoria, even transcendence.

It is apparent that many sportspeople do have extraordinary experiences when engaged in sport, but also that many others (or the same sportspeople at different times) will also be involved in the professionally routinized and the casually-ritualized activities that we also call sport.

Working at play and playing at work

There are many forms and experiences of sport, but the steady (and often spectacular) expansion in pay for play is the principal link between them. The commercialization and professionalization of sport has had the most profound consequences in systematically separating players and spectators, amateurs and (semi)professionals, the lovers of games from the employees of sports. The experience of sport is, once significantly remunerated, very different from that of casual play. The concept of 'voluntarism' rapidly disappears, to be replaced with contractual obligations, just as intensive training and competition progressively erode the idea of expressive physical play. The strict schedules of professional sports are most vividly represented by the global circuits in sports like tennis and golf, where competitors are constantly in transit as they move from tournament to tournament, exhibition to exhibition. The intense public gaze as sportspeople perform in front of huge audiences (from stadiums to lounge rooms) is magnified by increasingly intrusive media techniques of 'getting up close' in order to render the sports action in ever more realistic and compelling fashion. Some recent incidents have highlighted this enhanced surveillance of professional athletes. In Australia in 1993, for example, one of the largest 'live' television audiences of the year on the eastern seaboard was 'treated' to a string of expletives after an on-field camera crew relayed a pre-match motivational talk by one of the captains in the rugby league State of Origin series. In England at about the same time, long-range directional microphones picked up a conversation between the Australian cricket captain and one of his players in which, again, 'obscene' words were used. Both incidents generated further media discussion of declining standards of sports conduct, leading to even closer monitoring of the on-field (and, increasingly, extra-curricular) behaviour of professional athletes. The shrinking private space for sports performers makes increasingly available to a wider audience the tension, violence, ruthlessnesss and aggressiveness that are prevalent in contemporary competitive professional sports.

The outcome of the trade-off of higher remuneration for lesser privacy is increasing disillusion among professional sportspeople. At a 1994 press conference the declining champion tennis player Boris Becker, after losing to the world's 96th (and Britain's top!) ranked tennis player, stated that at the age of 26 and after 10 years on the circuit, playing tennis was 'like going to the office'. His experience is widely canvassed as a case of 'burn-out', which afflicts players who have entered strict training regimens and pressurized competitions in childhood, and have subsequently discovered other priorities. If the only lasting impact of burn-out was early retirement from competitive sport to a satisfying and materially comfortable life, then there would be little to remark on here. However, cases such as that of Jennifer Capriati, who joined the professional tennis circuit at the age of 13 and at 18 had suffered severe personal decline (including arrests for shoplifting and illegal drug possession) before returning to the court, suggest a degree of malignancy in the culture of contemporary professional sport. One such spectacular recent example of a high-profile sportsperson experiencing very public and spectacular decline is that of Argentinian soccer player Diego Maradona, who, while playing in Italy, was arrested on a variety of drugs charges. Maradona, another sporting prodigy (and of very humble origins), revealed in a previous interview (Huxley, 1990: 7A) the pressure of mass expectation: 'The people must understand that I'm not a machine that dispenses happiness or kisses . . . I have the right to play badly sometimes.' This is, in fact, a profoundly misleading statement, for while Maradona is clearly not a machine, as the 'the most extravagantly gifted and extravagantly rewarded player in the history of soccer' he was expected to function like one in always performing at the optimal level of efficiency. For fans and the media he simply did not have 'the right to play badly sometimes'. Such a luxury is only available to the amateur player (and is not always tolerated in that instance) because the 'world's best player' and his colleagues and competitors carry on their backs the enormous weight of national aspiration and economic accumulation. It is perhaps not surprising that Maradona's 'comeback' during the 1994 World Cup Finals in the USA was curtailed when he tested positive for performance enhancing drugs and was sent home 'in disgrace'. The under-researched but impressionistically high incidence of depression, suicide, unemployment, illness, degenerative injury, poverty and crime among retired sports stars also puts in serious doubt the widespread view of professional sport's culture of privilege and wellbeing.

The interlocking demands of sporting associations, clubs, sponsors, advertisers, media and fans leave little room for 'under-par' sporting performance. The transformation of physical play into local and regional amateur sport, and then into national and international professional sport, represents not only the extended commodification of the body (Fitzclarence, 1990), but also a major shift in the nature of sport as culture. The magnitude of this change is highlighted in briefly considering televised international one-day cricket, a sporting form that has developed from its origins on the village green, through the English public schools and the travelling exhibitions of paid professionals, to its current amateur basis in schools and communities and its professional form in local, regional and national teams. International (five-day) test match cricket, once unchallenged at the professional apex of the game, is no longer the principal cricket spectacle (Harriss, 1990). One-day cricket is now an essential component of international competition. No test series is complete without a parallel one-day competition, while various triangular and larger tournaments (including a 'World Cup') are crammed into the already hectic playing schedules of professional international cricketers. Live attendances and television audiences (especially in Australia) are usually greater for one-day cricket than for the five-day version of the game. It is not difficult to understand why – the five-day game is much longer and more conservative than its 'instant' equivalent, with players dressed in all white engaging in an often stately and intricate series of manoeuvres. In many passages of play there is little overtly dramatic action, and it is not uncommon for test matches to end in a draw. Not to produce a 'result' is increasingly rare in an era of 'penalty shoot-outs' and 'count backs', but the idea of a drawn contest after five days of play, some of it perhaps lost to rain or bad light, is unfathomable to most contemporary sports marketers.

The one-day game is entirely different. The players are in coloured uniforms, the play is fast and spectacular, and a result is almost guaranteed (there is an occasional 'tied' result or 'washout'). Crowds at one-day cricket generally behave much more boisterously than in tests, with a good deal of chanting, catcalling, can-throwing and 'Mexican waving'. The tactics of the game are rather less arcane than in full-length matches, and are explained by commentators to an expanded target audience of women and children. This colourful, noisy spectacle is likened in its structure by Ian Harriss (1990: 118) to 'a one-hour television melodrama', with its formulaic regularities of pace, plot, characterization and resolution. The television viewer, if watching on free-to-air commercial television (again, particularly in Australia, where levels of advertising and non-programme material are high), is bombarded not only with the relayed sights and sounds of the game, but also by spot advertisements roughly every four minutes, various 'crawl' messages across the screen, extensive stadium perimeter advertising, sponsors' logos on players and other sites, and a good deal of 'spruiking' by commentators (Lawrence, 1986b; Harris, 1988). Players are required to combine high levels of performance with pragmatic technical adjustments to a one-day game viewed by purists as an unfortunate economic necessity to support the 'real' five-day game. Harriss (1990: 120) regards one-day cricket's predominance as symptomatic of a general shift from the modern to the postmodern condition:

> In the transition, then, from techno-bureaucratic capitalism to late, mass-consumption, global capitalism, there is also a cultural transition from modernity to postmodernity. In the game of cricket this transition is from an emphasis on rationalism, depth, order and constraint to surface, spectacle and excess. While cricket in the era of modernity performed an ideological function in masking the contradiction and oppression inherent in the capital/labour relationship, cricket in the era of postmodernity performs a different ideological function, by presenting the act of consumption as though it were totally unrelated to the social relations of production.

This spectacularization of the notoriously staid game of cricket is a product of the interaction between sport and television (Whannel, 1992: 79). Each sport must make itself telegenic by adapting to the presentational requirements of the medium, which in turn introduces further refinements of the screen spectacle. The sports spectator's leisure is produced out of the increasingly visible and minutely-monitored labour of the sports star. This now unremarkable state of affairs reflects deep changes in the culture of sport – from the activity of playing to the act of performing, and from the practice of 'watching' to the task of 'spectating'. In the process, the 'sports text' itself is transformed in both form and content, although this should not be taken to mean that it is easily harnessed to a solid and immutable regime of signification. The cultural shifts produced by commercially-driven innovations in the packaging of sport for television (especially in the case of custom-made screen sports like one-day cricket) also have important ideological ramifications. As Harriss (1990) pointed out above, televised sport tends to obliterate asymmetries of power according to a de-politicizing logic of entertainment. Within this process of production, exclusive emphasis is placed on the effect (and affect) of spectacular consumption. This strategy is symptomatic (and reproductive) of the condition of postmodernity (Harvey, 1989), where the politics of consumption (Mort, 1989) cannot be conceived as epiphenomenal to those of production, but are central to the constitution of society and its structures of power.

If we consider, again, the phenomenon of one-day cricket (and other sports like rugby league and basketball) from the perspective of cultural exclusion, these politics of consumption come into focus. The domination of most sports – and certainly the culture of sport – by men has, as argued both above and below, been a crucial mechanism by which hegemonic masculinity has been transmitted and reproduced. A claim to mastery over sporting knowledge has been a vital way in which men have established their identity, the 'difference' that sets them apart from those women, children and other men who do not exercise central, institutionalized political, economic and cultural control. Under late/disorganized capitalism, however, it is difficult to hold the line against the expansion of capital. According to the logic of consumption, it is necessary to 'pitch' for consumers wherever they can be found or created. Consumer capitalism is no respecter of cultural legitimacy where it can be over-ridden by commercial imperatives. For this reason, televised sport cannot be sealed off from women, who constitute over half of the population and dispose of the greater proportion of discretionary income in advanced capitalist societies. At the same time, women themselves have demanded equal access to sport and greater recognition of their existing sporting activities, thereby seeking to erode and overturn its deep association with patriarchy (Bryson, 1990). The outcome is not the sudden 'equal-time' appearance of professional sportswomen on the screen and a uni-sex televisual culture of sport, but rather the strategic spectacularization and sexualization of screen sport. While the bodies of female athletes have always been (positively or negatively) sexualized, the overt sexual address of sportsmen is comparatively new (Lynch, 1993). Women and gay men may not be celebrated as sportspeople through this process – indeed, they might be seen to be co-opted in the celebration of the hegemonic masculine male body – but they gain recognition as consumers of the images and products of sport. Once a breach is made in the sports gender and sexuality orders, new possibilities are opened up for the appropriation of strategically significant sporting sites, including sporting clubs and associations, television screens and newspaper columns, and state-funded sports activities and infrastructure (Hall, 1995). The commercialized stimulation of women's interest in sport, may, therefore, have significant unintended and unanticipated consequences.

The experience of sport at various stages of mediation is, then, profoundly influenced by the social characteristics of the person 'doing the experiencing'. Key social variables such as gender and class mediate the ecstatic and the transcendent dimensions of the sports spectacle. If we consider, in greater detail, the relationship between prevailing modes of masculinity and sports participation and spectatorship, then a wider picture is obtained of the manner in which sports culture is fashioned out of the material of social life. Not only does this analysis demonstrate how sport is linked to other parts of the social formation, but it also reveals how sport works in tandem with other constituents of society and culture to fashion some of the most potent identity formations in contemporary society.

Man-for-man marking

If universalist, ahistorical descriptions of the experience of playing sport are set aside, different subjects can be seen as bringing a degree of specificity to each sporting 'moment'. Human subjectivity is constructed at the confluence of social agency and structure – that is, at the point where subjects are inscribed with and within prevailing discourses of power. If, for example, the notion of a transcendent sporting subject in search of euphoria is displaced, and its heavily gendered complexion acknowledged, then the ideological dimensions of sporting culture are made visible. Bob Connell (1983: 18) analyses this sports gender formation in describing the centrality of sport in the making of men, arguing that:

> Sport is, all considered, astonishingly important. It is the central experience of the school years for many boys, and something which the most determined swots have to work out their attitude to.

Connell links the practices of sport with particular expressions of hegemonic masculinity, in particular the assertion of presence, the occupation of space and the corporeal competitiveness of adult males, an emphasis that the novelist John Updike (1994: 24) calls the male sense of 'outer' space, the 'fly ball high against the sky, the long pass spiralling overhead . . .'. Sport is similarly described by Connell (1983: 18) as a 'sensuous experience', with pleasure and exhilaration arising from the acquisition of sport-specific combinations of:

> force and skill. Force, meaning the irresistible occupation of space; skill, meaning the ability to operate on space or the objects in it (including other bodies) . . . The combination of the two is a power – meeting Weber's definition, the capacity to achieve ends even if opposed by others.

The image of the male that is generated by the interdependence of sport and masculinity is, of course, heavily reliant on fantasy and aspiration. Most boys and men cannot even approach the sporting ideal, with its myths of omnipotence, indestructibility and obliviousness to pain. Yet the potency of male sporting culture and the weight of negative sanctions against those who renounce it are such that even males who are alienated from many of its aggressive, patriarchal and homophobic dimensions mostly acquiesce in its reproduction. Douglas Crimp (1993: 256), for example, records how he played basketball in his small home town largely as a matter of family tradition and gender-based expectation, covering over the locker room self-consciousness caused by his 'queerness'. Escape from sport came only with physical and cultural relocation, so that 'when I left my hometown and found there were places where playing basketball wasn't the only measure of worth, I rarely played or watched a basketball game again'. Michael Messner (1992: 30), in his study of males who were formerly athletes, discovered a similarly compelling male sporting socialization process through initiation by older brothers and fathers. As has often been remarked, the male sporting identity is established largely in opposition to that of the female, with boys and men routinely claiming a monopoly of sport's most celebrated values and most spectacular performances, with women's sport ritually denigrated as an aberration or impertinence and players' shortcomings attributed to their 'femaleness' (Messner, 1992; Sabo and Panepinto, 1990: 120). Among professional male sporting ranks, the hegemonic masculinity–sports nexus is particularly evident. Connell (1990: 94), in his analysis of the masculinity of a professional 'iron man' called Steve, notes that he:

> certainly enacts in his own life some of the main patterns of hegemonic masculinity: the subordination of women, the marginalization of gay men, and the connecting of masculinity to toughness and competitiveness. He has also been celebrated as a hero for much of his life, in school and in adult sport. He is being deliberately constructed now as a media exemplar of masculinity by the advertisers who are sponsoring him.

It is through the mass media that sports stars function as celebrity advertisements for masculinity. The requirement to fashion and sustain a marketable image does, however, problematize the projection of masculinity because, in spite of sporting appearances to the contrary, hegemonic masculinity is by no means stable or unified. Indeed, sport's widespread deployment as ideological support for hegemonic masculinity is as much an index of the vulnerability and contradictoriness of the male power formation as it is an articulation of its character. The aforementioned case of the media treatment of Magic Johnson's HIV status, for example, reveals how the pressures on hegemonic masculinity produced a defence strategy which could only function by stigmatizing the figure of the infective female sports groupie (Rowe, 1994a).

The culture of professional sportsmen does not exhaust the possible permutations of male sporting affectivity and identification. A much larger population of sports fans, supporters and appreciators of variable fervour sustains the cultural breadth and depth of sport, while various sub-groupings (such as those devoted to football 'hooliganism') can be located within that larger aggregation. The sports fan is essentially the creation of the emergence of industrialized, professionalized spectator sport. In pre-sport folk-games, competition was insufficiently regular and formalized to produce sports fans as such, while in historical periods when amateur sport has been preponderant and a universalist commitment to 'play up and play the game' evident, the absence of the cultural–industrial machinery devoted to the constant priming of sporting interest and consumption severely limited opportunities to display a wide-ranging sporting fandom. Although fans may currently be or have been players of some technical degree of attainment in certain sports, most will never have played any kind of representative sport and, even if they have, will often be keenly interested in a variety of sports that they have never or have barely played. Indeed, the common notion of the 'sports nut' strongly emphasizes the portability of a sporting affiliation quite distinct from any forms of physical participation. Sports spectatorship and fandom may take many forms, including a relatively detached or periodic attention to the sport that is made readily (indeed, unavoidably) accessible through the mass media. Absorption, partisanship and a propensity to extrapolate from sporting experiences to those of other social domains are more frequently recounted and analysed. Some of the most spectacular examples of such sporting affiliation are the autobiographical and observational accounts of young, male, British soccer fans, with particular emphasis on their expressive cultures of violence (Buford, 1991; Hornby, 1992; Robins, 1984; Ward, 1989). The introductions to sports anthologies are especially rich sources both of passionate declarations of sporting affectivity and of exhortations to record and produce adequate literary treatments of the love of sports (such as the work being introduced). Ian Hamilton (1992b: 2, 3), for example, confides to the reader some of the details of his 'own fan-autopsy' and 'hang-ups' while expressing the spectators' need for 'more access' to 'great soccer documentary' material. Ross Fitzgerald and Ken Spillman (1988: 4, 5), similarly, in their celebration of 'The Greatest Game' (Australian Rules Football), describe their 'relief' at compiling the collection of words that properly represents their deep commitment to the ideals of sport:

> How often do we turn to the sports pages and read about our own injured and depleted spirit? How often do we read the back page first for hope and confirmation of our fragile identity, for a sense of mythic self? This is the abiding reality of football, the life beyond the manufactured image.

The pleasures of sport for the spectator may, then, be intense. Miller (1990), for example, remarks on the homo- and hetero-erotic pleasures of gazing on the athlete's body and of the ecstasy of sporting patriotism. Whannel (1993: 346), in a similarly Barthesian mould, notes how the sports spectator may experience both *plaisir* and *jouissance* in encountering the drama of anticipation, tension, uncertainty, loss and victory. In these various examples of spectator involvement in sport, personal and local community structures and values are clearly of deep significance, but it is intertwined with the 'mediatization' of sport, from the parodying of condemnatory newspaper headlines (as in Robins' (1984) *We Hate Humans*) to the routine employment of the lexicon of sports journalism (as in Martin Amis' (1989: 91, 97) fictional work *London Fields*). Diffuse media-relayed forms of 'mythic identification' are, as Michael Real and Robert Mechikoff (1992: 324) argue, produced of necessity on occasions when the 'largest number of people ever in human history to engage in one activity at the same time are the television viewers watching the Olympic Games and the World Cup'. They are also present in the multiplicity of media forms constituting the discourse of sport, which, in incorporating both commentary and its own critique, renders a 'discourse on a discourse about watching others' sport as discourse' (Eco, 1986: 162).

The centrality of media representation to the domain of sport generates a dichotomous model which coalesces around the misleadingly simple notion of 'passive **versus** participatory' (Redhead, 1993b: 6). It is, nonetheless, important to examine the relationships between those who perform sport, those who watch it and those engaged in disseminating descriptive and analytical information about it. This task entails appraising those who professionally represent sport and interrogating the texts that they produce. Because of the pivotal position of television to the economics and 'availability' of sport, it has gained most attention (Barnett, 1990; Goldlust, 1987; Whannel, 1992; Wenner, 1989). Here we will concentrate on the historically prior and continually important activity of sports writing.

The making of 'sportuguese'

As we have seen, sporting culture goes far beyond the confines of playing and watching. Even when sport seems to be at its 'purest' – at the point of performance – there are signs everywhere of mediation. In children's mannerisms and gestures on the sporting field which mimic those of sports stars on television; in the heroic fantasies of amateur adult sportspeople, replaying great moments in sport; in the circulation via the media of the chants and catcalls of spectators at geographically dispersed sports events; and in many other instances, the general cultural features of sport are revealed. These sporting signifying codes are clearly not 'organic' to the activity itself, but are produced and mediated within the totality of the institution of sport. A central element of that institution is the industrial apparatus of sports commentary, which both draws on and moulds sports discourse. While it is apparent that sport will be spoken about 'at ground level', the development of the sports–media complex has provided massive impetus to the language and speech of sport that consume so much conversational space. Sport under advanced capitalism stimulates new permutations of leisure and work. The everyday discussions of sport which constitute a significant component of (mostly masculine) leisure are commonly prompted by the professionalized sporting activities of others. At the same time, sports journalists and other popular cultural 'translators' perform much of the symbolic labour of producing, interpreting and circulating sport's meanings in a variety of contexts. In the first instance, professional sports journalists operate within the structures of television, radio and print peopled by fellow journalists whose discipline is the 'hard' news of business, politics, crime and social affairs. Given sport's predominant status as lowbrow culture, the 'toy department of the news media' (Garrison and Salwen, 1989) is regularly called upon to justify itself as a legitimate journalistic specialism. There is a continuing conflict, however, between professional norms of objectivity, balance and critical distance and pressures to support local/regional/national teams and to display the credentials of the sports fan rather than of the professional observer and critic. As in other fields of journalism (like the police 'beat' discussed by Chibnall, 1977), sports journalists are both reliant on their sources (principally, sports stars and administrators) and ethically bound (according to their professional code) to be independent of them. Those sources are often suspicious of sports journalists, believing that they will 'misquote, misinterpret or misunderstand them' (Richman, 1991: 260), preferring the wider reach and less inquiring approach of television. The sports journalist is expected by many sportspeople (and fans) to demonstrate playing as well as writing expertise, with the former seeming to take precedence. As James Traub (1991: 36) notes:

> The idea that the press is the tribune of the citizenry, and the guardian of the principle of objectivity, has not made much much headway in the locker room. Bobby Knight, the chair-throwing basketball coach at Indiana University, once summed up the jock view of sportswriters with winning candor. 'All of us learn to write in the second grade,' said the parfit Knight. 'Most of us then go on to greater things.'

The sports journalist, as cultural worker, must 'broker' these transactions between other cultural workers (especially sportspeople) and the publics which consume their products. The interviews with personnel in the independent rock music industry presented and discussed earlier in this book evidenced analogous pressures to reconcile competing tasks and interests. Interviews with professional and semi-professional sports journalists in Britain, Australia and New Zealand revealed how sports journalism, as an integral component of sports culture, must accommodate the economic interests of the 'sportsbiz', occupational and professional norms, and the affective investments of sports publics (Rowe and Stevenson, 1994). If we examine, for instance, the relationships between sports journalists and their sources, the complex and conflicting underpinnings of sports print texts are revealed in the following comments by the sports editor of a British newspaper:

> A: One of my problems with the British sporting press in general is the policy that you have the manager available to you after the match and that's it, the manager appears. Sometimes he doesn't. If you really want a player you ask or you loiter outside hoping they'll pop out and you'll grab them. They tend to be dealing with the managers quite sycophantically, they're usually very intimidated. They're very scared of being called out on the fact that they've never played professional soccer, they never *played*.

Here, the dependency of the sports journalist on the source and their anxiety about critical credentials are asserted. Traub (1991: 37) argues that a 'malignant side effect' of television is the audience demand for the 'inside scoop', which in practice means asking 'stupid questions' of sportspeople shortly after the end of competitive events. The refusal of athletes, managers and coaches to provide attributable and non-attributable information to sports journalists can cause considerable professional problems for them. Once, for example, the post-game subject matter moves beyond banal, much-parodied questions like 'How do you feel?' and 'What will be your approach to the next game?' into more critical questions about mistakes, tactics and selections, sports reporters can be quickly judged to be troublesome or negative, and so shunned on future occasions. Similarly, if while travelling on tour with an international sports team a sports journalist observes and reports violent behaviour, drug-taking and so on, it is quite likely that ostracism (sometimes from fellow reporters) will result, as the Australian sports journalist Roland Fishman (1991) discovered when he published a book detailing sexual conduct on the Australian cricket team's tour of the West Indies in 1991. The deployment of prominent sporting figures in newspapers or heavy reliance on them for 'insider' information further erodes the possibility of genuinely critical sports journalism. As the above-quoted editor observed:

> A: There are a couple of complications with the tabloids. Very often, the stars of the game or one of the managers will be clients of their newspapers. They'll be writing columns, will be guest writing columns. Even if they're not, these are people who are contacts, they have their phone numbers, they phone them up and chat to them, they're relying on them. You know, if you've got a football manager you rely on him very heavily to leak you stories of when he's bought a player or done a big deal or something like that because that's news on the non-soccer days. It's what keeps, it's the main forward spin type thing. He'll feed you the big transfer stories, he's a source and they don't like upsetting them.

While sports stars and teams are also dependent on the media for publicity, they are attracted to those forms that provide maximum exposure with minimum potential embarrassment. Television, in the form of friendly interviews or advertisements, is best fitted for this role of favourably presenting sports personnel. Richman (1991: 260) has noted in the American context: 'Day-to-day publicity is still perceived as useful, but why deal with an unpredictable writer who may venture into undesirable areas – money, drugs, girlfriends? Television is harmless . . . Athletes might know nothing about sportswriting, but they sure grasp broadcasting.'

The vulnerability of the sports print journalist to a 'source strike' and the domination of television combine to create the culture of 'sycophancy' described above. The absence of an investigative and critical journalistic approach is also in part a reflection of the problem of the legitimacy of sports writing. Professional players and managers often demand that a critic should have played at the highest level of the sport in order to be qualified to comment on it. The sports journalist is, therefore, required to offer writing skills as primary credentials in a field which privileges the body's 'manual' labour over the 'non-manual' labour of the mind. The increasingly easy entry of sportspeople into the sports pages, either through 'ghosted' regular columns or through post-retirement careers as specialist sports correspondents, makes the establishment of secure professional status boundaries highly problematic. The 'fantasy' aspirations of sports journalists who have not played at an elite, representative level and a collusive, complacent attitude to problems in sport (such as financial corruption) often adopted by players-turned-journalists, are seen to negate the possibility of more challenging sports journalism:

> A: It may be that, I don't suppose police beat reporters want to be policemen, but soccer reporters wish they were or had been professional footballers. One of the most distressing things, the worst actually, are the ex-professional footballers, who really will say nothing, they won't break any of the rules.

Much of the copy in the sports pages is, however, antagonistic towards certain sporting figures. The tabloid *Sun*'s 1992 campaign against the former England soccer manager Graham Taylor, in which he was likened to a turnip and other vegetables, is an example of a highly-charged and vitriolic treatment of a prominent sports identity. Here, the newspaper may judge that the potential source is more newsworthy as a target, especially when regular news conferences are part of the job description of a significant sporting figure. The practical accomplishment of contact with the source in this case is seen to rely on the presentation of a publicly accommodating facade which is at considerable variance with what is actually written about players or managers:

> A: It's pretty disgusting after an England match when the England manager comes in and his team has lost, and they ask a few polite questions and he gives them a few polite answers, and they go off and write hatchet-wielding stories for their papers.

Where 'exposure' of the sport source's behaviour in the context of scandal is proposed, the story is often handled by non-sports journalists. It is argued by this sports editor that the reasons for this practice are two-fold: first, in order that the sports journalist can disclaim responsibility for the embarrassment (and possible breach of trust) involved; and, second, because of the inability of most sports journalists to engage in 'serious' and complex investigative journalism:

> A: Now what they do, then, if there's a financial problem, if there are some sort of sexual allegations against someone, they'll bring news reporters in to handle them. Often when they are faced with a genuine news story they don't react very well.

In spite of these claimed professional limitations which lead sports reporters to be regarded with some disdain by their colleagues from other journalistic disciplines – a dismissive attitude not unconnected to sport's association in middle-class, middle-brow intellectual culture with 'mindless' popular diversion – there is also recognition of the skill entailed in servicing particular audiences and of the possibilities for stretching the genre of sports writing beyond its self-imposed limits. As one freelance sports journalist stated:

> B: . . . there are people who have turned it into such an art . . . who recognize sport as being much more than just a knockabout between two competing sides of individuals but as [being] part of the culture of the country and society . . . They elevate their own sport to something bigger and greater really, and because they can write well and capture the atmosphere and the social reflections in sport, then I think they actually become recognized as rather better than your average results recorder.

While such sentiments are not universally held among sports journalists, the brief comments above point effectively to areas of tension, uncertainty and difference. There is a strong emphasis on the relationships of dependency and exploitation in sports journalism, as well as on the ethical difficulties of having professional sports personnel – as key subjects and sources – also operating as authors of newspaper articles. The use of third parties (general news reporters) to research and write stories based on inside knowledge from sports journalists reveals also how sports stories may move easily from the sports pages to other parts of the newspaper. The credentials of sports journalists are shown to be seriously questioned by sports personnel and 'serious' journalists alike, and to be ultimately established by appeal to their responsiveness as service providers to readers rather than to more abstract qualities of informational value. Within the print media, a distinction is made between the 'tabloids' and the 'qualities', a split that is replicated in the typology of 'sports reporters' and 'sports writers'. The 'writer-driven' style of the quality papers is routinely contrasted with its assumed opposite, the reader-driven tabloid paper seen as cynically exploitative of sport and its personnel according to the demands of market-based profit maximization.

Fiske (1992) has argued that this quality/tabloid journalistic hierarchy is an ideological inflection of class relations. The difference in style between broadsheet and tabloid sports journalism is, indeed, often dramatic. If we select at random a short paragraph from Hugh McIlvanney (1993: 10), who is repeatedly identified as the consummate British sports writer, the complexity of language, especially vocabulary and syntax, is readily apparent in the following description of the play of the Irish soccer player Paul McGrath:

> His pervasive authority helped the man alongside him, Alan Kernaghan, to rise above the worryingly flawed form of his earlier appearances in the team and perform impressively. Kernaghan deserved special praise, since he was a special target for the screaming, gesticulating viciousness of the most bigoted sections of the Windsor Park crowd.

The writing here has its own 'pervasive authority' in addressing 'worryingly flawed form' and 'gesticulating viciousness' in linguistically dense, slightly elliptical fashion. This individualistic, 'signature' style contrasts sharply with the more direct populist voice of the tabloids. Selections from a back-page article in one of the more notorious tabloid British papers, *Daily Sport*, briefly demonstrate this difference of language and approach:

> DAVID PLATT will today join Sampdoria – and take his Italian wheel of fortune spinning towards £10 million . . .
> . . . The midfield star's golden trail to becoming the richest-ever British footballer started with his £5.5m move to Bari from Aston Villa in 1991 . . .
> . . . With two years left on his loadsalira contract, Platt was loathe to ask for a move as he would forfeit his right to be paid off by the Italian super-club. (Maddock and Dunn, 1993: 32)

In such sports articles 'that misery of stringer's clichés' (Amis, 1989: 98; see Rowe, 1991c) is set in play in constituting the genre of tabloid sports journalism. The 'sportuguese' of the 'wheel of fortune', the 'midfield star's golden trail', and its 'loadsalira contract' from the 'Italian super-club' provides a familiar framework for the interpretation of events and the formation of rhetorical responses. Fritz Spiegl (1983: 10) notes that this 'disembodied' style is one in which 'Words, phrases, whole sentences even, appear to be mass-produced like plastic kitchen utensils, each one identical to the next. It is a language of its own, never encountered in real life.' The very 'redundancy' (that is, predictability) of much sports tabloid 'newsspeak' does, however, create its own linguistic authenticity, as its judicious selection from the stock of everyday words and constructions, when melded with its own vernacular style, provides a readily available resource for the various utterances that comprise sports chatter. Both the development of expansive sports writing and of the tabloid form are generated as much by commercial judgements of the 'pulling power' of sport as by any discernible reader demand. There is some hostility among sports fans to the idea that professional writers, be they purveyors of 'high literature of the Mailer-in-Esquire school' (Diamond, 1994: 16) or 'hacks' whose clichéd writing 'panders to the lowest tastes of readers' (Richman, 1991: 337), are paid handsomely to write about favourite teams and sports. The very nature of the cash nexus and the routine dependence of sports journalists on peak sports organizations and significant individuals set them apart (materially and symbolically) from 'the people'. It is for this reason that, as with the aforementioned case of punk music, fanzines emerged as amateurist or semi-professional responses to the mainstream rationalization of popular culture.

Fanzine culture

Fanzines are most closely identified with British soccer, although they can be found outside that country and there are some devoted to other sports (such as the rugby codes). The extent of the phenomenon in Britain may be gauged from the May 1992 edition of *AFN Distribution*, a catalogue of scores of fanzines for sale which includes those covering large soccer clubs such as Arsenal and tiny ones like Wealdstone. As Richard Haynes (1993b: 68) states, the 'actual production of fanzines relies on the humour and sense of fun they provide, thriving on the misuse of language, revitalising conventional football media speak, using puns and clichés to convey a multiplicity of meanings'. This irreverent tone is typified in the fanzine entitled *Talk Us through It, Ray* (1992), which is subtitled 'The magazine that doesn't know the meaning of the word etepimeletic'. The major (and some minor) media are the target of humour or criticism. The name of the fanzine parodies the questions put to soccer players by television journalists immediately after matches, and one unsigned article, 'John Motshon'sh Shpot, I Fanshy', consists entirely of an imaginary pastiche of television sports commentary. A more serious piece by Simon English (1992: 7–8) condemns both the provincial commercial press and the local fanzines in questioning the tactics of one (now retired) prominent manager, Brian Clough of Nottingham Forest, whose:

> strange decision not to give a team talk was hardly criticised at all, especially not in the sycophantic local press. And the reason why this article appears in a Surrey-based mag, rather than a Forest fanzine is because in Nottingham there is no considered criticism of the man, only blind faith.

Apart from direct criticisms of the sports media, the constant use of self-deprecating humour, irony and vernacular language sets fanzines apart from mainstream print media. This is a style associated with *When Saturday Comes*, a pioneering fanzine with fairly high production values and some professional contributors which is subtitled 'The Half Decent FOOTBALL Magazine'. It is useful to consider aspects of the history of this key fanzine in analysing the relationships between cultural production, professionalism, industry and the construction of taste 'constituencies' addressed in the foregoing discussion of independent record companies. In his sympathetic critique of *When Saturday Comes*, Haynes (1993a: 46) notes that 'From its "bedsit origins" in March 1986, the first issue of 200 copies had twelve pages and cost 15p, the magazine (as its editors have always preferred to call it) has a readership approaching 40,000'. Haynes documents the origins of the magazine in a record shop; the modest allowances its founders paid themselves; its move towards greater permanency, regular publication and commercial distribution; the gradual expansion of its full and part-time staff; the production of books and merchandising; and, significantly, its decision to accept some paid advertising. This is a protypical history of an independent cultural enterprise, hinging as it does on 'managing the conflict between progress and principle' (Haynes, 1993a: 47).

Opportunities for expansion pose difficult challenges for the ethos of such organizations which, having developed informally as a 'fan-driven' alternative to the commercial media, come to generate capital and consumption at significant commercial levels. These developments bring the enterprise closer to the mainstream, as the early chaotic (and, in most cases, small-scale and short-lived) activity is stabilized and rationalized. Issues of consolidation extend beyond the realm of the commercial. In the case of *When Saturday Comes*, the contributed articles and letters which are so important to the magazine's function as a forum for non-professional writers and 'critics' are governed by an editorial policy which requires that any that are 'offensive, either racist, sexist, or of a sectarian type, are immediately dismissed' (Haynes, 1993a: 50). Such a politically progressive stance may be seen by emerging 'players' (like the Manchester United fanzine *Red Issue*) as an attempt to impose ideological orthodoxy and to prescribe moral standards for a sector of the sports print media founded on its unpredictability and poly-vocalism. In achieving a degree of sectoral leadership in the sports marketplace, the established alternative enterprise also necessarily activates contestation consistent with the discourse of resistive oppositionalism. Far from being rendered obsolete by the notion of unalienated cultural production, discursive struggle is able to be invoked at any point where resistive, alternative and oppositional qualities are to be measured and evaluated.

Whatever the judgement of a particular sports fanzine's level of radicalism, the rationale for the phenomenon itself is that the mainstream sports print (and electronic) media have in some significant sense failed (Rowe, 1992). Professional sports journalists – at least when they are not 'moonlighting' on fanzines – are held to be too remote from the 'common' fan and too compromised by their membership of the sports–media complex. It is this failure to engage with the 'ills of the game' (Haynes, 1993a: 48) which is seen to condemn sports 'hacks' and to commend fanzine writers. The problems raised by grass-roots supporters, as they are presented in one anthology of fanzine writing entitled *Whose Game is It Anyway?* (Shaw, 1989), include compulsory identity cards, police conduct, ground safety, racism, hooliganism, property development and sports business ethics. As Phil Shaw (1989: n.p.) argues in the introduction to the collection:

> The message from virtually all these magazines, so varied in quality and allegiance, is clear. It is that football belongs not to television, to an elitist clutch of clubs, to rapacious agents or sensation-hungry tabloids, or to the shareholders and sponsors, but to the people whose pounds and partisanship sustain the sport.

This populist polemical quality of much fanzine writing is identified by Shaw as providing a challenge to the commercial sports magazines and newspapers (a domain in which he also operates). This is not to suggest that fanzines are serious business rivals to the established media, although fanzine sales in Britain by the late eighties had exceeded one million per year. The fanzine weapons of rhetoric and ridicule can, however, be effective in challenging the division of cultural labour between professional interpreters of sport and non-professional consumers of it. Fanzines are seen by their supporters not only as desirable models for communication between aficionados, but also as essential correctives to the failings of the mainstream commercial press:

> It is true that many fanzine 'attacks' walk a fine line between irreverence and name-calling. But in the context of the dominant football press – the tabloids' fantasy world of 'now-I-must-tell-all' revelations, verbal sniping, plus fiction masquerading as transfer news, and the sometimes po-faced or pretentious posturing of the broadsheets – they perform the function of a disarmingly blunt antidote. (Shaw, 1989: n.p.)

The role of fanzines in helping to 'demystify the notion that "fans" and "writers" are, of necessity, breeds apart' followed closely the precedent of punk rock fanzines like '*Ripped & Torn, Sniffin' Glue, 48 Thrills, Temporary Hoarding . . .*' (Shaw, 1989: n.p.). This strong streak of populism which sustains fanzines is fuelled rather than dissipated by the expanding sports copy of the major sports publications. It would, however, be inaccurate and misleading to present sports fanzines as magically overcoming, by force of cultural populist will, the deep structural divisions that still substantially segregate leisure tastes and experiences. The following description of the readership of *When Saturday Comes* by its current editor reveals its highly selected nature:

> . . . the average reader is probably someone in their 20s, may be ex-student, or quite likely to be a student, and the *Guardian/Independent* reader . . . Someone that grew up watching football in the late sixties, early seventies. Predominantly male. We have got some women readers, but not that many really. But in a way there's not a great deal you can do about that. Probably not that many readers over fifty. Probably not that many under sixteen. An adult readership . . . We only ever really thought about stuff that we find interesting ourselves; if other people are interested then fair enough. (quoted in Haynes, 1993a: 49–50)

The class, gender, educational and age profile of the magazine revealed here is quite specific, but in essence not much different from the sports page readerships of the 'quality' British daily and Sunday newspapers. Other, more partisan and localized sports fanzines, such as the aforementioned *Red Issue*, seem to mirror the more working-class readerships of the tabloids. Hence, as with the music independents (and their own non-mainstream publications), the sports fanzines may be seen to be 'rounding out' the range of sports publications by occupying complementary niche markets, rather than presenting a fundamental alternative to the established sports press. Indeed, while some professional sports journalists and writers express hostility or display indifference towards fanzines, several have welcomed and even promoted their activities. This range of attitudes towards fanzines is displayed in interviews with sports journalists and editors. One senior sports journalist on a London-based tabloid newspaper stated:

> H: I'll be honest, I don't think I've ever read one in my life, you know, I don't think it has any effect on sports journalism *per se* . . . If they're selling then they must be [filling some sort of need] and maybe newspapers should have a look at them, I don't know. Maybe I'm wrong not to look at them and not to take more interest in what they're up to – some papers do.

A sports columnist on a nationally-circulated, British broadsheet newspaper similarly argued:

> D: I don't read them so I can't really give you a first-hand view . . . I'd like to see more before I could say what information is provided by these magazines that the papers aren't providing.

From this perspective, sports fanzines are regarded as largely irrelevant to the professional practice of sports journalism and as barely worthy of even a casual reading. In contrast, a sports journalist on a provincial newspaper found fanzines to be a 'good entertaining read', but, while understanding the impulse that leads supporters of a local soccer club to set up their own fanzines, believed that their lack of access to key sources within the organization meant that they could not provide superior analyses to those of professional sports journalists. In answer to a question about criticisms of local newspapers for being too closely aligned with soccer club administrators rather than supporters, he argued:

> G: . . . it's the supporters who have these feelings and think, 'OK, the journalists aren't really doing the job the way we like to see it done, so let's have a crack at it ourselves.' Obviously, they go along to the far extreme, because there would be no point in taking the middle line, you know, because in that way they would be almost trying to compete with the newspaper, so they wouldn't be looking to do that, so they go to the other extreme and produce the fanzine. Some of them can be quite good entertaining publications, whether or not it's valid criticism, I don't know. Again, it comes back to being able to obtain the information you need to keep close to the club. You are not going to find out, you might hear rumours on the terraces but you're not going to find the stories on the terraces, you'll find them in the club tea room and the VIP rooms afterwards.

This more positive view of fanzines confines them to the role of the external polemic, 'gingering' rather than deeply influencing orthodox print journalism and its analysis of sport. A sports editor on a magazine saw more of value in this view from the outside, accepting contributions from several:

> T: fanzine editors who can actually write and what they're writing is very different. It's this thing about not being party line, not being the view of the jaded hack who has watched football for 40 years. It's the view of somebody predominantly young, standing on the terraces or sitting in the seats with more of a fan's eye view . . . The fact that there's a new, different knowledge coming into writing about sport and their opinions are as valid as those who have watched it and played it and become experts who, in many cases, aren't experts.

This positive assessment of fanzines is, obviously, shared by those who produce them, such as the fanzine writer and coordinator who sees them as being 'run on love really, love of football' rather than for careerist or monetary reasons. Another sports editor had a generally favourable attitude towards fanzine writers, seeing them also as closer to grass-roots sports supporters and as much less 'politically' compromised than professional sports journalists. A 'punk attitude' that 'you could express yourself, you just need a printer and a typewriter and you could do it' is combined with deep popular resentment about the power structures of sport in creating the climate for the rise of the critical sports fanzine. Soccer fanzine writers are seen to be:

> A: disillusioned with the board [of directors], with their particular club, with the local press . . . they meet a need. I think it's generally accepted by most football fans that they are being fucked over by the club in various ways, that their interests are not taken in, and increasingly they have a stake in the club . . . They're filling a need that the national press really can't fill, and it's fun. It's a lot of fun, anybody can do it. I can sit down on a Saturday night feeling angry and contribute to a fanzine or buy a fanzine – great fun.

It is notable that sports editors appear to be more favourable towards fanzines than staff sports journalists, probably for the reason that they can accept or commission freelance material, while rank-and-file sports journalists are positioned in some way as competing both for space and for professional authority with, according to one journalist, the increasing number of 'people who started on fanzines [who] have now been assimilated into mainstream journalism, perhaps with no journalistic qualifications'. This resistance to the easy entry of 'amateurs' into the professional sports writing labour market is analogous to that of some musicians signed to major or established independent record companies who see the markets for skills and texts saturated by aspiring producers. If sports fanzines function (like some small independent record labels) as nurseries for mainstream organizations (in this case major newspapers and magazines), as popular safety valves for frustrated sports fans, or as specialist niche publications which comfortably co-exist with the more general outlets, then they can be understood as useful but hardly radical conversations within the general flow of 'sports chatter'. Some fanzines do, however, as noted in the previous chapter, provide a more thoroughgoing and potentially disruptive alternative when they explicitly cater to readerships largely or wholly neglected by the established commercial media (such as *The Football Pink* and *Against the Tide*). Fanzines dedicated to the specific sporting interests of women, gays, lesbians and non-Anglo cultures greatly extend the depleted range of human subjects imagined by the mainstream sports press. They seek to mobilize subordinate groups in pursuit of neglected interests and to celebrate their difference in the face of their erasure or marginalization. These may, on the other hand, be judged simply as small-scale, marginal alternative media which confirm the subordinate status of their readerships. The tentative use of specialist features on 'women's and ethnic sport' in the enlarged sports supplements (Trelford, 1993: 17) might, it could be argued, be more effective in disturbing the seemingly secure male, white, heterosexual character of sport and sports coverage. In fact, both perform important functions in the face of a dominant sporting culture which, in spite of state-sanctioned 'Sport for All' rhetoric and the commercially-driven desire to expand sports markets to hitherto neglected groups of consumers, is experienced by many as oppressive and exclusionary.

In sport there is no real equivalent of the independent rock band, the emergent force which may threaten the majors' domination of the industry. Amateur and semi-professional sport do compete with professional sport for public and private resources, but the hierarchical power structure of sport is more soundly established even than its pop music counterpart. It is for this reason that contest over the representation of sport is so central to the state of sports culture. Sport on the page and screen is not the unalloyed product of an over-determining patriarchal–capitalist logic of commercialization and professionalization, in spite of the strength of those forces in the sports–media complex. The dynamism and multi-accentuality inherent in all forms of popular culture are present in sport. Sports culture is also subject to the collapse of high–low boundaries so often proclaimed by proponents of postmodernism – exemplified, perhaps, by the literary imprint Granta's book on English soccer player Paul Gascoigne (Hamilton, 1994). It is important, however, not to overestimate its resistive present or its liberatory future. Sport culture, on the evidence available, is neither more nor less free of asymmetries of power than any other domain of the popular. Nor can it be insulated from other forms – the developing role of the sports fanzine, as noted above, is based on a model imported from independent rock music. Indeed, one important consequence of the rapid turnover and 'cannibalization' of style under conditions of rapid-fire image production and circulation is a blending and cross-referencing of formerly separate spheres of popular culture such as rock and sport.

Sound and motion

The relationship between rock and sport as cultural forms is many-sided. As noted earlier, rock's emergence as dissenting youth culture in the sixties set it apart from sport, with its multi-generational following and endorsement by conservative elements of the state apparatus. Yet, there has always been a degree of cross-fertilization between rock and sport, which is not altogether surprising given the close proximity between male-dominated youth subcultures devoted to rock (such as biker gangs – see Willis, 1978) and to sport (such as football gangs – see Ward, 1989), with, of course, some instances of cross-membership. The collisions and convergences of rock and sport culture have occurred in a number of settings and in a variety of ways. In the sixties, for example, the pop-based image of 'Swinging London' melded with that of the leading stylist soccer clubs like Chelsea and Queens Park Rangers. In the seventies, the influence of British (specifically, Scottish) soccer 'terrace' culture was evident in the tartan scarf motif employed by the Bay City Rollers and Rod Stewart and The Faces, with the latter regularly performing soccer 'tricks' on stage. In the 'glam' rock and pop of that period, the declamatory vocal style and the chanted choruses used by Gary Glitter, Slade, The Sweet and others were directly related to the sounds of soccer supporters, while in the punk era not only did the chanted football chorus re-appear, but also particular bands (like Sham 69 and The Stranglers) associated themselves with individual football clubs (respectively, West Ham United and Arsenal). In the eighties, a further and more generalized integration of rock and sport occurred. A striking instance was the publication in 1986 by the *New Musical Express* of a full, front-page colour picture of black British decathlete Daley Thompson beneath the headline 'Revolt into Sport: The Tracksuit Rebellion'. The following article declared:

> The sporting rebel is a modern folk devil in sponsored training shoes who is at permanent war with the authorities of sport . . . By comparison with sport, rock music is an exhausted old corpse hardly capable of controversy. (Cosgrove, 1986: 24–5)

This rather dramatic re-positioning of the traditional resistive functions of rock and sport was, according to Steve Redhead (1991; 1993b), part of a general blurring of the boundaries of styles and subcultures. Redhead (1991: 16) notes how the development in Europe of 'casual' style on 'the soccer terraces gave a new direction to sportswear and menswear and fixed a notion of a crossover between football and dance clubs which was to long outlive this particular development in youth culture'. He goes on to compare directly the 'micro' processes in rock and sport that have been extensively discussed in this book:

> From 1985 what captured the imagination of thousands of football fans (of both sexes) in their teens, 20s and 30s was the explosion of football fanzines exploiting the accessibility of desktop technology and constituting an excess of print addiction to rival the rush of independent record labels and music fanzines in the wake of punk in the 70s. (Redhead, 1991: 16–17)

By 1990, the rock–sport crossover in Britain was so well established that New Order, probably the 'hippest' independent rock band of the post-punk era, composed and performed 'World in Motion', the official theme for the English World Cup finals campaign in Italy. It would be unwise to ignore the specifically British dimension of these developments, but it would be equally ill-advised to discount the global character of the interpenetration of rock and sport cultures. The most striking example of the moment is that of American basketball culture, with its inseparable melange of 'cool' style, rap music and sport (echoed, it should be noted, in 'World in Motion's' video presentation of the black footballer John Barnes). There are now few sports in which the leading players do not attend systematically to presentational codes in a manner formerly associated with rock and pop stars, while, by the same token, there is an increasing number of rock and pop icons (including Mick Jagger, Iggy Pop and Madonna) who proclaim their bodily fitness through rigorous exercise and dietary regimens. In this way, the figure of the sports star has merged with that of the rock star as embodiments of style, just as rock, pop and sports cultures interact to produce increasingly short-lived and unpredictable hybrid forms. This state of affairs is the outcome both of the 'flattening' effect of a (hyper)commodifying logic of culture industries which are no guarantors of stylistic and subcultural boundaries, and also of initiatives emanating from within cultural groupings whose impulse is as much towards innovation and synthesis as it is towards the marking out of separate, consistent identities and styles. Rock and sports cultures, it may be concluded, articulate and interweave in a mutual process of re-articulation and re-formulation which is now prevalent in the making of late-twentieth-century popular culture.

Conclusion

In this chapter I have traced some of the key developments and features of the sprawling conceptual entity of contemporary sports culture. In analysing the social, cultural, economic and political constituents of sport, it is apparent that dominant processes such as the commodification of athletic competition and the ideological deployment of sporting identification are to some degree countered by forces which obstruct or resist the smooth incorporation of sport into everyday capitalist enterprise and systems of value. The reasons for this theoretical and empirical inconclusiveness lie in the uneven and contradictory nature of change within and outside sport. If we consider, for instance, the notion of a global sports culture, the move towards a universalist sporting order spreading out from the centres of economic, military and political power is often not smoothly accommodated at the local level, while the 'contra-flow' of sports culture from the periphery to the centre both promotes and confuses a sense of global sporting uniformity (Rowe et al., 1994). A similar assessment was offered in Chapter 2 of the rock and popular music industries. As has often been remarked, it is the very restlessness of capital, as well as the stubborn persistence of popular difference, inertia and resistance, that prevents the establishment of anything more than a provisionally ascendant hegemonic order. In the era of, according to analytical

taste, postmodernity, postmodernization, neo/post-Fordism, flexible accu-
mulation/specialization, reflexive accumulation or disorganized capitalism,
sports culture is inescapably subject to the kinds of transformations and
uncertainties that characterize all contemporary social formations (Crook et
al., 1992; Hall and Jacques, 1989; Harvey, 1989; Lash and Urry, 1994;
McKay and Miller, 1991).

Sport, then, has been inevitably caught up in the macro- and micro-
changes that have made so much of late-twentieth-century culture profoundly
different from previous formations. Garry Whannel (1992: 162) effectively
summarizes the shifts in the shape and practice of the culture(s) of sport
thus:

> The traditional amateur paternal forms of sport organisation were of course them-
> selves always profoundly contradictory, containing a class-ridden elitism, an uneven
> degree of semi-democratisation, a commitment to voluntarism and service, and
> the economic function of distributing resources to the less commercially viable sec-
> tors of sport and thus maintaining a broad base. The commercial challenge is
> equally contradictory in that, while providing the means of economic survival for
> many sports, and producing an entertaining and pleasurable spectacle, it has con-
> centrated resources at the elite levels, made sport a branch of the advertising
> industry, made sports over-conscious of image and the needs of television, and
> heightened the tensions between the uncertainties inherent in sport and the need of
> entrepreneurs to offer guaranteed entertainment. This whole process, profoundly
> re-making sporting cultures, should lead us to ask the question 'Who is sport for?'

This latter question is, of course, necessarily unanswerable in the abstract.
Sport can only be 'for' any individual or group under highly specific and variable circumstances, even assuming that the concept of sport itself holds for all
uses. The sport that is 'for' corporations and entrepreneurs in the pursuit of
profit may in quite different ways be 'for' or 'against' professional athletes,
amateur players, committed spectators, casual observers and hostile commentators. The pronounced industrialization of sport in the late twentieth
century cannot be denied, but what it has done, apart from creating a
sports–media complex of daunting proportions, is to create the conditions for
some surprising re-configurations of economics and cultural politics. This
assessment applies to the entire unstable domain where signs, codes and practices are exchanged within and outside popular culture. It is in this way that
rock and sport develop unanticipated syntheses and 'hybridities'. Any
account which is not attuned to these shifts and multi-level transformations
cannot begin to understand the diverse forms of the contemporary popular
and their many-sided politics of pleasure.

References

Adorno, T. (1967) *Prisms*. London: Neville Spearman.

Adorno, T. and Eisler, H. (1979) (originally published, 1947) 'Eye, ear and the function of music', extracts reprinted in M. Solomon (ed.), *op. cit.* pp. 378–82.

Against the Tide: The Voice of Women Who Just Love Football (1993) Issue 2. Cleveland, UK.

Alomes, S. (1991) 'Politics as sport: reality and metaphor in Australian politics and political coverage', in S. Alomes and D. den Hartog (eds), *Post Pop: Popular Culture, Nationalism and Postmodernism*. Melbourne: Footprint. pp. 67–87.

Althusser, L. (1971) *Lenin and Philosophy and Other Essays*. London: Monthly Review Press.

Amis, M. (1989) *London Fields*. London: Jonathan Cape.

Anderson, B. (1983) *Imagined Communities: Reflections on the Origin and Spread of Nationalism*. London: Verso.

Anderson, D. (1993) 'Cultural diversity on campus: a look at collegiate football coaches', *Journal of Sport and Social Issues*, 17 (1): 61–6.

Appadurai, A. (1990) 'Disjuncture and difference in the global cultural economy', *Public Culture*, 2 (2): 1-24.

Attali, J. (1985) *Noise: The Political Economy of Music*. Manchester: Manchester University Press.

Australian Sports Commission and Office of the Status of Women (1985) *Women, Sport and the Media*. Canberra: Australian Government Publishing Service.

Banerji, S. and Baumann, G. (1990) 'Bhangra 1984-8: fusion and professionalization in a genre of South Asian dance music', in P. Oliver (ed.), *op. cit.* pp. 137–52.

Barnett, S. (1990) *Games and Sets: the Changing Face of Sport on Television*. London: British Film Institute.

Barthes, R. (1977) 'The grain of the voice', in *Image–Music–Text*. London: Fontana. pp. 179–89.

Bassett, J. (1982) quoted in The *New Musical Express*, 17 July, p. 5.

Baudrillard, J. (1983a) *Simulations*. New York: Semiotext(e).

Baudrillard, J. (1983b) 'The ecstasy of communication', in H. Foster (ed.), *The Anti-Aesthetic: Essays on Postmodern Culture*. Port Townsend, WA: Bay Press. pp. 126–34.

Baudrillard, J. (1988) *Selected Writings*. Stanford, CA: Stanford University Press.

Baudrillard, J. (1990) *Cool Memories (1980–85)*. London: Verso.

Bayton, M. (1990) 'How women become musicians', in S. Frith and A. Goodwin (eds), *op. cit.* pp. 238-57.

Bayton, M. (1993) 'Feminist musical practice: problems and contradictions', in T. Bennett et al. (eds) (1993) *op. cit.* pp. 177–92.

Belz, C. (1969) *The Story of Rock*. New York: Oxford University Press.

Benjamin, W. (1973) *Illuminations*. London: Fontana.

Bennett, H.S. (1980) *On Becoming a Rock Musician*. Amherst, MA: University of Massachusetts Press.

Bennett, T. (1986) 'The politics of the "popular" and popular culture', in T. Bennett et al. (eds) (1986) *op. cit.* pp. 6–21.

Bennett, T. (1992) 'Putting policy into cultural studies', in L. Grossberg, C. Nelson and P. Treichler (eds), *Cultural Studies*. New York: Routledge. pp. 23–37.

Bennett, T., Frith S., Grossberg, L., Shepherd, J. and Turner, G. (eds) (1993) *Rock and Popular Music: Politics, Policies, Institutions*. London: Routledge.

Bennett, T., Mercer, C. and Woollacott, J. (eds) (1986) *Popular Culture and Social Relations*. Milton Keynes: Open University Press.

Berman, M. (1983) *All That is Solid Melts into Air: the Experience of Modernity*. New York: Simon & Schuster.

Bhabha, H. (ed.) (1990) *Nation and Narration*. London: Routledge.

Birch, M. (1984) 'The politics of popular music', *Meanjin*, 4: 513–24.

Blue, A. (1987) *Grace under Pressure: the Emergence of Women in Sport*. London: Sidgwick & Jackson.

Bourdieu, P. (1977) *Outline of a Theory of Practice*. Cambridge: Cambridge University Press.

Bourdieu, P. (1984) *Distinction: a Social Critique of the Judgement of Taste*. London: Routledge.

Bourdieu, P. (1988) 'Program for a sociology of sport', *Sociology of Sport Journal*, 5 (2): 153–61.

Brackenridge, C. (ed.) (1993) *Body Matters: Leisure Images and Lifestyles*. Eastbourne: Leisure Studies Association.

Brake, M. (1980) *The Sociology of Youth Culture and Youth Subcultures*. London: Routledge.

Breen, M. (ed.) (1989) *Our Place, Our Music*. Canberra: Aboriginal Studies Press.

Breen, M. (1994) 'One for the money: the commodity logic of contemporary culture in Australia', *Media Information Australia*, 72: 62–73.

British Phonographic Industry Yearbooks (1976–92). London: BPI.

Brown, P. (1993) 'Who gets the coverage and who is counting?: a methodological review of selected studies of newspaper coverage of women in sport', in A. Boag, C. Lamond and E. Sun (eds), *Proceedings of the Inaugural Conference of the Australian and New Zealand Association of Leisure Studies*. Brisbane: ANZALS. pp. 196–203.

Bryson, L. (1985) 'Why women are always offside', *Australian Society*, 4 (6): 33–4.

Bryson, L. (1990) 'Challenges to male hegemony in sport', in M. Messner and D. Sabo (eds), *op. sit.* pp. 173–84.

Buckingham, L. (1994) 'Lights, cameras and bankroll', *The Guardian*, 27 August, p. 36.

Buck-Morss, S. (1978) 'Review of "The Civilizing Process"', *Telos*, 37: 181–98.

Buford, B. (1992) 'Taking the city', in I. Hamilton (ed.) *op. cit.* pp. 317–27.

Caillois, R. (1961) *Man, Play and Games*. New York: Free Press.

Caine, B., Grosz, E. and de Lepervanche, M. (eds) (1988) *Crossing Boundaries: Feminisms and the Critique of Knowledges*. Sydney: Allen & Unwin.

Caldwell, G. (1976) 'Sport and the Australian identity', in T. Jaques and G. Pavia (eds), *Sport in Australia: Selected Readings in Physical Activity*. Sydney: McGraw-Hill. pp. 140–7.

Callinicos, A. (1989) *Against Postmodernism: a Marxist Critique*. Cambridge: Polity.

Cashmore, E. (1982) *Black Sportsmen*. London: Routledge & Kegan Paul.

Cashmore, E. (1990) *Making Sense of Sport*. London: Routledge.

Castles, J. (1992) 'Tjungaringanyi: Aboriginal rock', in P. Hayward (ed.) *op. cit.* pp. 25–39.

Chambers, I. (1985) *Urban Rhythms: Popular Music and Popular Culture*. London: Macmillan.

Chapple, S. and Garofalo, R. (1977) *Rock 'n' Roll is Here to Pay: the History and Politics of the Music Industry*. Chicago: Nelson Hall.

Chibnall, S. (1977) *Law-and-Order News*. London: Tavistock.

Clarke, J. and Critcher, C. (1986) '1966 and all that: England's World Cup victory', in A. Tomlinson and G. Whannel (eds), *Off the Ball: the Football World Cup*. London: Pluto. pp. 112–26.

Clarke, J., Hall, S., Jefferson, T. and Roberts, B. (1976) 'Subcultures, cultures and class: a theoretical overview', in S. Hall and T. Jefferson (eds), *op. cit.* pp. 9–74.

Cohen, G. (1993) *Women in Sport: Issues and Controversies*. Newbury Park, CA: Sage.

Cohen, Sara (1991) *Rock Culture in Liverpool*. Oxford: Clarendon Press.

Cohen, Stan (1980) (originally published, 1972) *Folk Devils and Moral Panics: the Making of Mods and Rockers*. Oxford: Martin Robertson.

Common Knowledge (1980) London.

Connell, R.W. (1983) 'Men's bodies', in *Which Way is Up? Essays on Class, Sex and Culture*. Sydney: Allen & Unwin. pp. 17–32.

Connell, R.W. (1990) 'An iron man: the body and some contradictions of hegemonic masculinity', in M. Messner and D. Sabo (eds), *op. cit.* pp. 83–95.

Conway, R. (1983) 'High time to knock the rock', *Quadrant*, 187, March: 42–7.

Coon, C. (1977) *1988: The New Wave Punk Rock Explosion*. London: Omnibus.

Cooper, B. (1991) *Popular Music Perspectives: Ideas, Themes, and Patterns in Contemporary Lyrics*. Bowling Green, OH: Bowling Green State University Press.

Cosgrove, S. (1986) 'Impure genius', The *New Musical Express*, 30 August, pp. 24–5, 28.

Costello, M. and Wallace, D. (1990) *Signifying Rappers: Rap and Race in the Urban Present*. New York: Ecco.

Creedon, P. (ed.) (1994) *Women, Media and Sport: Challenging Gender Values*. Thousand Oaks, CA: Sage.

Crimp, D. (1993) 'Accommodating Magic', in M. Garber, J. Matlock and R.L. Walkowitz (eds), *Media Spectacles*. New York: Routledge. pp. 255–66.

Critcher, C. (1993) 'In praise of self abuse: reviewing body theory', in C. Brackenridge (ed.) *op. cit.* pp. 225–35.

Crook, S., Pakulski, J. and Waters, M. (1992) *Postmodernization: Change in Advanced Society*. London: Sage.

Cunningham, S. (1992) *Framing Culture: Criticism and Policy in Australia*. Sydney: Allen & Unwin.

Cunningham, S. and Miller, T. (with Rowe, D.) (1994) *Contemporary Australian Television*. Sydney: University of New South Wales Press.

Curran, J. (1990) 'The new revisionism in mass communication research: a reappraisal', *European Journal of Communication*, 5: 135–64.

Curtis, J. (1987) *Rock Eras: Interpretations of Rock and Society, 1954–1984*. Bowling Green, OH: Bowling Green State University Popular Press.

Cuthbertson, I. (1992) 'Footy fanatics', *Campaign*, 197: 16–20.

Dahlgren, P. and Sparks, C. (eds) (1992) *Journalism and Popular Culture*. London: Sage.

Daly, J. (1985) 'Structure', in *Australian Sport: A Profile*. Canberra: Australian Government Publishing Service. pp. 12–19.

Davis, J. (1990) *Youth and the Condition of Britain: Images of Adolescent Conflict*. London: Athlone.

de Certeau, M. (1984) *The Practice of Everyday Life*. Berkeley, CA: University of California Press.

Denisoff, R. (1975) *Solid Gold: The Popular Music Industry*. New Brunswick, NJ: Transaction.

Denisoff, R. and Peterson, R. (eds) (1972) *The Sound of Social Change*. Chicago: Rand McNally.

Denselow, R. (1980) 'Why it's beautiful to be small', *The Guardian*, 30 July, p. 8.

Denselow, R. (1989) *When the Music's Over: the Story of Political Pop*. London: Faber & Faber.

Diamond, J. (1994) 'Match of the day, every day', *The Guardian*, 11 April, p. 16.

Docker, J. (1984a) *In a Critical Condition*. Ringwood: Penguin.

Docker, J. (1984b) 'Popular culture: a middleclassist response', *Arena*, 60: 192–5.

Docker, J. (1989) 'Popular culture, postmodernism and the death of the left', *Social Alternatives*, 8 (3): 5–7.

Dorfman, A. and Mattelart, A. (1975) *How to Read Donald Duck: Imperialist Ideology in the Disney Comic*. New York: International General.

Downing, J. (1976) *Future Rock*. St Albans: Panther.

Duncan, M. (1990) 'Sports photographs and sexual difference: images of women and men in the 1984 and 1988 Olympic Games', *Sociology of Sport Journal*, 7 (1): 22–43.

Dunning, E. (1986a) 'Sport as a male preserve: notes on the social sources of masculine identity and its transformations', in N. Elias and E. Dunning (1986a) *op. cit.* pp. 267–83.

Dunning, E. (1986b) 'The dynamics of modern sport: notes on achievement-striving and the social significance of sport', in N. Elias and E. Dunning (1986a) *op. cit.* pp. 205–23.

Dunning, E., Maguire, J. and Pearton, R. (eds) (1993) *The Sports Process: a Comparative and Developmental Approach*. Kingswood: Human Kinetics.

Durant, A. (1984) *Conditions of Music*. London: Macmillan.

Durant, A. (1990) 'A new day for music? Digital technologies in contemporary music-making', in P. Hayward (ed.), *Culture, Technology and Creativity in the Late Twentieth Century*. London: John Libbey. pp. 175–96.

Eagleton, T. (1990) *The Ideology of the Aesthetic*. Oxford: Basil Blackwell.

Eco, U. (1986) 'Sports chatter', in *Travels in Hyperreality*. New York: Harcourt Brace Jovanovich. pp. 159–65.

Edwards, H. (1969) *The Revolt of the Black Athlete*. New York: Free Press.

Egger, G. (1981) *The Sport Drug*. Sydney: Allen & Unwin.

Eisen, J. (ed.) (1969) *The Age of Rock*. New York: Random House.

Eisen, J. (ed.) (1970) *The Age of Rock 2: Sights and Sounds of the American Cultural Revolution*. New York: Random House.

Elias, N. (1986) 'The genesis of sport as a sociological problem', in N. Elias and E. Dunning, *op. cit*. pp. 126–49.

Elias, N. and Dunning, E. (1986a) *Quest for Excitement: Sport and Leisure in the Civilizing Process*. Oxford: Basil Blackwell.

Elias, N. and Dunning, E. (1986b) 'Folk football in medieval and early modern Britain', in N. Elias and E. Dunning (1986a) *op. cit*. pp. 175–90.

Ellis, C. (1985) *Aboriginal Music: Education for Living*. St Lucia: University of Queensland Press.

Ellison, M. and Donegan, L. (1993) 'Singer risks all in court fight with record firm', *The Guardian*, 11 October, p. 5.

English, S. (1992) 'A Clough round the ear', *Talk Us through It, Ray*, 3: 7–8.

Enzensberger, H.M. (1976) *Raids and Reconstructions*. London: Pluto.

Falk, P. (1994) *The Consuming Body*. London: Sage.

Featherstone, M. (1991) 'The body in consumer culture', in M. Featherstone, M. Hepworth and B. Turner (eds), *The Body: Social Process and Cultural Theory*. London: Sage. pp. 170–96.

Featherstone, M. (1993) 'Global and local cultures', in J. Bird, B. Curtis, T. Putnam, G. Robertson and L. Tickner (eds), *Mapping the Futures: Local Cultures, Global Changes*. London: Routledge. pp. 169–87.

Ferguson, H. (1990) *The Science of Pleasure: Cosmos and Psyche in the Bourgeois World View*. London: Routledge.

Ferrante, K. (1994) 'Baseball and the social construction of gender', in P. Creedon (ed.), *op. cit*. pp. 238–56.

Finnegan, R. (1989) *The Hidden Musicians: Music-Making in an English Town*. Cambridge: Cambridge University Press.

Fishman, R. (1991) *Calypso Cricket: the Inside Story of the 1991 Windies Tour*. Sydney: Margaret Gee.

Fiske, J. (1989) *Understanding Popular Culture*. Boston: Unwin Hyman.

Fiske, J. (1992) 'Popularity and the politics of information', in P. Dahlgren and C. Sparks (eds), *op. cit*. pp. 45–63.

Fitzclarence, L. (1990) 'The body as commodity', in D. Rowe and G. Lawrence (eds), *op. cit*. pp. 96–108.

Fitzgerald, R. and Spillman, K. (1988) 'Preface', in R. Fitzgerald and K. Spillman (eds), *The Greatest Game*. Melbourne: Heinemann. pp. 3–5.

Fletcher, S. (1984) *Women First: the Female Tradition in English Physical Education 1880–1980*. London: Athlone.

The Football Pink (1992) Issue 6. London.

Foucault, M. (1979) *Discipline and Punish: the Birth of the Prison*. Harmondsworth: Penguin.

Foucault, M. (1980) *Power-Knowledge: Selected Interviews and Other Writings, 1972–77*. Ed. Colin Gordon. New York: Pantheon.

Foucault, M. (1981) *The History of Sexuality, Volume 1: an Introduction*. Harmondsworth: Penguin.

Frankel, B. (1993) *From the Prophets Deserts Come: the Struggle to Reshape Australian Political Culture*. Melbourne: Arena.

Frankovits, A. (ed.) (1984) *Seduced and Abandoned: the Baudrillard Scene*. Sydney: Stonemoss.

Frith, S. (1976) 'The A and R men', in C. Gillett and S. Frith (eds), *Rock File 4*. St Albans: Panther. pp. 25–44.

Frith, S. (1978) *The Sociology of Rock*. London: Constable.

Frith, S. (1981) *Sound Effects: Youth, Leisure, and the Politics of Rock 'n' Roll*. New York: Pantheon.

Frith, S. (1986) 'Art versus technology: the strange case of popular music', *Media, Culture and Society*, 8 (3): 263–79.

Frith, S. (1988) *Music for Pleasure: Essays in the Sociology of Pop*. Cambridge: Polity.

Frith, S. (ed.) (1989a) *World Music, Politics and Social Change*. Manchester: Manchester University Press.

Frith, S. (1989b) 'Introduction' and 'Editor's note', in S. Frith (ed.) (1989a) *op. cit.* pp. 1–6; 198–9.

Frith, S. (1990) 'Review article', *Screen*, 31 (2): 231–5.

Frith, S. (1993) 'Popular music and the local state', in T. Bennett et al. (eds) (1993) *op. cit.* pp. 14–24.

Frith, S. and Goodwin, A. (eds) (1990) *On Record: Rock, Pop and the Written Word*. London: Routledge.

Frith, S. and Horne, H. (1987) *Art into Pop*. London: Methuen.

Gardner, C. (ed.) (1979) *Media, Politics and Culture: a Socialist View*. London: Macmillan.

Garnham, N. (1990) *Capitalism and Communication: Global Culture and the Economics of Information*. London: Sage.

Garrison, B. and Salwen, M. (1989) 'Newspaper sports journalists: a profile of the profession', *Journal of Sport and Social Issues*, 13 (2): 57–68.

Gee, G. (1981) *Music Business Yearbook*. London: Eccentric.

Geertz, C. (1973) *The Interpretation of Cultures*. New York: Basic Books.

George, S. (1976) *How the Other Half Dies: the Real Reasons for World Hunger*. Harmondsworth: Penguin.

Giddens, A. (1984) *The Constitution of Society*. Cambridge: Polity.

Giddens, A. (1985) *The Nation-State and Violence*. Cambridge: Polity.

Giddens, A. (1991) *Modernity and Self-Identity: Self and Society in the Late Modern Age*. Cambridge: Polity.

Gillett, C. (1971) *The Sound of the City*. London: Sphere.

Gillett, C. (1974) *Making Tracks*. New York: Dutton.

Glyn, D. (1979) 'Class strategies for a new cinema', in C. Gardner (ed.), *op. cit.* pp. 71–80.

Goldlust, J. (1987) *Playing for Keeps: Sport, the Media and Society*. Melbourne: Longman Cheshire.

Goodwin, A. (1990) 'Sample and hold: pop music in the digital age of reproduction', in S. Frith and A. Goodwin (eds), *op. cit.* pp. 258–73.

Goodwin, A. (1992) *Dancing in the Distraction Factory: Music Television and Popular Culture*. Minneapolis, MN: University of Minnesota Press.

Gould, S. (1977) *The Attack on Higher Education*. London: ISC Study Group. *Grapevine* (1980) London: BBC.

Greig, C. (1989) *Will You Still Love Me Tomorrow? Girl Groups from the 50s On*. London: Virago.

Grossberg, L. (1988) *It's a Sin: Postmodernism, Politics and Culture*. Sydney: Power.

Grossberg, L. (1990) 'Is there rock after punk?', in S. Frith and A. Goodwin (eds), *op. cit.* pp. 111–23.

Grossberg, L. (1993) 'The framing of rock: rock and the new conservatism', in T. Bennett et al. (eds) (1993) *op. cit.* pp. 193–209.

Gruneau, R. (1982) 'Sport and the debate on the state', in H. Cantelon and R. Gruneau (eds), *Sport, Culture, and the Modern State*. Toronto: University of Toronto Press. pp. 1–38.

Gruneau, R. (1993) 'The critique of sport in modernity: theorising power, culture, and the politics of the body', in E. Dunning, J. Maguire and R. Pearton (eds), *op. cit.* pp. 85–109.

Guilliatt, R. and Dwyer, C. (1994) 'Why Sydney is hot', *The Sydney Morning Herald*, 15 October, pp. 1A, 4A.

Habermas, J. (1987) *The Philosophical Discourse of Modernity*. Cambridge: Polity.

Hall, M.A. (1985) 'How should we theorize sport in a capitalist patriarchy?', *International Review for History of Sport*, 1: 109–13.

Hall, M.A. (1993) 'Gender and sport in the 1990s: feminism, culture, and politics', *Sport Science Review*, 2 (1): 48–68.

Hall, M.A. (1995) 'Feminist activism in sport: a comparative study of women's sport advocacy organizations', in A. Tomlinson (ed.), *op. cit.* pp. 217–50.

Hall, S. (1981) 'Notes on deconstructing "the popular"', in R. Samuel (ed.), *People's History and Socialist Theory*. London: Routledge & Kegan Paul, pp. 227–40.

Hall, S. (1985) 'Authoritarian populism: a reply to Jessop et al.', *New Left Review*, 151: 115–24.

Hall, S. (1989) 'The meaning of New Times', in S. Hall and M. Jacques (eds), *op. cit.* pp. 116–34.

Hall, S. and Jacques, M. (1986) 'People aid: a new politics sweeps the land', *Marxism Today*, July: 10–14.

Hall, S. and Jacques, M. (eds) (1989) *New Times: the Changing Face of Politics in the 1990s*. London: Lawrence & Wishart.

Hall, S. and Jefferson, T. (eds) (1976) *Resistance through Rituals: Youth Subcultures in Post-War Britain*. London: Hutchinson.

Hamilton, I. (ed.) (1992a) *The Faber Book of Soccer*. London: Faber & Faber.

Hamilton, I. (1992b) 'Introduction', in I. Hamilton (ed.), *op. cit.* pp. 1–3.

Hamilton, I. (1994) *Gazza Italia*. London: Granta.

Hardy, P. (1984) 'The fall and rise of the British record industry', *The Listener*, 24 May , pp. 7–10.

Hargreaves, Jennifer (1993) 'Bodies matter! Images of sport and female sexualisation', in C. Brackenridge (ed.), *op. cit.* pp. 60–6.

Hargreaves, Jennifer (1994) *Sporting Females: Critical Issues in the History and Sociology of Women's Sports*. London: Routledge.

Hargreaves, John (1986) *Sport, Power and Culture*. Cambridge: Polity.

Harker, D. (1980) *One for the Money: Politics and Popular Song*. London: Hutchinson.

Harris, K. (1988) 'What do we see when we watch the cricket?', *Social Alternatives*, 7, (3): 65–70.

Harriss, I. (1990) 'Packer, cricket and postmodernism', in D. Rowe and G. Lawrence (eds), *op. cit.* pp. 109–21.

Harron, M. (1988) 'McRock: pop as a commodity', in S. Frith (ed.), *Facing the Music: Essays on Pop, Rock and Culture*. London: Mandarin. pp. 173–220.

Harvey, D. (1989) *The Condition of Postmodernity: an Enquiry into the Origins of Cultural Change*. Oxford: Basil Blackwell.

Harvey, D. (1993) 'Class relations, social justice, and the politics of difference', in J. Squires (ed.), *op. cit.* pp. 85-120.

Hatch, D. and Millward, S. (1987) *From Blues to Rock: an Analytical History of Pop Music*. Manchester: Manchester University Press.

Hawkes, T. (1992) *Meaning by Shakespeare*. London: Routledge.

Haynes, R. (1993a) 'Vanguard or vagabond? a history of *When Saturday Comes*', in S. Redhead (ed.), *op. cit.* pp. 45–54.

Haynes, R. (1993b) 'Every man(?) a football artist: football writing and masculinity', in S. Redhead (ed.), *op. cit.* pp. 55–73.

Hayward, P. (ed.) (1992a) *From Pop to Punk to Postmodernism: Popular Music and Australian Culture from the 1960s to the 1990s*. Sydney: Allen & Unwin.

Hayward, P. (1992b) 'Sound commodities: copyright, sampling and cultural politics', *Media Information Australia*, 64: 42–7.

Hebdige, D. (1979) *Subculture: the Meaning of Style*. London: Methuen.

Hebdige, D. (1987) *Cut 'n' Mix: Culture, Identity and Caribbean Music*. London: Comedia.

Hebdige, D. (1988) *Hiding in the Light: On Images and Things*. London: Routledge.

Hebdige, D. and Stratton, J. (1982/3) 'Interview', *Art and Text*, 8: 21–30.

Held, D. (1989) 'The decline of the nation state', in S. Hall and M. Jacques (eds), *op. cit.* pp. 191–204.

Herman, G. and Hoare, I. (1979) 'The struggle for song: a reply to Leon Rosselson', in C. Gardner (ed.), *op cit*, pp. 51–60.

Hewison, R. (1987) *The Heritage Industry*. London: Methuen.

Hill, C. (1992) *Olympic Politics*. Manchester: Manchester University Press.

Hirsch, P. (1970) *The Structure of the Popular Music Industry*. Ann Arbor, MI: University of Michigan Survey Research Centre.

Hirsch, P. (1971) 'Sociological approaches to the pop music phenomenon', *American Behavioural Scientist*, 14: 371–87.

Hirst, P. (1989) 'After Henry', in S. Hall and M. Jacques (eds), *op. cit.* pp. 321–29.

Hoberman, J. (1984) *Sport and Political Ideology*. Austin, TX: University of Texas Press.

Hornby, N. (1992) *Fever Pitch*. London: Victor Gollancz.

Hustwitt, M. (1984) 'Rocker boy blues: the writing on pop', *Screen*, 25 (3): 89–98.

Huxley, J. (1990) 'Diego: soccer's tarnished deity', *The Sydney Morning Herald*, 2 June, p. 7A.

INGI Labour Working Group (1991) 'Unjust but doing it', paper presented at the International NGO Forum on Indonesia Conference, Washington, DC.

Jackson, S. (1993) 'Even sociologists fall in love: an exploration in the sociology of the emotions', *Sociology*, 27 (2): 201–20.

James, P. (1986) 'The ideology of winning: cultural politics and the America's Cup', in G. Lawrence and D. Rowe (eds), *op. cit.* pp. 136–47.

Jameson, F. (1979) 'Reflection and utopia in mass culture', *Social Text*, 1: 130–48.

Jameson, F. (1991) *Postmodernism: Or the Cultural Logic of Late Capitalism*. London: Verso.

Jarvie, G. (1993) 'Sport, politics, and South Africa (1948-1989)', in E. Dunning, J. Maguire and R. Pearson (eds), *op. cit.* pp. 265–79.

Jary, D. and Horne, J. (1993) 'The figurational sociology of sport revisited', paper presented at the Third International Conference of the Leisure Studies Association, Loughborough University.

Johnson, V. (1992) 'Be my woman rock 'n' roll', in P. Hayward (ed.), *op. cit.* pp. 127–38.

Jones, Stella (1993) 'Body images: the objectification of the female body in sport', in C. Brackenridge (ed.), *op. cit.* pp. 136–40.

Jones, Stephen (1989) *Sport, Politics and the Working Class*. Manchester: Manchester University Press.

Jones, Steve (1992) *Rock Formation: Music, Technology and Mass Communication*. Newbury Park, CA: Sage.

Keil, C. (1966) *Urban Blues*. London: University of Chicago Press.

King, N. (1990) 'Mapping Hebdige', *Southern Review*, 24 (1): 80–91.

King, S. (1993) 'The politics of the body and the body politic: Magic Johnson and the ideology of AIDS', *Sociology of Sport Journal*, 10 (3): 270–85.

Kroker, A., Kroker, M. and Cook, D. (1989) *Panic Encyclopedia: the Definitive Guide to the Postmodern Scene*. London: Macmillan.

Kuhn, A. (1993) 'Muscles, the female body and cinema: Pumping Iron II', in C. Brackenridge (ed.) *op. cit.* pp. 67–72.

Kuhn, T. (1970) *The Structure of Scientific Revolutions*. Chicago: University of Chicago Press.

Laing, D. (1969) *The Sound of Our Time*. London: Sheed & Ward.

Laing, D. (1978) 'Interpreting punk rock', *Marxism Today*, April, pp. 123–8.

Laing, D. (1985) *One Chord Wonders: Power and Meaning in Punk Rock*. Milton Keynes: Open University Press.

Lane, M. (1980) *Books and Publishers: Commerce against Culture in Postwar Britain*. Lexington, MA: Heath.

Larson, J. and Park, H. (1993) *Global Television and the Politics of the Seoul Olympics*. Boulder, CO: Westview.

Lash, S. and Urry, J. (1987) *The End of Organized Capitalism*. Cambridge: Polity.

Lash, S. and Urry, J. (1994) *Economies of Signs and Space*. London: Sage.

Lawe Davies, C. (1993) 'Aboriginal rock music: space and place', in T. Bennett et al. (eds) (1993) *op. cit.* pp. 249–65.

Lawrence, G. (1986a) 'In the race for profit: commercialism and the Los Angeles Olympics', in G. Lawrence and D. Rowe (eds), *op. cit.* pp. 204–14.

Lawrence, G. (1986b) 'It's just not cricket!', in G. Lawrence and D. Rowe (eds), *op. cit.* pp. 151–65.

Lawrence, G. and Rowe, D. (eds) (1986) *Power Play: Essays in the Sociology of Australian Sport*. Sydney: Hale and Iremonger.

Leonard, J. and Shannon, D. (1984) *Bands' Guide to the Music Industry*. Ilford: International Music Publications.

Leonard, W. and Reyman, J. (1988) 'The odds of attaining professional athlete status: refining the computations', *Sociology of Sport Journal*, 5 (2): 162–9.

Lewis, G. (1983) 'The meanings in the the music and the music's in me: popular music as symbolic communication', *Theory, Culture and Society*, 1 (3): 133–41.

Lloyd, A. (1975) *Folk Song in England*. London: Paladin.

Loy, J., Andrews, D. and Rinehart, R. (1993) 'The body in culture and sport', *Sport Science Review*, 2 (1): 69–91.

Lueschen, G. (1993) 'Doping in sport: the social structure of a deviant subculture', *Sport Science Review*, 2 (1): 92–106.

Lydon, M. (1970) 'Rock for sale', in J. Eisen (ed.) (1970) *op. cit.* pp. 51–62.

Lynch, R. (1993) 'The cultural repositioning of rugby league football and its men', in A. Veal and B. Weiler (eds), *op. cit.* pp. 105–19.

Lyotard, J. (1984) *The Postmodern Condition*. Minneapolis, MN: University of Minnesota Press.

Macherey, P. (1978) *A Theory of Literary Production*. London: Routledge & Kegan Paul.

MacInnes, C. (1986) (originally published, 1959) *Absolute Beginners*. Harmondsworth: Penguin.

Maddock, D. and Dunn, A. (1993) 'Gold Platted', *Daily Sport*, 14 July, p. 32.

Maguire, J. (1990) 'More than a sporting touchdown: the making of American football in England 1982-1990', *Media, Culture and Society*, 7 (3): 213–37.

Mandell, R. (1971) *The Nazi Olympics*. New York: Macmillan.

Manuel, P. (1988) *Popular Musics of the Non-Western World: an Introductory Survey*. New York: Oxford University Press.

Marcus, G. (1989) 'We are the world?', in A. McRobbie (ed.), *op. cit.* pp. 276–282.

Marcuse, H. (1972) *One Dimensional Man*. London: Abacus.

Marks, A. (1990) 'Young, gifted and black: Afro-American and Afro-Caribbean music in Britain 1963–1988', in P. Oliver (ed.), *op. cit.* pp. 102–17.

Marre, J. and Charlton, H. (1985) *Beats of the Heart: Popular Music of the World*. London: Pluto.

Marsh, P. (1977) 'Dole-queue rock', *New Society*, 20 January, pp. 112–14.

Marshall, G. (1990) *In Praise of Sociology*. London: Unwin Hyman.

Martin, B. (1981) *A Sociology of Contemporary Cultural Change*. Oxford: Basil Blackwell.

Martin, D.S. (1990) 'Incidental advertising of beer and cigarettes in TV broadcasts of the Adelaide Grand Prix', *Media Information Australia*, 57, August: 6–11.

Matlock, G. (1990) *I was a Teenage Sex Pistol*. London: Omnibus.

Mattelart, A. (1979) *Multinational Corporations and the Control of Culture*. Brighton: Harvester.

May, A. and McHoul, A. (1989) 'Writing pop/pop writing', *Southern Review*, 22 (3): 175–83.

McClary, S. and Walser, R. (1990) 'Start making sense! Musicology wrestles with rock', in S. Frith and A. Goodwin (eds), *op. cit.* pp. 277–92.

McIlvanney, H. (1993) 'Need of Glory at Twilight', *The Observer*, 21 November, p. 10.

McIntosh, F. (1992) 'That's why Neighbours became good friends', *Daily Mirror*, 14 September, p. 9.

McKay, J. (1986) 'Hegemony, the state and Australian sport', in G. Lawrence and D. Rowe (eds), *op. cit.* pp. 115–35.

McKay, J. (1990) 'Sport, leisure and social inequality in Australia', in D. Rowe and G. Lawrence (eds), *op. cit.* pp. 125–60.

McKay, J. (1991) *No Pain, No Gain? Sport and Australian Culture*. Sydney: Prentice Hall.

McKay, J. (1994) '"Just do it": corporate slogans and the political economy of "enlightened racism"', paper presented at the Fifth Congress of the International Association for Semiotic Studies, University of California, Berkeley.

McKay, J. and Kirk, D. (1992) 'Ronald McDonald meets Baron de Coubertin: prime time sport and commodification', *ACHPER National Journal*, Winter: 10–13.

McKay, J. and Miller, T. (1991) 'From old boys to men and women of the corporation: the

Americanization and commodification of Australian sport', *Sociology of Sport Journal*, 8 (1): 86–94.

McKay, J. and Smith, P. (1995) 'Exonerating the hero: frames and narratives in media coverage of the O.J. Simpson story', *Media Information Australia*, 75: 57–66.

McKay, J. Rowe, D. and Miller, T. (1994) 'Sport and postmodern bodies' (unpublished paper).

McRobbie, A. (ed.) (1989) *Zoot Suits and Second-Hand Dresses: An Anthology of Fashion and Music*. London: Macmillan.

McRobbie, A. (1991) *Feminism and Youth Culture: From 'Jackie' to 'Just Seventeen'*. Basingstoke: Macmillan.

Meggyesy, D. (1992) 'Agents and agency: a player's view', *Journal of Sport and Social Issues*, 16 (2): 111–12.

Melly, G. (1970) *Revolt into Style: the Pop Arts in Britain*. Harmondsworth: Penguin.

Menzies, H. (1980) 'Content analysis: one week's coverage of sport on all television, and in all daily newspapers in all capital cities' (unpublished paper).

Mercer, C. (1986) 'Complicit pleasures', in T. Bennett et al. (eds) (1986) *op. cit.* pp. 50–68.

Messner, M. A. (1992) *Power at Play: Sports and the Problem of Masculinity*. Boston: Beacon Press.

Messner, M. and Sabo, D. (eds) (1990) *Sport, Men and the Gender Order: Critical Feminist Perspectives*. Champaign, IL: Human Kinetics.

Middles, M. (1988) *The Smiths: the Complete Story*. London: Omnibus.

Middleton, R. (1990) *Studying Popular Music*. Milton Keynes: Open University Press.

Miliband, R. (1970) 'The capitalist state: reply to Nicos Poulantzas', *New Left Review*, 59: 53–60.

Miller, L.K, Fielding, L.W. and Pitts, B.G. (1992) 'A uniform code to regulate athlete agents', *Journal of Sport and Social Issues*, 16 (2): 93–102.

Miller, T. (1990) 'Sport, media and masculinity', in D. Rowe and G. Lawrence (eds), *op. cit.* pp. 74–95.

Miller, T. (1993) *The Well-Tempered Self: Citizenship, Culture and the Postmodern Subject*. Baltimore, MD: Johns Hopkins University Press.

Mills, C.W. (1970) *The Sociological Imagination*. Harmondsworth: Penguin.

Milner, A. (1993) *Cultural Materialism*. Melbourne: Melbourne University Press.

Moore, A. (1993) *Rock: the Primary Text: Developing a Musicology of Rock*. Buckingham: Open University Press.

Morley, P. and Thrills, A. (1979) 'Independent discs', The *New Musical Express*, 1 September, pp. 23–6.

Morris, M. (1988) *The Pirate's Fiancée: Feminism, Reading, Postmodernism*. London: Verso.

Morris, M. (1990) 'A small serve of spaghetti: the future of Australian studies', *Meanjin*, 49 (3): 470–80.

Mort, F. (1989) 'The politics of consumption', in S. Hall and M. Jacques (eds), *op. cit.* pp. 160–72.

Mowbray, M. (1993) 'Sporting opportunity: equity in urban infrastructure and planning', in A. Veal and B. Weiler (eds), *op. cit.* pp. 120–41.

Mukerji, C. and Schudson, M. (eds) (1991) *Rethinking Popular Culture: Contemporary Perspectives in Cultural Studies*. Berkeley, CA: University of California Press.

Murdock, G. (1982) 'Large corporations and the control of the communications industries', in M. Gurevitch, T. Bennett, J. Curran and J. Woollacott (eds), *Culture, Society and the Media*. London: Methuen. pp. 118–50.

Murdock, G. (1993) 'Leisure, participation and cultural rights', paper presented at the Third International Conference of the Leisure Studies Association, Loughborough University.

Murphie, A. and Scheer, E. (1992) 'Dance parties: Capital, culture and simulation', in P. Hayward (ed.), *op. cit.* pp. 172–84.

Murphy, M. and White, R. (1978) *The Psychic Side of Sport*. London: Addison Wesley.

Murray, R. (1989) 'Fordism and Post-Fordism', in S. Hall and M. Jacques (eds), *op. cit.* pp. 38–53.

Nava, M. (1992) *Changing Cultures: Feminism, Youth and Consumerism*. London: Sage.

Negus, K. (1992) *Producing Pop: Culture and Conflict in the Popular Music Industry*. London: Edward Arnold.

Nettleton, B. (1985) 'Education', in *Australian Sport: a Profile*. Canberra: Australian Government Publishing Service. pp. 86–97.

Nixon, H.L. (1976) *Sport and Social Organization*. Indianapolis, IN: Bobbs-Merrill.

Norris, C. (1992) *Uncritical Theory: Postmodernism, Intellectuals and the Gulf War*. London: Lawrence & Wishart.

Norris, C. (1993) 'Old themes for new times: postmodernism, theory and cultural politics', in J. Squires (ed.), *op. cit.* pp. 151–88.

Novak, M. (1976) *The Joy of Sport*. New York: Basic Books.

Oliver, P. (ed.) (1990a) *Black Music in Britain: Essays on the Afro-Asian Contribution to Popular Music*. Milton Keynes: Open University Press.

Oliver, P. (1990b) 'Introduction' and 'Conclusion' in P. Oliver (ed.) *op. cit.* pp. 3–15; 166–75.

Palmer, R. (1985) 'Rock's new respectability', *The Sydney Morning Herald*, 21 May, p. 13.

Palmer, T. (1977) *All You Need is Love: the Story of Popular Music*. London: Futura.

Pattison, R. (1987) *The Triumph of Vulgarity: Rock Music in the Mirror of Romanticism*. Oxford: Oxford University Press.

Peterson, R. and Berger, D. (1975) 'Cycles in symbol production: the case of popular music', *American Sociological Review*, 40: 158–73.

Pronger, B. (1990) 'Gay jocks: a phenomenology of gay men in athletics', in M. Messner and D. Sabo (eds), *op. cit.* pp. 141–52.

Ramet, S. (1994) *Rocking the State: Rock Music and Politics in Eastern Europe and Russia*. Boulder, CO: Westview.

Real, M.R. and Mechikoff, R.A. (1992) 'Deep fan: mythic identification, technology, and advertising in spectator sports', *Sociology of Sport Journal*, 9: 323–39.

Redhead, S. (1990) *The End of the Century Party: Youth and Pop towards 2000*. Manchester: Manchester University Press.

Redhead, S. (1991) *Football with Attitude*. Manchester: Wordsmith.

Redhead, S. (ed.) (1993a) *The Passion and the Fashion: Football Fandom in the New Europe*. Aldershot: Avebury.

Redhead, S. (1993b) 'Always Look on the Bright Side of Life', in S. Redhead (ed.), *op. cit.* pp. 1–10.

Reynolds, S. (1989) 'Against health and efficiency: independent music in the 1980s', in A. McRobbie (ed.), *op. cit.* pp. 245–55.

Richman, A. (1991) 'The death of sportswriting', *GQ*, September: pp. 254–61, 334–7.

Rijven, S. (1989) 'Rock for Ethiopia', in S. Frith (ed.), *op. cit.* pp. 199–204.

Riordan, J. (1980) *Soviet Sport*. Oxford Blackwell.

Roberts, K., Asturias, L. and Brodie, D. (1993) 'Health and the leisure factor', in A. Veal, P. Jonson and G. Cushman (eds), *Leisure and Tourism: Social and Environmental Change*. Papers from the World Leisure and Recreation Association Congress. Sydney: Centre for Leisure and Tourism Studies. pp. 366–9.

Robins, D. (1984) *We Hate Humans*. Harmondsworth: Penguin.

Robinson, D.C., Buck, E.B. and Cuthbert, M. (1991) *Music at the Margins: Popular Music and Global Cultural Diversity*. Newbury Park, CA: Sage.

Rojek, C. (1985) *Capitalism and Leisure Theory*. London: Tavistock.

Rose, C. (1981) 'Always read the label', *The Sunday Times Magazine*, February, n.p.

Rosselson, L. (1979) 'Pop music: mobiliser or opiate?', in C. Gardner (ed.), *op. cit.* pp. 40–50.

Rowe, D. (1991a) 'Play on words', *Media Information Australia*, 59: 59–66.

Rowe, D. (1991b) 'Player's worktime: sport and leisure in Australia', *ACHPER National Journal*, 131: 4–10.

Rowe, D. (1991c) '"That misery of stringer's clichés": sports writing', *Cultural Studies*, 5 (1): 77–90.

Rowe, D. (1992) 'Modes of sports writing', in P. Dahlgren and C. Sparks (eds), *op. cit.* pp. 96-112.

Rowe, D. (1994a) 'Accommodating bodies: celebrity, sexuality and "Tragic Magic"', *Journal of Sport and Social Issues*, 18 (1): 6–26.

Rowe, D. (1994b) 'The federal republic of Sylvania Waters', *Metro*, 98: 14–23.

Rowe, D. (1995) 'Big defence: sport and hegemonic masculinity', in A. Tomlinson (ed.), *op. cit.* pp. 123–33.

Rowe, D. and Brown, P. (1994) 'Promoting women's sport: theory, policy and practice', *Leisure Studies*, 13: 97–110.

Rowe, D. and Lawrence, G. (eds) (1990) *Sport and Leisure: Trends in Australian Popular Culture*. Sydney: Harcourt Brace Jovanovich.

Rowe, D. and Stevenson, D. (1994) 'Negotiations and mediations: journalism, professional status and the making of the sports text', paper presented at the International Communication Association Conference, Sydney.

Rowe, D. Lawrence.G, Miller, T. and McKay, J. (1994) 'Global sport? Core concern and peripheral vision', *Media, Culture and Society*, 16 (4): 661–75.

Ryan, B. (1991) *Making Capital from Culture: the Corporate Form of Capitalist Cultural Production*. Berlin: de Gruyter.

Sabo, D. and Panepinto, J. (1990) 'Football ritual and the social reproduction of masculinity', in M. Messner and D. Sabo (eds), *op. cit.* pp. 115–26.

Said, E. (1983) *The World, the Text, and the Critic*. Cambridge, MA: Harvard University Press.

Savage, J. (1991) *England's Dreaming: Sex Pistols and Punk Rock*. London: Faber & Faber.

Schiller, H. (1969) *Mass Communication and the American Empire*. Boston: Beacon Press.

Schumpeter, J. (1954) *Capitalism, Socialism and Democracy*. London: Allen & Unwin.

Schwichtenberg, C. (ed.) (1993) *The Madonna Connection: Representational Politics, Subcultural Identities, and Cultural Theory*. Boulder, Co: Westview.

Scraton, S. (1990) *Gender and Physical Education*. Geelong: Deakin University Press.

Shaw, P. (1989) 'Introduction', in P. Shaw (ed.), *Whose Game is It Anyway? The Book of the Football Fanzines*. Hemel Hempstead: Argus. n.p.

Shepherd, J. (1987) 'Towards a sociology of musical styles', in A. White (ed.) *op. cit.* pp. 56–76.

Shilling, C. (1991) 'Educating the body: physical capital and the production of social inequalities', *Sociology*, 25: 653–72.

Shilling, C. (1993) *The Body and Social Theory*. London: Sage.

Shoemaker, A. (1994) 'The politics of Yothu Yindi', in K. Darien-Smith (ed.), *Working Papers in Australian Studies, Nos 88–96*, London: Sir Robert Menzies Centre for Australian Studies. pp. 19–37.

Simpson, S. and Stevens, G. (1986) *Music: the Business and the Law*. Sydney: Law Book Company.

Simson, V. and Jennings, A. (1992) *The Lords of the Rings: Power, Money and Drugs in the Modern Olympics*. London: Simon & Schuster.

Sissons, R. (1988) *The Players: a Social History of the Professional Cricketer*. Sydney: Pluto.

Solomon, M. (ed.) (1979) *Marxism and Art; Essays Classic and Contemporary*. Brighton: Harvester.

Sparks, C. (1992) 'Popular journalism: theories and practice', in P. Dahlgren and C. Sparks (eds), *op. cit.* pp. 24–44.

Sparks, R. (1988) 'Ways of seeing differently: complexity and contradiction in the critical project of sport and leisure studies (response to Rosemary Deem)', *Sociology of Sport Journal*, 5 (4): 355–68.

Spiegl, F. (1983) *Keep Taking the Tabloids! What the Papers Say and How They Say It*. London: Pan.

Sport in the GDR: Past and Present (1984). Berlin: Panorama.

Squires, J. (ed) (1993a) *Principled Positions: Postmodernism and the Rediscovery of Value*. London: Lawrence & Wishart.

Squires, J. (1993b) 'Introduction', in J. Squires (ed.), *op. cit.* pp. 1–13.

Stanley, L. (1993) 'On auto/biography in sociology', *Sociology*, 27 (1): 41–52.

Staudohar, P.D. (1992) 'McNeil and football's anti-trust quagmire', *Journal of Sport and Social Issues*, 16 (2): 103–10.

Steinberg, L. (1992) 'Agents and agency: a sports agent's view', *Journal of Sport and Social Issues*, 16 (2): 113–15.

Stell, M. (1991) *Half the Race: a History of Australian Women in Sport*. Sydney: Allen & Unwin.

Steward, S. and Garrett, S. (1984) *Signed, Sealed and Delivered: True Life Stories of Women in Pop*. London: Pluto.

Stewart, B. (1990) 'Leisure and the changing patterns of sport and exercise', in D. Rowe and G. Lawrence (eds), *op. cit.* pp. 174–88.

Stilwell, F. (1977) 'Political economy of sport and pop music', *Journal of Australian Political Economy*, October: 83–6.

Stoddart, B. (1986) *Saturday Afternoon Fever: Sport in the Australian Culture*. Sydney: Angus & Robertson.

Stoddart, B. (1994) *Invisible Games: a Report on the Media Coverage of Women's Sport*. Canberra: Sport and Recreation Ministers' Council.

Stove, R. J. (1983) 'Rock and its audiences', *Quadrant*, September, 193: 39–41.

Stratton, J. (1983a) 'Capitalism and romantic ideology in the record business', *Popular Music*, 3: 143–56.

Stratton, J. (1983b) 'What is popular music?', *The Sociological Review*, 31 (2): 243–309.

Stratton, J. (1985) 'Youth subcultures and their cultural contexts', *Australian and New Zealand Journal of Sociology*, 21 (2): 194–218.

Straw, W. (1989) 'Rock for Ethiopia', in S. Frith (ed.), *op. cit.* pp. 204–9.

Street, J. (1986) *Rebel Rock: the Politics of Popular Music*. Oxford: Basil Blackwell.

Struthers, S. (1987) 'Technology in the art of recording', in A. White (ed.), *op. cit.* pp. 241–58.

Stubbs, D. (1989) 'Fear of the future', in A. McRobbie (ed), *op. cit.* pp. 267–75.

Swingewood, A. (1977) *The Myth of Mass Culture*. London: Macmillan.

Tait, G. (1993) 'Youth, personhood and 'Practices of the Self": some new directions for youth research', *Australian and New Zealand Journal of Sociology*, 29 (1): 40–54.

Talk Us through It, Ray (1992) Issue 3. Redhill, Surrey.

Tatz, C. (1986) 'The corruption of sport', in G. Lawrence and D. Rowe (eds), *op. cit.* pp. 46–63.

Taylor, I. Walton, P. and Young, J. (1973) *The New Criminology: For a Social Theory of Deviance*. New York: Harper.

Thompson, D. (ed.) (1964) *Discrimination and Popular Culture*. Harmondsworth: Penguin.

Tomlinson, A. (ed.) (1995) *Gender, Sport and Leisure: Continuities and Challenges (Topic Report 4)* Brighton: Chelsea School Research Centre.

Traub, J. (1991) 'Please don't mash the sportswriter', *Washington Journalism Review*, July/August: 34–7.

Treichler, P. (1987) 'AIDS, homophobia and biomedical discourse: an epidemic of signification', *Cultural Studies*, 1: 263–305.

Trelford, D. (1993) 'The long and the sport of it', *The Guardian*, 18 October, pp. 16–17.

Troitsky, A. (1987) *Back in the USSR: The True Story of Rock in Russia*. London: Omnibus.

Tumas-Serna, J. A. (1987) *An Investigation of the Primitive in Rock and Roll Performance*. Ann Arbor, MI: University Microfilms International.

Turner, B. (1992) *Regulating Bodies: Essays in Medical Sociology*. London: Routledge.

Turner, G. (1990) *British Cultural Studies: an Introduction*. Boston: Unwin Hyman.

Updike, J. (1994) 'The American male: why a man's best friend is his body', *The Observer Magazine*, 2 January, p. 24.

Veal, A. and Weiler, B. (eds) (1993) *First Steps: Leisure and Tourism Research in Australia and New Zealand*. Sydney: ANZALS Leisure Research Series 1.

Vignolle, J. (1980) 'Mixing genres and reaching the public: the production of popular music', *Social Science Information*, 19 (1): 79–105.

Wallis, R. and Malm, K. (1984) *Big Sounds from Small Peoples: the Music Industry in Small Countries*. London: Constable.

Ward, C. (1989) *Steaming In: Journal of a Football Fan*. London: Sportspages, Simon & Schuster.

Wearing, B. and Wearing, S. (1990) 'Sport for all? Gender and policy', in D. Rowe and G. Lawrence (eds), *op. cit.* pp. 161–73.

Weber, M. (1965) *The Protestant Ethic and the Spirit of Capitalism*. London: Allen & Unwin.

Weber, M. (1970) *From Max Weber: Essays in Sociology*. London: Routledge & Kegan Paul.

Wells, J. (1991) 'Putting the squeeze on a magic model', *The Australian*, 28 November, p. 32.

Wenner, L. (ed.) (1989) *Media, Sports and Society*. London: Sage.

Wenner, L. (1994) 'The Dream Team, communicative dirt, and the marketing of synergy: USA basketball and cross-merchandising in television commercials', *Journal of Sport and Social Issues*, 18 (1): 27–47.

Whannel, G. (1992) *Fields in Vision: Television Sport and Cultural Transformation*. London: Routledge.

Whannel, G. (1993) 'Sport and popular culture: the temporary triumph of process over product', *Innovation*, 6 (3): 341–9.

White, A. (ed) (1987a) *Lost in Music: Culture, Style and the Musical Event*. London: Routledge & Kegan Paul.

White, A. (1987b) 'Popular music and the law – who owns the song?', in A. White (ed.), pp. 164–90.

Whiteley, S. (1992) *The Space between the Notes: Rock and the Counter-Culture*. London: Routledge.

Whitson, D. and Macintosh, D. (1993) 'Becoming a world class city: hallmark events and sport franchises in the growth strategies of western Canadian cities', *Sociology of Sport Journal*, 10 (3): 221–40.

Wicke, P. (1990) *Rock Music: Culture, Aesthetics and Sociology*. New York: Cambridge University Press.

Wickham, G. (1990) 'Sport and the formation of manners', paper presented at the Australian Sociological Association Conference, University of Queensland, Brisbane.

Widgery, D. (1986) *Beating Time: Riot 'n' Race 'n' Rock 'n' Roll*. London: Chatto & Windus.

Williams, C., Lawrence, G. and Rowe, D. (1986) 'Patriarchy, media and sport', in G. Lawrence and D. Rowe (eds), *op. cit.* pp. 215–29.

Williams, L. (1994) 'Sportswomen in black and white: sports history from an Afro-American perspective', in P. Creedon (ed.), *op. cit.* pp. 45–66.

Williams, R. (1966) (originally published, 1958) *Culture and Society 1780–1950*. Harmondsworth: Penguin.

Williams, R. (1968) (originally published, 1962) *Communications*. Harmondsworth: Penguin.

Williams, R. (1975) (originally published, 1961) *The Long Revolution*. Harmondsworth: Penguin.

Williams, R. (1977) *Marxism and Literature*. London: Oxford University Press.

Williams, R. (1981) *Culture*. London: Fontana.

Willis, P. (1977) *Learning to Labour: How Working Class Kids Get Working Class Jobs*. Farnborough: Saxon House.

Willis, P. (1978) *Profane Culture*. London: Routledge and Kegan Paul.

Willis, P. (with Jones, S., Canaan, J. and Hurd, G.) (1990) *Common Culture*. Milton Keynes: Open University Press.

Wilson, B. (1990) 'Pumping up the footy: the commercial expansion of professional football in Australia', in D. Rowe and G. Lawrence (eds), *op. cit.* 27–39.

Wilson, N. (1988) *The Sports Business: the Men and the Money*. London: Piatkus.

Wonsek, P. (1992) 'College basketball on television: a study of racism in the media', *Media, Culture and Society*, 14 (3): 449–61.

Yeates, H. (1992) 'Women, the media, and football violence', *Social Alternatives*, 11 (1): 17–20.

Yetman, N.R. and Berghorn, F.J. (1993) 'Racial participation and integration in intercollegiate basketball: a longitudinal perspective', *Sociology of Sport Journal*, 10 (3): 301–14.

Index